A PLACE IN EL PASO

A Mexican-American Childhood

A PLACE IN

Gloria López-Stafford

University of New Mexico Press
Albuquerque

A MEXICAN-AMERICAN CHILDHOOD

EL PASO

First Edition

LIBRARY OF CONGRESS CATALOGING-IN-PUBLICATION DATA
Lopez-Stafford, Gloria, 1937-
A place in El Paso : a Mexican-American childhood
Gloria Lopez-Stafford. – 1st ed.

p.   cm.

ISBN 0-8263-1687-5

1. Lopez-Stafford, Gloria, 1937- –Childhood and youth.
2. Mexican Americans–Texas–El Paso–Biography.
3. El Paso (Tex.)–Biography.   I. Title.

  F394.E4.L67 1996
  976.4'96–dc20
  [B]   95-32451
  CIP

Designed by Sue Niewiarowski
Title page photograph: Gloria and Roy Rogers, 1949

To my daughters, Michele, Heather, Katherine

and my brother Charlie "Carlos" Palm

and

For all those who have known and loved El Paso,

the place in the sun!

CONTENTS

PART I

THE PROJECTS

1   Prologue, 1949

"Remember the Alamo!"

The banner slogan was draped across the blackboard of my social studies class in El Paso, Texas. The black letters jumped off the white background. The slogan on the banner was appropriate because the elementary school was named after Sam Houston, first president of the Republic of Texas. The colors were the colors of the school.

It was September and we were going to the auditorium to see the movie, *The Battle of the Alamo*. Texas history was the course of study for the year and the whole week before the film we made salt maps of the state. I was very proud of my carved Ivory Soap model of the Alamo. I had compared it to the other kids' models before recess and after shaving off more of the soap mission, it looked better and more like the others. I did not want to be different since I was particularly sensitive to laughs and pokes. I wanted it to look as good as Michael's because his was carefully carved and it looked like the mission I had seen in Ysleta, Texas.

That year, my class at Houston School was about half Anglo and half Mexican. It would become predominantly Mexican-American in the 1970s because of the Mexican population's moving up from the south side and pushing the Anglos to the east side and west side. Houston Elementary was in Five Points, which in the 1940s and 1950s was predominantly Anglo, Syrian, and Mexican. The area was named for the intersection of five streets that were in the center of the city at the time. It was partly residential and partly a business district.

The Battle of the Alamo was an old film, very dark and gray. The battle brought together small, overdressed Mexican men and big white men dressed in buckskins. As you probably know, the battle was fierce and it was won by a villain named Antonio López de Santa Anna. He was portrayed as a small ruthless man who made martyrs of the Anglos that day at the Alamo. There were 187 Anglos killed and 600 Mexicans killed.

After the film was over, the dark shades on the windows were lifted and the lights turned on. I felt uncomfortable as I looked around the auditorium, a huge cream colored room that had pictures of American presidents on the walls. George Washington's head and shoulders were on top of some clouds. On this afternoon, no one said anything. The film had a quieting effect on all the kids. I avoided the looks of my friends because I couldn't understand my confused feelings. I felt sick. I was painfully aware of being Mexican. And it wouldn't be the last time that year.

We started down the hall to our classroom. Some kids shoved when the teacher was not looking. I didn't want to be pushed or to have to push back. I walked back quietly until my friend Linda ran up to me. Linda's family was from Monterrey and she didn't live far from me.

"Gloria, who did you cheer for?" she asked in a quiet tone.

I looked at her and looked around before I answered.

"The Mexicans," I replied softly.

Linda shrieked, "Me, too," her pigtails framing her face as she jumped with joy. Her wide smile showed the milk teeth she still had. I stared at them as if seeing them for the first time. Her joy did not make me feel any better.

"Just be quiet, Linda," I said as I pushed her. Her enthusiasm left her face as she realized that I was annoyed at her. She jerked away and scooted up in line to get away.

When we were back in the classroom, the teacher stood in front of the room directly beneath the banner. She was a slender, very white woman with sky blue eyes. Those eyes were red and wet just then. I became concerned. What could be the problem? I watched her as she blotted her nose with a lace handkerchief. She forced a smile.

"The men at the Alamo were heroes—true Texans," she said in a soft voice. She was quiet for a while.

"Did they all come from Texas?" asked Amad.

"No, but they were real Texans that day," the teacher whispered. I could tell emotion filled her chest.

"The Mexicans did not fight fair," Michael protested.

"Don't let that bother you, Michael," the teacher reassured him. "As you will learn, later we beat them at San Jacinto."

"Yeah. And Texas is for Texans," yelled a voice from the back of the classroom. I didn't turn around to see who was speaking; I didn't care. Even though I was born in Mexico, I had been a Texan since I was two years old. I am also a Mexican. Joe pushed me from behind and uttered a chant of mockery. My friend José across the aisle slugged him. He gestured to Joe with his fists to leave me alone.

The teacher told us to open our textbooks to the section on the battle. She dreamily called out the names of the heroes in a tone like Padre Luna's when he recited the saints' names during mass. Her voice became low and harsh when she spat out the name of Santa Anna just the way Padre Luna's did when he uttered Judas' name during Lent.

I looked down at the gum wrapper whose silver paper I was removing. I felt both angry and sad; I felt bad. All the Mexicans in the classroom were quiet. I wondered how they felt. The teacher held her head high and said in a musical voice, "Remember the Alamo!" Angry and confused, I put my head down so that no one could see me cry.

But, I am getting ahead of my story. Houston School was located in the middle of the city. It was not in the Segundo Barrio, the Second Ward, the place I want to tell you about first. It wasn't that far away really, but as you will see, it was for me.

2   The Second Ward and My Parents

My childhood is tucked away in a special place in my mind. In my memory, everything is huge compared to what it was in reality. The Segundo Barrio in South El Paso is basically the place it has always been. Its people are the living energy. The poverty is still there, and while many come and go, many stay for generations. In the physical sense, most of the changes are on the periphery. Some of the buildings have been modified or their names have been changed. For me, it is the same as it was in the 1940s, even if it is true that the part close to the Río Grande changed when they built the permanent, cement river bed.

The Río Grande was a great river in the thirties, forties and fifties. It was like a long, thin, silver snake that would not lie still. During dry weather when parts of the river dried, many people immigrated during the night by walking across the cracked river bed. There were dead animals that came all the way from Colorado. Once I saw a swollen animal that looked like a huge fish to me until Diego, the local drunk, told me it was a rat that had had too much to drink. We could also collect interesting driftwood.

There were two bridges downtown between El Paso and Juárez—the Stanton Street Bridge and the Santa Fe Bridge. The Stanton Bridge has never been as interesting as the Santa Fe Bridge, my own personal favorite. The Santa Fe Bridge, in the time prior to the cementing of the Río Grande, had the money boys—young Mexicans who would stand in the water under the bridge. They would be dressed in cut-off pants or shorts and they would carry long poles that had cylindrical containers on the end. The boys would yell and whistle at the pedestrians crossing the bridge back from Juárez and when people leaned over to look into the river, they would yell, "Give us some money!" As soon as the money was tossed into the river, the boys would maneuver themselves in the water, catching the coins with the poles, looking like awkward giraffes. There seemed to be some agreement as to who would get each coin. Some people would toss the coins in creative arches, challenging those money boys of the muddy Río Grande. I bet the river kept few of the missed coins. Those jovial boys were there on the hottest and coldest days, day and night. They became a memory when the river was channeled.

Many times, when I was a very young child who did not speak English and when in the company of Mexican nationals, immigration officers would detain me at the river. They did so because my "American" declaration was not convincing enough. My father would have to come to the bridge to claim me. And he always complained about the fact that I didn't speak English. I learned to fear the "migra." When my life is not going smoothly I dream of this bridge and the walk across it. In my nightmare, I seem never to finish the walk; it seems to have no end. I am frightened that I can never return to El Paso. In the nightmare, *la Llorona* appears in the middle and Charon of the River Styx in Hades is at the immigration station. The migra, *la Llorona*, and Charon are suddenly all one and the same. It is the kind of dream that makes me appreciate waking up.

In the old days of El Paso and Juárez, the Río Grande would change its course. Sometimes it was in Mexico and sometimes it was in the United States. These changes would cause a political incident over the location of the border. Not that the change was always dramatic, but it caused problems. Was it Mexican land or gringo land? It was an age-old problem that reached out of the past. Men on both sides of the border would set their jaws. The Anglo would grind his teeth, and the Mexican *se chupaba los dientes*, the equivalent Mexican expression of the same disgust.

It was decided in the sixties that the river must remain stable and permanent, at least through the two cities. The river would be channeled in cement. El Paso, or the Segundo Barrio, would give up the land south of Tenth Street. Who would complain? It was useless land with some tenements housing Mexicans who wanted to live as close to Mexico as they could. On the Mexican side, some uninhabited farm land was given up. Later, a beautiful park, the Chamizal, would be built there. That is how I remember the cementing of the Río Bravo, as the Mexicans call the Río Grande.

In the early 1940s, the Segundo Barrio had Alamo, Douglass, Aoy Elementary, and Bowie High School. Some names reflected El Paso's pride in the Battle of the Alamo. "La Bowie" was named after Jim Bowie, the hero of the battle against the Mexicans.

The two largest churches in the Segundo Barrio were St. Ignacius on Park Street, the east end, and Sacred Heart on Oregon Street, the west end. In the barrio there was the Second Baptist Church at the end of Virginia Street, which was listed under the heading "Colored Churches" in the Coles Directory. There was also the Mormon church on St. Vrain across from where I lived.

The Segundo Barrio was and is made up of tenements, small houses, grocery stores, and some small restaurants. At the heart of the barrio are the Alamito Government Housing Projects, again named for that famous battle. This is the place I would call home from 1940 to 1947. When we first immigrated from Mexico, we lived in a tenement on Florence Street. But all I remember is my beloved Alamito project apartment on St. Vrain.

The population in the barrio was predominantly Mexican or American of Mexican descent. I call myself Mexican-American because I am both. A small percentage of the barrio's population was of other ethnicities, as indicated by some of the unusual surnames. They usually spoke Spanish as fluently as any Mexican. One of those persons was an old Anglo of Swedish descent named Palm. He was my father.

The Segundo Barrio has always been a temporary place for many persons when they first come to the country, a kind of Ellis Island for Mexicans. From there many people migrated to different parts of the United States. Many went to Chicago or California, the most popular destinations in the 1940s and 1950s. This barrio was the environment of my childhood, a world all its own. It was Little Mexico in the city of the pass, in the elbow of the state of Texas, at the bottom of the United States.

My father, Palm, was a skinny, yellowish-gray–haired, blue-eyed old gringo who had dropped out of a Baptist middle-class life in South Texas. On one of his trips to Piedras Negras, across Eagle Pass, he met a young Mexican woman—my mother. He continued to commute back and forth to his home. In the late 1920s, he apparently wanted more than the Republican party, the mercantile business, and his family in South Texas, so he left. His deserted children's hatred was so intense that at his death one of them was quoted as saying, "You can throw him into the Río Grande for all we care." It made me cry when Palm's youngest son by that first marriage told me this many years later. Palm's abandoned wife did not give him a divorce but eventually the state granted him one in 1939.

Palm took up chicken farming in Piedras Negras. There my oldest brother, Oscar, was born. A storm destroyed my father's chicken coops, so he took his family to Juárez, Chihuahua. There my brother Carlos was born in 1936, and seventeen months later, I was born to Palm and Francisca López. She was in her late twenties and Palm was sixty-five years old. In August of 1939, after he married my mother, we were able to enter the United States as citizens because Palm was a *norteamericano*.

In El Paso, Palm became a *ropa usada* man, a used clothing dealer. His customers were poor Mexicans on both sides of the river. He bought clothing in huge cardboard boxes from many places in the United States—clothes for all seasons, shoes, underwear, hats, even corsets. Whenever he got a shipment, we would be as excited as children on Christmas morning. Sometimes he would get great stuff; at others, he would get junk no one would buy. In the summer of 1945, I remember he got three huge boxes for a good price. He was all excited until he opened them and found nothing but old shoes. There must have been a million of them! Except when my mother died, I don't think I ever saw him so discouraged. I'll tell you later what happened to the shoes.

My mother, Francisca "Panchita," was a tiny, high cheek-boned, handsome woman who suffered insults for having married Palm. Many Mexicans called him *pan*, bread. Some called him that to be funny, and others called him that to emphasize that he was white and an outsider.

Let me tell you about my neighborhood's custom of nicknames. Some come from the way people look: tall, thin, fat. Others reflect character traits. Behavior, work, and status can get you a nickname, too. Sometimes, when you do not know a person and someone calls them by their nickname, you look for why the person has the nickname when you meet them. Although it isn't fair, people don't consult a person before they *bautizar* her, give her a name. I didn't like that part. I had many nicknames. Some of mine were *la pirinola*, spinning top, *la pecosa*, the freckled one, and *la güerita*, the fair one. I would acquire other nicknames as I grew up.

Another custom was to call people by informal names: Jesús is Chuy, Ignacio is Nacho, José is Pepé. Guadalupe is Lupe for both men and women. They called me Yoya as they do all Glorias. All these diminutives communicate affection and closeness. Teachers and immigration officers called you by your Christian name if they could pronounce it; if not, you got another kind of christening. I remember a girl called Lolita, whose given name was Dolores. She was pretty but not very bright.

People would teach her songs and jokes to amuse themselves, in turn, Lolita would constantly try to get attention. One day, Lolita's mother was in the grocery store on Fourth Street and she dropped the *blanquillos*, eggs, on the floor. She was very upset and called upon the holy family, "*Jesús, María y José!*" And as Lolita was standing by, she rescued the moment by yelling so that everyone on St. Vrain could hear, "Ayyy! *Chuy, Mariquita y Pepé (Jesús, María y José).*" Needless to say, the grocer repeated the story to the amusement of the *chusma*, the people. That was the *pilón* for the day. A *pilón* is an old tradition of giving customers a gift for their patronage such as a small piece of candy or gum. Some merchants allowed you to choose. I loved the custom!

But, let's go back to Francisca "Panchita" López Palm. She was a sickly woman who had a *curandero* for a father. Old man López sometimes was a genuine *brujo*. What made him a *brujo* in the eyes of the barrio was that he also used his gift for healing to fulfill his carnal wishes. One of the best stories about López was the one my godmother told me years later. There was a young married woman in the neighborhood who thought herself *embrujada*, hexed. My grandfather performed a *limpia*, a cleansing, with his herbs and massages. He also swept around her with a broom and rubbed her body with an egg as part of the treatment. But because the woman was passionate, the cleansing got out of hand and her husband walked in and caught them in each other's arms. My grandfather fled toward Juárez with the husband in pursuit. On Stanton Bridge, the man fired a shot from his gun at my grandfather. Fearing the Mexican Custom officers at the end of the bridge, the jealous husband threw the gun into the río and my grandfather escaped into the streets of Juárez. Needless to say, not even this close encounter cured my grandfather of seeking out women. After all, he was a man first.

During the war, López made some extra money buying groceries in Juárez for people in the barrio. He lived in Juárez, off Calle Lerdo and down Mejía. As long as he was traveling back and forth every other day to visit my mother, he tried to make it profitable. In those war days, everyone had tokens or stamps for scarce merchandise like sugar, coffee, and shoes. Many people in the Segundo Barrio shopped in Juárez because they could buy those items cheaply and without limitations. Of course that meant the sugar was brown and the shoes were huaraches.

López was like a bumblebee. He would go around to all the women who had problems getting to Juárez on a regular basis and take their orders for sugar, coffee, or huaraches for the kids. He always made his rounds after the children and the men had gone for the day. Often I would hear him buzzing away with the ladies, whose laughter was like wind chimes in the ever-present West Texas wind. He would go to Juárez and return in the afternoon after haggling with *los Chinos*, Chinese merchants, by the cathedral in Juárez. Sometimes he was even successful in smuggling a mango or two for his favorite customers. He got caught once when it was very hot and the delicious aroma of the mango gave the deed away. *La Migra* confiscated the fruit and fined the old Indian five dollars.

López came over to El Paso practically every day to see my mother, Panchita. She was always ill and depressed over being ill. López had been a widower twice and was married a third time to a querulous woman who was determined to outlive him. So he got away to visit my mother, his child from the first marriage. She was his *consentida*, his favorite one. When his wife was pregnant with her he wanted a son whom he could name Francisco after the two Mexican revolutionaries— the martyr Madero and the hero Villa. When his wife gave birth to a daughter, he named her Francisca. When she became ill, he tended to her with all kinds of herbs and ceremonies. He prepared potions for her to drink and smelly pastes to cover her body. He always prayed with Francisca, and many times his herbs and prayers helped. At other times he got carried away.

In 1942, Panchita's stomach problems got worse. Palm said it was all the *mugre*, dirt, that López gave her. My father talked her into going a doctor downtown who put her in the county hospital, an old building on Alameda Street. Being very poor, she didn't get the best care, but they operated on her and she came home in a few days. After that she was doing well and was happy, which made us all happy.

My godmother told me later that Panchita became sick again the following year. When she visited my mother, she saw that she was pale and depressed. She would always try to cheer Panchita up and since the two women liked to have a couple of beers together, it usually worked. My godmother always brought the *frescas* and cigarettes when she visited.

By springtime, my godmother heard that Francisca was not well and that López had become frantic in his care for her. She went to the projects to satisfy herself on the condition of my mother. When my godmother arrived, some of the neighbors were standing outside the apartment. Inside she found a group of women in the living room with their rosaries in hand. Their frantic praying sounded like a swarm of bees. It annoyed my godmother because she was not religious.

She went upstairs and looked down the short hall toward my parents' bedroom. There she saw the dancing contrasts of candlelight and she could smell the heavy odor of wax and the herbal packs. She approached the doorway quickly and became alarmed that perhaps she was already too late.

Francisca was lying on the bed in her white nightgown. She was surrounded by flowers and religious objects. A crucifix lay on her chest. López was dressed in a strange gown that he wore over his clothes; he was praying on his knees while his body leaned against the bed. There were two women seated by the window praying silently and another by the door as if standing guard. My godmother asked my grandfather what was wrong. He declared that my mother was ill and neglected by my father. My mother added that her father said she was at death's door.

My godmother quickly looked my mother over and concluded that this was *puro papelitos*, sheer dramatics, on the part of the old man. She pulled the crucifix off my mother. She ordered the woman near the door to turn on the light and then she removed all the flowers and religious objects from the bed. She softly asked my mother to sit up and lean against the pillow, then she ordered López to tell the hysterical women downstairs to go home.

"Francisca is not dying. But what you are doing is going to send her off before it is her time." My godmother was angry now. And because of the social status that López knew she had, he respected her orders and left the bedroom.

My mother recovered herself and was smiling in a short time. Seeing the improvement on Francisca's face, my godmother produced the bag of beers for them. She opened a bottle of Mitchell's and handed it to my mother, who did not object. My godmother took out her ivory cigarette holder and inserted a Chesterfield. She lit the cigarette with her lighter and gave it to my mother. Then she lit one for herself. They spent a couple of hours chatting and laughing quietly about the antics of López. By the time I entered the room, my godmother was preparing to leave. She kissed me and told me to take care of my mother.

"*Madrina*, can I go with you?" I said. Although I don't remember this conversation, it made me happy when my godmother Martha would retell the story.

"No, *mi'jita*. You need to stay with your mother."

"But I want to go with you," I whined.

My mother pulled me towards her and said softly,

"You stay with me. The time is coming when you can go with your *madrina*," my mother said sadly. According to my godmother, she realized later that it meant that someday I would become her little girl.

That June, Francisca despaired of her illness and decided on someone's advice to go to Juárez for another operation. Palm protested and begged her not to go. She didn't listen and went to a clinic in downtown Juárez. She died on the operating table. My godmother went to the clinic with every intention of talking Panchita out of the operation, but this time she was too late.

The day of the funeral people came to the house. I didn't understand why. I somehow knew something was wrong, but because I was always afraid that it was something I did, I didn't ask. Palm was not there. He had not been home in two days. A neighbor stayed with us.

Around noon, I was having a *birote*, small roll, with some coffee when Padre Luna knocked on the screen door. I was so happy to see him and ran to let him in. He did not smile but looked at me strangely. He appeared tired and hot.

"*Buenas tardes*, Padre Luna," I said.

"I just came from Juárez and I am hot and I need a glass of water, please!" he said as he removed his straw hat.

As he was talking to me I wondered why he looked different. Then I realized that he didn't have on his black shirt and white collar. He had his black suit on, but he was wearing a white shirt and no tie. I went into the kitchen to get the water.

"Doña Lupe, Padre Luna is here, and he is hot, and he doesn't have on his white collar. He wants some water." I listed the things that were on my mind.

"*Calla, niña*." She put her index finger across her mouth. "Padre Luna cannot wear a collar when he is in Juárez. It is against Mexican law. They would probably only tell him to take it off since the Constitution says he can't wear it in public. . . ." She paused to catch her breath as she handed me the glass of water. I rushed out of the kitchen saying that one doesn't keep a padre waiting, but in truth I wasn't in the mood for a long story from her. Most of the time I loved her stories—they helped me pass the time—but not today.

Padre Luna had already sat down in Palm's big brown chair with the chenille cover. He was leaning his head back and had his eyes closed. I stood in front of him with the glass of water, not wanting to bother him. Maybe he was talking to God in his head. I waited respectfully until he opened his eyes and smiled at me.

"Ay, Yoya. You are such a good little girl." He paused. "And you are also a brave one. Your mother would be very proud of you." He drank the water quickly.

"No, Padre, she's angry at me. I cried when she went to Juárez because I didn't want her to go." I bowed my head.

He looked at me with a confused look and he was about to say something to me when the screen door opened and López and Palm came into the house. The two old men looked very tired. López staggered and Palm had a blank look on his face. Padre Luna stood up and went to the door. He grabbed López's arm and helped steady him. Then the trio moved toward Palm's big chair. There my father collapsed into the brown chair. I wondered what was going on.

"I'm all right, it's just the heat and . . ." López said to Padre Luna. "The ride on the streetcar was hard. It's too hot! Please, *mi'ja*, get me some water."

I turned only to meet Doña Lupe carrying two glasses of water for López and Palm. They both took the water and gulped it down. Palm looked terrible; his body was a shell and he looked so old.

Just then the screen door opened and in came two couples—friends and relatives from Chihuahua. They were dressed like country people whom you see in the streets of Juárez. The men took off their big straw hats and I stared at them. I couldn't believe that anyone could wear such big hats. Doña Lupe told me to take the hats from the men and to put them in the bedroom upstairs. I took them, one in each hand. They were as big as I was. One of the women was amused by this and started to giggle but her husband gave her a look that could have turned her into stone. Naturally I was delighted. Somehow I managed to grab the cones of the hats and my tiny hands dug in. I went upstairs to the boys' bedroom and placed the hats on the bed. I tiptoed to the door and closed it. I put one of the hats on my head and I disappeared into it. I laughed and took it off. I danced with the hats for a little while until I could hear the voices downstairs. I remembered that there were visitors and I didn't want to miss out on anything. Just as I entered the living room, I heard one of the paisanos say to Padre Luna:

"You are the *cura*, priest, aren't you?" I guess since Padre wasn't wearing his clerical collar, it wasn't easy to see that he was a priest. Padre nodded.

"Aren't you Juan Luna de la Torre?" the other one asked. Padre looked uncomfortable and surprised for a moment. As if remembering the name, he answered in a soft voice,

"Yes, *por favor*, just Luna. I don't use the de la Torre. It confuses immigration and seems out of place here in the barrio. Have we met before?"

"*Sí, hace muchos años*, many years ago." The paisano stretched the *muchos* out like pulling a long string of gum from his mouth. His tone was harsh.

"*¿Es español, que no?* You're a Spaniard, right?" The question was sharp.

"*Mis padres* are Spanish by birth. But I was born in the republic of Mexico and I consider myself a Mexican, señor." Padre's voice was the one he used when giving a serious lecture to his parishioners.

"A Mexican! I hardly think that someone who changes his *chaqueta*, jacket, can be considered a Mexican. I, sir, I am a Mexican. I live in *la patria*, the fatherland." The paisano's chest went out as if he were about to sing the Mexican national anthem to prove his loyalty.

"No man loves *la patria* more than I do," declared Padre Luna in a loud voice. "But señor, the government does not love the church. They proved that during the revolution and in the Constitution." Padre caught his breath, "War also makes victims of innocent people. That's why I left. *Primero Dios*, God first!"

"No, Padre, *primero la patria*!" The paisano's face was turning bright red as he declared his love.

Both López and Palm moved towards the men. López grabbed the paisano's arm and said in a stern voice,

"Señores. This is not the time or the place to be discussing this. We are here for another matter. My son-in-law is grieving. The question of who is a better Mexican is not for this day."

The women came over and separated the trio. Padre Luna apologized to López and then engaged Palm in a soft and private conversation.

The day was to be a long one. People came and left including my godparents. No one told me, but I knew by dusk that my mother had died. No one discussed it with me. They just rubbed my head and told me what a brave little girl I was. That night, after Palm had turned off the light in the living room and as we were all going upstairs, my brother Carlos asked my father,

"My mother is never coming back, Papí?"

"No, son. She's not," he said in an empty voice. He picked me up in his arms and I looked at the light at the top of the stairs. I let out a sigh and hugged Palm's neck. We went upstairs to bed. All night long I dreamed of big Mexican hats chasing me and Padre Luna. And no one was there to help us.

A precious person and a child's memory of her were buried that day. It was as if pain and anger entered my brain and erased the memories of my mother. I must have felt so abandoned by her that I decided to abandon her memory in turn. My godmother would tell me stories about my mother, but that didn't bring her memory back. It seems strange that I remember even the most trivial events of my childhood but I don't remember one of the persons whom I loved the most. I only have two photographs to remind me that I did have a mother. I think Padre Luna understood how I felt whenever I talked to him about it.

3   St. Vrain Street

The winter of 1944 arrived on St Vrain Street much as it had always done except for the war. We knew about the war because some families had sons in the fight. Some of their sons came home on furlough dressed in their military uniforms; others came home for burial. There were marines, sailors, fly boys, and soldiers. The family across the street had two, a year apart, who came home to be buried at Fort Bliss cemetery.

When the widow's son Ignacio joined the Air Force and left for the war, he parked an old black convertible on St. Vrain in front of our mulberry tree and our street light. My friends and I looked the convertible over every day after they came home from school. I was still at home because children had to be six years old as of the first of September to start the first grade and I turned six on September 12. That meant that I was left alone in the apartment with minimal care from the neighbors and, sometimes, my grandfather López. No one complained unless I kept asking for food; there was never any food in my apartment. If there was anything in the refrigerator, it was a can of evaporated milk. I was always hungry.

We kept an eye on the *tartana*, the convertible jalopy, and played around it at first. By fall we realized that the widow, who did not drive, did not care if we got into the car. So we started out by leaning on the convertible to organize our play. Then we used it as the observation post to watch over our mulberry tree and our lamppost. Soon we took possession of the convertible. It became what tree houses and club houses were for other children.

We examined and fiddled with every knob, every pedal, and the shift stick, just as if we were learning to drive. We would take turns sitting in the driver's seat and pretending to drive. We would hold out our hands as we turned the steering wheel. Flaco, Pelón, Prieto, my brother Carlos, and I became masters of the jalopy. It pleased the neighbors because it removed us from the front of the apartments. The car became our metal playpen. Anyone looking for us found us there. And the widow was relieved to have us out of her flower garden.

Inside the jalopy we would sing, pretend, *charlar*, chat, and conspire. Generally, we acted out what we saw at the Wigwam theater or at the Alcázar. The Alcázar was known to us as the *calcetín parado*, the standing sock, because it was dirty and smelled so bad. It showed cowboy serials on Saturdays. If I went with the boys and was able to sit through the movie, we would have the material for our play. We had a whole repertoire of characters—Cantinflas, whom we had seen at the Colón theater, Jorge Negrete, the handsome cowboy singer and actor, Johnny Weismuller as Tarzan, and our beloved Joe Louis, the Brown Bomber. We would also take characters out of the comics such as Dick Tracy, Joe Palooka and Steve Canyon. Carlos and the boys would read the comics and create the scripts. We would spend a while before each play to set the general story, and we had a fixed way to begin each drama, which made it easy. Most of the time I was Tarzan's Jane, Roy Rogers' Dale, or the singer Toña la Negra. Some of our material came from events on St. Vrain Street. Once, the most famous *matador* in all of Mexico came to our block to visit a young pretty woman who lived across from us. The *runrún*, gossip, was that she claimed the bullfighter was the father of her *hija natural*, illegitimate daughter. She would tell how she had gone to a bullfight in the Juárez downtown ring and had caught the eye of the most popular bullfighter. No one believed her. Old López, who *le echaba flores*, wanting to flatter her, would humor her. Naturally, she was grateful to him for believing her.

One day, a big car pulled up behind our *tartana*. We thought someone had died. Instead of the mortician, an entourage of *caballeros bien vestidos*, well-dressed men, emerged from the black limousine. We looked them over. One of them seemed very familiar. Suddenly Carlos yelled that the man was the darling of the bullring. He was a superstar of the times. It was an occasion to be remembered by all the neighbors, and it was to be our drama for the week. I played the beautiful woman and Flaco was the bullfighter. Carlos would play bullfighting music on his comb covered with toilet paper and the others played the fierce bulls. Pelón's grandmother's red shawl was the matador's cape and a broomstick the killer sword. The neighbors who passed by could easily guess our plot.

When we tired of pretending we would relax in the jalopy and watch the *borregitos*, sheep-like clouds, as they scattered across the Segundo Barrio sky. We would take turns interpreting the big puffy clouds of spring and convince each other of what the shapes looked like. Many were ships, witches, animals, human faces, any imaginable thing. We would laugh like crazy when they would break up, for instance, when a nose broke off an identified clown.

By April the neighbors started to complain that I was dirty, neglected, and in need of supervision. They took this message to Palm with the suggestion that in the mornings I go to the nearby *asilo de niños*, a shelter run by nuns. Then Señora Alma the neighbor, who had lost her two sons in the war, could keep me until school let out for the summer. Palm thanked her for her kindness.

In the mornings I went to the *asilo*. The nuns taught me to color and would hit me with a ruler if I misbehaved: I was hit every day. After a lunch of pea soup and some french bread, I went to Señora Alma's. I hated the food with the nuns, but I knew that dinner at Señora Alma's would be good. Her daughters were in their twenties and preparing for marriage by cooking at home. Every evening, when Señora Alma said the dinner prayer, she thanked God that she had daughters and no more sons for the army to take.

Apparently, I had deplorable eating manners and the family couldn't stand it. So they set up a small table with a red and white checkered oil cloth in the pantry that all the apartments had. They explained why I couldn't eat with them, but told me I could rejoin them as soon as I learned manners. I was so unhappy. Sometimes I would try to sneak out to their table, but it never worked. I hated sitting by myself in the pantry where I could only hear and not participate in the wonderful conversations.

Even though I was with Señora Alma and her family, I played every afternoon until dusk with my friends in the jalopy. By May, the mulberries were ripe on our tree. We didn't like to eat them, but we loved to squash them with our *huaraches*. Each day before we played with tops or *baleros*, we would smash all the mulberries that the birds had caused to drop that day. The squashed mulberries would leave big purple spots on our sidewalk under our lamp post. It would be late summer before they would begin to fade. In the summer, those purple spots formed colorful designs for our *a la pata coja*, hopscotch, that we drew with caliche rock.

That June I returned home because my brothers were out of school and there were many kids to play with. Flaco's family became a source of interest for us. Flaco, who was Kiki, was the youngest in his family. López said that Kiki's birth had been a surprise; he was their *pilón*, small gift. There were already three older sons and an older sister who lived in L.A. Flaco's big brother, Juan, who had gone into the army two years before, had some distinguishing behaviors. He chewed Dentyne gum and he could pop the gum each time his molars met and he could do it as he talked. He wore taps on his shoes. When he walked, the taps would click as he popped his gum. We were in awe of his talents!

That July we heard that Juan had been injured in the war and his mother, Señora Olga, had received his purple heart. Flaco said that his mother had the purple heart but wouldn't show it to anyone because she was so bitter.

One day when we were talking in the jalopy, we planned a commando raid on Flaco's apartment—we wanted to see the purple heart. We talked about it and tried to figure out what it looked like. Pelón said he had seen a cow's heart in the Chinos market in Juárez. It was big. We could all just speculate on what the purple heart looked like.

In the afternoon, we made our plan as we ate some *cajeta*, soft caramel candy that came in a round wooden box, that López had brought from Juárez. As we scooped the caramel out with a broken part of the lid, we watched the apartment out of the corners of our eyes. Flaco said that Señora Olga was going over to the Canton Grocery on Stanton Street and she would be gone for a while. We were all afraid of Señora Olga. She was a mean, loud, dark brown woman with a large body that shimmered like a Russian brown bear dancing on its hind legs when she walked. And, like the bear, her face showed no expression. It was only when she opened her mouth that you realized she was angry. And by then, it was too late!

We waited until we saw her leave the apartment and disappear into the distance. Flaco opened the back door for us. The house smelled of beans and meat with chile that was pushed to the back of the stove top. This was for the men when they got home from work in the afternoon. Most of the women on the block did the same thing. The tortillas were made and wrapped up in a white cotton cloth by the sink, ready to become plates. We noticed the food and were tempted to take some, but we were in search of the purple heart.

"Where does she keep it?" I asked Flaco

"I think in the closet by the kitchen," he answered.

We opened the closet door. The odor of moth balls hit our noses and some roaches ran out. I let out a shriek. We looked everywhere in the closet and finally we saw a small, thin box. This couldn't be it. A purple heart would be in a bigger box.

"This is it. There is nothing new in here except this." Flaco held the slender box in his hand. We told him to open it, and he did. Inside the box was a medal and a folded letter. Flaco, who could read, looked at the letter and told us,

"This is it. A medal! This is a purple heart!" We stared in disbelief at a small gold medal with a silhouette of Washington hanging from a purple ribbon.

"*Chale*! No!" We all yelled angrily. Then we heard a loud roar behind us. "*Chale*! I'll give you *chale*!" The big bear grabbed for anyone she could. Since I was so small, I hit the floor and crawled past her. She got Flaco and Pelón. I ran outside, jumped into the jalopy and hid under the dashboard. After a long time the boys came to find me.

"What a *maderista*, liar, you are Flaco. That was no purple heart. It was just a medal." We yelled at him as we let him have it. "And you know what Flaco? From now on, your mother is *la Tamalera*, quarrelsome woman."

"She really gave me some blows!" complained Pelón.

We all started keeping an eye out for *la Tamalera*. That wasn't hard to do because she was everywhere and knew everything that was going on in our small neighborhood. The day would come when I would be glad she did.

Sunsets in El Paso are spectacular and intriguing. The sun does not bounce playfully like a Mexican persimmon on the horizon as it does on flat land like the south plains of Texas or on the west horizon of the ocean. In El Paso, the sun steals away like a truant child at recess. Old Sol dips behind Mount Franklin or Mount Cristo Rey. When I was young, it was as if the sun took refuge from me and my friends behind the huge figure of Christ when we weren't looking. We only became aware of its departure after the sky turned the color of a freshly sliced cantaloupe on a warm summer day. It was on one of these beautiful late afternoons that I chased the devil!

We were playing in our convertible. My friends and I laughed and tried to out talk each other until we were spitting everything we said. We all wiped our faces and laughed harder. The only world that existed at that moment was inside our jalopy.

Our block light came on suddenly, triggered by the setting sneaky sun, and caught our attention. We all looked up and then looked back at each other and started laughing and shrieking again. After the giggles subsided, I leaned back on the driver's seat, of which I was in command, looked up at the light, and smiled at my old faithful friend. We took its coming on and going off as naturally as we took the motions of Old Sol. Once, the summer before, the summer my mother died, it did not come on for two nights. Juanito said it was because someone had forgotten to pay the electric bill. Of course, I cried as any five-year-old would. That night Palm found me glued to the window that looks out on the light. He said that the light had blown out and that it only needed a new lamp.

"You must not cry about everything, Yoya. You can't listen to those *tontos* when they tell you stupid things," he said in a tired voice that I knew meant he was through discussing the situation. "They like to see you upset."

Palm went into the living room as was his custom when he returned from work. He lowered his lanky, tired old body into the brown uphol-stered chair with the fringed chenille cover. As usual, he turned on the brown wooden radio to some cowboy music. More often than not, I would make my way over to him and he would invite me to sit on his lap. I would braid the fringe on the chenille cover while we both waited to hear one of his favorite songs in English that I didn't understand. Two of his favorite songs were "No Letter Today" and "Born to Lose." I didn't care what they said. I knew he liked them and he tried to teach them to me. But I had no use for English, even though Palm told me that if I learned English, I would understand the cowboy songs and the movies at the Wigwam. I didn't care to learn.

Let's go back to that Saturday at twilight when one could hear the dogs barking in the distance, creating a hollow sound. The sun had got-ten away and my companions and I became aware of our surroundings—there were some pachucos standing next to our lamp post. They must have been standing there for quite some time but we had been oblivious to their silent presence. These *tirilongos*, dressed up gang members, were the older brothers of one of my friends in the convertible. They were waiting for night to begin so that they could go looking for *huisas*, girl-friends. Since they had nothing better to do, they were listening to our childish chatter. Then the *tirilis* began to laugh and talk to each other. We couldn't hear them well so we decided to get out of the jalopy and join them.

"*Póngansen trucho*, be alert!" whispered Prieto. "*Mis carnales son largo*," he warned us of his devious brothers. I did not understand. I was enjoying the feeling of being a girl in the midst of six *batos* under our lamp's vigilance. The pachuco Chato, who loved to tease me, spoke.

"*Watcha*, Gloria. Here comes a man." He gestured with his face in the direction of the street south of us. "He doesn't look like he's from around here," he said in a low, wet voice. "Ask him for some money."

"No, I don't want to," I answered sharply.

"*Andale, pirinola*, do it, little top," Chato urged me. By this time, the man was approaching us. You could tell by the way he carried himself that he wasn't from our barrio and was intimidated by the pachucos. He was just about to pass us when I was hit by an urge to be tough. All of a sudden I blurted out,

"Señor, will you give me some money, *por favor?*" I asked shyly with a winning smile.

The man stopped and nervously looked at my big smile. He returned a faint grin and looked around at the group. Annoyed, he put his hand into his pants pocket and drew out some coins. As I brazenly looked on, he picked out several coins, gave them to me, and walked away.

"*Gracias*, señor!" I said to the man's back. Clutching my coins in my hand, I looked at my companions and we all started laughing. We formed a huddle under our lamp to examine the money. Prieto counted the coins and told me I had twenty-five cents—enough for twenty-five pieces of gum!

"Yoya . . . Mira, look . . . the man is almost at the end of the projects. How could he have gone so far?" Chato yelled at me. "Maybe . . . maybe he is not a man." He paused as I stood frozen. "He must be *el diablo!* Only the devil could have walked that far in such a short time," he said in a pachuco singsong tone.

"*El DIABLO!* I took money from the devil!" I gasped.

I began running in my dried-out *huaraches* after the man. Crying and sobbing I yelled at the man as I nearly reached him. Wiping my tears, I cried out for *el diablo* to stop. He did and gave me a questioning look.

I stopped running and threw the coins that several minutes before had given me pure joy.

"Take your money! I don't want money from *el diablo*!" I screamed at him. I headed back toward my friends. They reached me as I walked, drained from the crying and sobbing.

"Yoya, he's not the devil!" shouted Carlos with a concerned look on his face. "He is not *el diablo*!"

"*Sí*, he is." I cried. "Look how far he went in a such a short time."

"He is a man. He walks fast," he said as he put his arm around my shoulders and tried to comfort me.

I cried all the way back to our lamppost. Trying to calm me down, my friends stayed and leaned against our jalopy for a while. Then someone's mother yelled in a loud voice for one of them to come home. Two dogs in the next block answered with continuous defensive barks. We looked at each other and they decided to walk me to my door. Carlos went off with the boys. Since there was no one at my house, I waited outside on the step. I did this almost every evening if I was the first one in. It had been over a year since I could go into the house by myself. My eyes were glued to the Virginia Street approach. I knew Palm would be coming that way. Soon I saw him. I felt my chest becoming heavy again. I had to control myself because I knew it would upset Palm if he saw me crying. I put my widest, minus-two-teeth smile on my face. He instantly recognized my *mascara*, mask.

"*¿Qué pasó, mi'ja?*" he asked in a tired voice.

Well, that was all this old man who looked like Gary Cooper needed to ask. (The only reason I had stayed and seen some of the Sergeant York movie at the Wigwam was because Cooper resembled Palm.)

"The pachucos scared me." I began to tell Palm my story. I told him about the man, the money, and the devil. The man was the devil even though Carlos said he wasn't. I explained that the devil had walked all the way to the end of the projects, three blocks, just like that. I snapped my fingers.

"Ay, Máma." Palm would call me Máma and Carlos, Pápa—I don't know why. He looked very seriously at my face. "*Mi'jita*, there is no devil," he reassured me. "Why do you listen to those pachucos. They are stupid. They just want to tease you."

"I know . . . but a man can't walk that fast." I said.

"*¡Basta!* You were deceived again. Just like the time after your *mamasíta* died and the *chavalos* got in the closet. You remember?" he asked in a firm voice. He looked straight into my eyes and said, "That time they brought you in the house where they had the radio in front of the closet door. One of those *tontos* talked and said it was your mother and the voice seemed to be coming from the radio. Do you remember?"

"*Sí*, Papá." I said with my head bowed. It *was* my mother.

Palm raised his voice and continued, "It was days before you could go back into the living room. All because you listened to those *pendejos!*" Eehh! He was angry! He never said that word.

"You were sick for a week! All because you believed your mother could be in the radio. Even after Padre Luna talked to you about death and your mother dying, you still were afraid of the radio." Palm was irritated with me.

Yes, Padre Luna had talked to me. He wanted to know what the voice had said. I told him she said she knew what my friends and I had been doing. He asked me in a very gentle voice if I had done something I didn't want my mother to know. I said that there wasn't anything. The only bad thing lately we had done was to wrap up some dog *caca* in some beautiful paper with a bow that Pelón had been given by his aunt and leave it on the doorstep for *la Tamalera*, Flaco's mother. Padre Luna nodded and said that maybe I felt bad about that. I said that it had not been my idea. We were afraid of her and we wanted to fool her.

"*Mi'jita*." Palm said softly to me. He seemed to understand that I was thinking about the past. I let out a big sigh. He kissed my head and patted it and then went inside. I waited a little and then I followed.

Inside, Palm walked over to his chair. He sat deep, the radio by his side. He pulled out his bag of tobacco. I ran over and sat on his lap.

"Let me, Papá," I said excitedly. I proceeded to make his cigarette. I slowly turned the paper to shift the tobacco more to one end. I laid it gently on the arm of the chair and I rolled the paper with the tobacco inside. I took care not to slobber and I carefully licked the free edge of the paper and slowly pressed the cigarette. Then I held my arm in a dramatic arch as I brought the cigarette up to my face and my mouth. Pretending to smoke it, I hoped to make Palm laugh.

"*¡Payasa!*" He smiled sweetly at me. He was relaxed. He put the cigarette down and got up from the chair and went into the kitchen. Palm poured some pure alcohol from Juárez into some water and he added a teaspoon of sugar. Palm said the sugar made the liquid taste better. He returned to the living room and found his spot in the chair again.

He picked up the cigarette I had made and prepared to light it with a wax match from a small box. My father puffed and puffed on the cigarette. The paper lit first, then the fire reached the tobacco and once again Palm had a smoke. He sighed a deep breath and I rushed over to blow out the match he held out for me. And, as always, he hiccupped after his first puff. And, as always, I asked "*Por qué te da hippo*, why do you hiccup?" And he would pretend that I was asking it for the first time. "Because I need to sip my drink." Then we would both laugh and he would hug me. I nestled in his arms, smelling the smoke of the cigarette and the faint odor of alcohol.

After he finished his drink and cigarette, Palm went into the kitchen and began fixing us some supper. I watched him since there wasn't much else to do. Whatever he brought home was what we would eat.

"*Mi'ja*," he began after a while. "When someone dies, they do not come back. Your *mamásita* died. She isn't coming back. And, at least, not in the radio." I felt uncomfortable again as Palm talked about the radio incident again. Then I felt bold for the second time that day.

"But you say that you talk to my mother every night."

"What?" he asked startled.

"*Sí*, Papá." If he wanted to talk about it, we would. "Every night when we go to sleep and you're changing clothes in front of the trunk in your closet in your bedroom, you talk. And when I ask you who you are talking to, you say . . . 'your *mamásita*.'

"*¡Ay Dios!*" he said. "I'm sorry, *preciosa*. I didn't think. I'm just talking to her memory in my head. I didn't know you would think that she was here."

"I thought she was in the trunk for a long time. I never wanted to go into your room. Then you opened the trunk and I saw only her clothes." I whispered, "I was afraid that she was going to be in there."

"Why didn't you ask me?" He looked at me with his white eyebrows in a puzzled arch.

"I did! You said you were talking to mamá," I said.

Palm gave up. He rubbed my arm and kissed my shoulder. His pale blue eyes were sad and he seemed so far away. I watched him silently.

"Gloria, people don't come back after they die. They're gone forever. I guess I should have taken you to the funeral. But, since it was in Juárez, I just couldn't think. It was too hard. But we have each other. And I love you and your brothers." He tried to comfort me. We sat in the living room listening to the radio until the clock struck nine. Palm was tired

and couldn't wait for my brothers. They would come home whenever
they did. I felt my fears less because we had talked.

In 1944, life in the projects was predictable and ordinary most of the
time. As the sky would begin to lighten up at dawn, the project apartments stuck straight up like black stalagmites against the pale yellow sky.
Mornings were always cool in the desert. By five, the *lechero* would pull
up in his milk truck sometimes in front of the jalopy or behind it. Our
jalopy was our evening sentry. By six, most of the men who worked in
construction or in the fields in Anthony, New Mexico, were walking with
their bodies tight to ward off the coolness of the dawn, their lunches
pinned under their armpits, toward the designated pick up corner. At
seven, Señora Elena walked out of her apartment with her pail of freshly
cooked *maíz*. She was on her way to the *molino* to get her corn ground
just like she wanted for tortillas or tamales. The slam of her screen door
was my wake up call. I would rush to the window to wave at her and then
dash to the living room to have Palm braid my hair. By eight, I was
already on the back cement step warming up my jacks game while the
señora on the corner hung up her wash after wringing it through the
robot-looking washer in her yard. It was just ordinary life.

In the projects, everyone knew everybody's business. The *huirihuri*,
idle talk, always seemed to convey the big picture but maybe not the
exact details. It was hard to be private when you lived in such close
proximity to others. For privacy, people drew their curtains if they had
them. Others didn't want privacy and opened their curtains so as not to
miss anything.

As I told you before, *la Tamalera* had three grown sons. Juan was the
recipient of the purple heart we tried to hunt down. The next son was
Eduardo, a pachuco who wore his hair in a pony tail as a *manda*, religious vow. He promised to wear his hair in that manner until God
brought back his brother from the war. The whole business of the
manda caused him problems with the other pachucos who wore their
hair slicked back with *pomada*. The pachucos teased Eduardo in order
to get him to wear his hair as they did. To avoid conflict with the
gang and the possible draft, Eduardo decided to go to live with an
uncle in Monterrey. Eduardo was as angry a person as his mother.
He wasn't like his father, a very quiet man who worked at night with
the Santa Fe railroad.

La Tamalera also had a younger son named Luís. He was eighteen, ten years older than my friend Flaco. A quiet and sensitive young man, Luís did not want to have anything to do with the gangs. When he graduated from high school in May, he got a job with a grocery store chain downtown. He didn't make much money, but he was very happy with his new job. He played the guitar and sang the songs of Augustín Lara and Jorge Negrete equally well. Many a Sunday evening we could hear him singing and playing his guitar. Like a big fat brown hen who is proud of her *pollito*, *la Tamalera* watched over her son. Luís wanted his music to help his mother forget about the war and her worries about Juan, who was in a military hospital in Denver. Whenever we had a blackout drill in the barrio and they turned the lights off, Luís would softly strum his guitar to calm his family and neighbors. I could be found sitting on my father's lap.

On July 4, some people at the grocery store where Luís worked gave a party. He invited Teresa from across the street to go with him. I don't think he had ever had a date before this one. Teresa was a pretty and sweet country girl from Zaragosa across the river from Ysleta. She was delighted to go with him, according to the neighborhood talk. Luís fell in love with her immediately and she seemed to like him, too. Luís took *gallo*, morning serenade, to Teresa outside her apartment. It was wonderful to wake up to the singing of the *gallo*. Eduardo and the group of musicians sang such beautiful songs to Teresa. That's the way you do it, the older people would say.

By August, Chillo, a cocky, slick pachuco, became interested in Teresa and *y se la ganó*, he won her away from Luís. She was flattered by the attention being Chillo's girl brought. All the boys and I were angry at her. Luís continued to seek her out until Chillo beat him up and Teresa told Luís to forget her. Then Chillo *se la robó*. He stole her virginity and made her his. Luís was heartbroken.

Luís was sick for about two weeks. By the end of the summer, he had quit his job; he lost weight and *la Tamalera* was beside herself. She took him to a clinic downtown and was told that Luís was sad. But she already knew that. Then she asked López to use his herbs or give him a treatment. I tagged along with López when he went to see the boy.

"Luisito, forget her. There are so many women in the world. *Esta no más es una*, this is just one woman." López told Luís. "Soon, another will be yours. *Sóbran mujeres*, there are many women."

"I appreciate your concern Señor López, but I don't think that you understand. *Ella se burló de mi*, she laughed at me," Luís said sadly.

"No, I understand. But what I'm trying to tell you is *no vale la pena.* Laugh back at her! Look at the *mierda* she ended up with! That should tell you something," López argued.

"No one knows what I feel . . . it's easy to give *consejos.*" Luís tried to end the conversation and he excused himself and went upstairs to his room. López talked with his mother and reassured her that time would heal Luís. Then he gave her some herbs and they said a prayer together. On the way across to our apartment, López sighed and was very serious.

"Ay, Yoya," López said in a low voice. "There is nothing more bitter than rejection."

"Has that ever happen to you, Tata?" I asked.

"Hmmmmm, *que si no*, and how!" He hummed that answer. "But, *carajo*, at my age, I know that there are many flowers on a bush. There is rarely only one. It's a matter of time."

"And, Luís, Tata?" I was worried about him.

"Ay, Luís is young. He will learn the hard way." López sighed and shook his head.

Luís listened to the radio in his bedroom all day and night. Because it was summer, the upstairs windows were open. The boys and I would sit on the ground, eating our cherry *nieve raspadas* thinking that we were keeping Luís company. It was hard when we would hear him cry. We usually left so as not to intrude on his privacy. Once in a while, we would hear *la Tamalera* talking to him sweetly, which shocked us since we were unfamiliar with that voice. Everyone on the block knew Luís's troubles. Every man would stop and give some advice. Nothing worked.

Then in September, Luís began leaving the apartment. He was unkempt and morose. He was playing his guitar again and sang painful love songs until midnight. No one complained. On September 16, Mexican Independence Day, he sang all night long. He sang only one song, "*Por un amor.*" It was a very popular song in 1943 about a person who is heartbroken. Even if people were aware he was singing only one song, they didn't care because they were too busy having fun.

At first no one realized that he planned to sing all night because there was a celebration going on. There was beer in ice in big tin tubs. There were also tamales, menudo, and *nieve raspadas.* There were also my favorite, *gorditas*, meat-stuffed corn tortillas. The next day, López talked to *la*

Tamalera for a long time and they agreed to ask Padre Luna to talk to Luís. Maybe he could reason with him. López was in the kitchen when Padre talked to Luís in the living room. My grandfather later told everyone what the two had talked about.

"Luisito, *qué te pasa?*" Padre asked, even though he already knew. He wanted to hear it from Luís.

"*Soy un hombre enganado, Padre*, I am a deceived man," he said sadly. "Life is not worth it."

"Don't say that, Luisito. It hurts me to hear you say that. Life is always worth it. It's a gift from God." Padre was trying to say something hopeful. "We all lose something in life. We have to find something to replace it. When I was young I had to leave Mexico, I thought I would die. . . ."

"Please Padre, don't bother yourself over me. I'll be fine. I'm just having a hard time accepting it." Luís tried to smile.

"Luís, you have a gift for singing. Use it to find meaning in your life. God shuts one door and opens another. You and Teresa were not meant to be. She's not the girl you thought she was." Padre would not give up.

"You're right, Padre," Luís smiled weakly.

Padre and Luís continued to talk until dusk. Luís agreed to see a doctor downtown. Padre would set up the appointment and come by later in the day to tell Luís what time the doctor would see him. Padre blessed Luís and then he left.

The next morning, Palm came into the kitchen from outside where he had been talking to someone. He seemed lost in thought. Carlos asked him what was wrong.

"Luís is dead," Palm said softly.

"What? How?" I blurted as I stopped eating a leftover tamale from Saturday's party.

"He went to Juárez and they say he darted into traffic and he was hit by a car. He died instantly." That was all they knew. Later, Flaco said that Luís had not been drinking. But it was better if people had thought that he had. People knew that Luís didn't want to live any longer, but they didn't want Padre Luna to know. I bet he knew anyway.

That evening, Palm told me to bathe and put on a clean dress because we had to go and sit with the family. They would leave for Monterrey tomorrow after the body was prepared in Juárez. I was full of curiosity and I didn't complain that Palm and I wouldn't have our time together. We crossed the breezeway between the apartments.

Palm wore his hat and I had my braids freshly made—I was in a party mood. Was I in for a surprise.

When we walked into the living room of the apartment, the atmosphere was very unfamiliar to me. Everyone was quiet and sad—the people who had been drinking and singing and happy two evenings before. I had to extinguish my smile when I saw Luisito's picture near the wall with the pictures of the family's favorite saints. El Santo Niño de Atocha and the Virgen de Guadalupe. On the table some short prayer candles were lit. The women were seated on the few available chairs; the men were standing with their hats on their chests or by their sides. Most of the women wore black and some had scarves on their heads. None wore any makeup. Most of them had rosaries in their hands and were praying silently. No one spoke. They only nodded in greeting as we entered the room. I could hear some dull sounds coming from upstairs, but I didn't pay much attention. I was confused because I could smell the food in the kitchen that people had brought over, just like they do for a party. It wasn't a party.

The room was full and I was holding Palm's hand. I kept thinking of Luís and the accident. Then from around the corner of the wall next to the stairs, there was a movement. A horrible cry shook the living room. I grabbed for Palm's leg and cried out to him.

"*¡Apá!*" I squeezed his leg hard.

"*Mi'ja*, it's all right. It's Luís' mother," he said.

I leaned forward past the legs of the grownups. I saw the large body of Luís' mother coming toward us. She was supported by her husband and my friend Flaco. They could barely handle her. Her face was a fountain of tears and she continued to cry at the top of her voice. She called out to God and the Virgin in the most agonizing voice. Then she collapsed to the floor. Her huge body crumbled into a heap.

"Ammonia, somebody get ammonia!" yelled one of the women who rushed to attend her. Just then, Padre Luna and my grandfather López entered the house. Padre went to the fainted woman and spoke gently to her. López went up to Palm and scolded him for bringing me along. My father said sharply that he couldn't leave me alone. López took me by the hand and told Palm that he was leaving with me.

"There are a lot of people there, Tata. They almost stepped on me," I said to López as we walked to my apartment. "Is it always like that?"

"*Sí, mi'ja.* There are always a lot of people when we are born.

There should be a lot of people when we die. The two are equally important." He seemed to be having a private talk with himself. "Now me, it'll be just as my father used to say. *Yo voy a morir sin sol, sin luz, y sin moscas*, I am going to die alone. Ha, ha, ha!" His laugh confused me. But indeed he was right. He contracted tuberculosis in 1949 and died alone in a remote *colonia* in Juárez.

La Tamalera wore black clothes for a year. She was in *luto*. *Estar de uto* is the traditional custom of grieving and it required black clothes and no joy. My friends and I would not play the radio whenever we saw *la Tamalera* coming our way. A couple of times, she became ill during the year. López said it was because of the *luto*. He said it was a dreadful custom that served little purpose.

I had nightmares for weeks. In my dreams, I would find myself looking for Luís near the railroad on Second Sreet. It was a place I feared because of the many trains that crossed there. In the nightmare, I was frantically looking up and down, trying to figure out where the trains were coming from and how I could avoid being hit. I would step onto one of the tracks to avoid a train only to find that I was in the path of another. Then suddenly I would hear Luís singing. I would see him in the distance, safely clear of the maze of tracks. He was dressed in a white shirt and black pants just like boys when they make their first holy communion. He had his guitar and he was singing the song he sang at the party.

Palm would hear my groans and come into my room. He would gently shake my arm to bring me out of the dream. And as always, morning would come to the projects and I would awaken again.

4   A Motherless Child

When it rains in El Paso, there is the most wonderful smell in the world.
It's a warm desert perfume that rises from the mixture of sands from
Mexico, New Mexico, and West Texas. In a good year, it rains about nine
inches. Because it rained so seldom, humidity was a strange experience
the first time I became aware of it. I recall feeling uncomfortable and
confused. I just didn't feel right. I thought something was wrong with
me until Palm assured me nothing was. It was just sticky, he told me, the
way it always was in South Texas where he was born.

The West Texas rain falls on the scrubs and cactus that have been here
ever since this area turned into a desert. A long time ago, someone
brought the Russian thistle to North America. It spread to the South-
west desert, where it found true love—lots of sun and little water, except
for the unexpected cloudburst. The Russian thistle has a cycle known to
all desert lovers. It first must grow and have a deep green life. Then it
dies. It becomes a blanched, dried-up plant and waits for the next
phase. The constant wind of the desert turns fierce when the days
warm up and it pulls the willing thistle skeleton out of the ground
offically to become the tumbleweed. It rolls at the speed of the wind.
Sometimes small tumbleweeds fly high in the air when a capricious
whirlwind gets a hold of them. Tumbleweeds roll, run, skip, and hop
until they get run over or get stuck in a doorway or under some steps.
In the spring, a child has to keep an eye out for the tumbleweeds that
roll into El Paso to race with cars and adventurous children. They
hurt when you collide with them.

April of 1945 brought the brief, gentle rains of spring that tease the
dusty earth. If it rained hard, I was to go to Señora Alma's house after
school because I couldn't stay dry in our jalopy. If it was a gentle rain,
I would dance my rain dance in the yard and let the drops fall on my
face. Rain was a treat!

One day that spring I went to Señora Alma's house because I knew they were having *chicharrones con chile verde*, pork skins in green chile. Señora Alma had invited me to come by after school and keep her company while she made dinner. Because I was always hungry I told her I would be there.

At five o'clock, Señora Alma arrived, crying and upset. She looked trashed and her dress was torn. She had fallen when she got off the streetcar and had smashed her groceries. I helped her take her things out of her *bolsa de red*, net shopping bag. I pulled the Purity bread out and was shocked to find it squashed completely flat. Señora Alma began crying again when she saw it. She had fallen on it and since it was so soft, it stood no chance.

"President Roosevelt is dead. That is why I am so upset," she said. "My eyes were full of tears after I saw the newspaper Extra that said he had died," she sighed. "What a tragedy!"

"What happened to him?" I asked innocently.

"He just died, Yoya!" she answered, annoyed by my question. "He had been ill and he died."

"But he is younger than Palm," I said in a halting voice. "Palm told me that he was ten years older than the president."

"Yes, but the president was ill." Señora Alma tried to reassure me when she sensed my concern.

"Now Truman will be president," she said to me. Then I remembered that López had told me how someone become president in Mexico— they killed the old one off and then they became president! I knew that Truman was responsible for what happened to Roosevelt. When Palm came home with the Extra edition that reported Roosevelt's death, I let him in on the secret.

"I know Truman made it happen."

"Ay, Gloria. No! That is not true. *Qué tontería*, what a stupid thing to say."

"Papí, you're older than the president. Are you going to die?" I asked, watching for any change in his face. "You're as old as López." I was shocked by my own words, especially because I would take offense when people asked me if Palm was my grandfather. I always answered sharply that he was my father.

"No, *mi'ja*. I'm just tired. But I'm fine. I have to be around to take care of you," he answered gently.

I looked at the picture on the wall behind Palm's brown chair. The picture showed an Indian on a horse at the end of a ride; they both looked exhausted. I thought that Palm and President Roosevelt were tired, too. Only, the president didn't have to worry about a seven-year-old little girl, so he died. Palm has a reason to live. Me! I hugged Palm and kissed his old face.

In May two terrible things happened to me. The first happened at the beginning of the month, one day when I was supposed to go to Señora Alma's after school. She wasn't there, so I sat on her front step and played with my *balero*, a small toy that consists of a stick, a string and a block of wood with a hole in it. López brought it from Juárez and for hours I would try to catch the block of wood on the stick. Pelón could do it almost every time. I couldn't.

Across the street next to our jalopy stood a cute pachuco from the neighborhood. He called out to me and asked me to come over and show him my *balero*. I went across the street and we sat in the jalopy. We played with the *balero* and time passed. Then he pulled out some ink and asked me if I would like him to put my initials on my upper arm. He said it would impress the boys.

"*Sí*, if it washes off," I said.

"*Simón*. It'll come off with soap and water. You can wash it off before you go to bed tonight," he convinced me.

He pulled out a needle and put my initials, GP, on the top of my right arm. It hurt but, I acted real tough. When the boys came, we began our *balero* competition. I forgot all about the initials on my arm because my dress sleeve covered it, but that night, after I took my dress off, I remembered them. I went to the bathroom and tried to remove them with soap and water. They wouldn't come off. I cried myself to sleep. In the morning, I looked again, hoping they would be gone; they weren't. After I made him swear on his mother's name to secrecy, I told Pelón about the initials. He said that the pachuco had used Indian ink. They would never come off.

The second bad thing happened on the last day of school in May. The sky was gray and noisy. I saw flashes of lightning and heard thunder as I walked to Señora Alma's apartment. There was a silver glow to the atmosphere that happens seconds before it rains in West Texas. I stopped at Señora Alma's but she wasn't there. Since I could see it was about to rain hard, I knew I should go to my apartment. I saw Pelón running to

beat the rain to his place; I laughed and yelled at him at the top of my
voice. I was excited and happy because of the silver magic of the impend-
ing rain. I sang a silly rhyme about Pelón loudly as I ran home.

Pelón,pelonete,
Cabeza de cuete,
Sale a la calle,
Y espanta la muerte.

Everyone on the block must have heard me. A dog barked and a
señora looked outside her door. It was not a smart thing to do, as I was
to find out. I reached my apartment and I closed the door. When I
turned around I saw *la Tamalera*'s son Eduardo in the living room.
He was the one with the pony tail who was supposed to be in Monterrey.
    "*Quiubole*, Yoya," he said *muy fresco*, real cool.
    "Are you here with my brother?" I asked as I looked around.
    "No, I just came in the back door, it was open," he said.
    "Well, my brother isn't home. I'll tell him that you're looking for
him." I was trying to figure out why he was there. "When did you come
back from Monterrey?" I was getting nervous. Outside I could hear the
rain beginning to fall.
    "Yesterday. Didn't Flaco tell you?" he asked.
    "No, it was the last day of school and I didn't see him." I kept won-
dering why he was in my apartment. I turned and started for the door
when he rushed to stop me. He grabbed my hands and he said in an
angry voice, "Let's go upstairs to the bedroom," he said as he dragged
me up the stairs. I knew I was in real trouble.
    "No, please Eduardo, no," I cried and begged.
    "*¡Callate!* If you don't, I'll hurt you. *Vale mas que coperes*, you better
cooperate," he said in a harsh voice.
    When we got upstairs, he took me into the boys' bedroom. He threw
me onto the bed and pulled my dress up. He was about to remove my
panties when he let out a yell. I opened my eyes, which I had closed out
of fear and because I was praying, and saw his head being pulled back by
his pony tail.
    "*Sinvergüensa, aprovechado*, shameless one, abuser!" *La Tamalera*
screamed as she pulled Eduardo off me. She slapped him and kept yelling at him. Then she took him downstairs and they went out the back
door. I straightened my clothes and went downstairs. I looked out the

window at the rain coming gently down. It made cups and saucers in the puddles just as Palm told me it does. Soon it stopped and because I was afraid of being in the apartment alone, I stepped outside and looked toward the jalopy. The boys were gathering to play in the water in the street or jump into the *charcos*, puddles. I took off my huaraches and threw them into the apartment. Doing my best Tarzan scream, I ran to join them at the curb. I jumped into the water that had become a big river and we were all Tarzans. Later, as I sat on the curb. I thought about what Eduardo had tried to do. I would never tell anyone; I was so embarrassed.

We played until it began to get dark and mothers were calling one by one for the boys to come home. The dogs were barking as the apartment lights were coming on. I went to sit outside my apartment on the cement step. When Palm came home, we went inside. He scolded me for staying outside while my clothes were wet. I went upstairs slowly and then ran into the bathroom. I took a bath and I thought about what had happened to me during the month. I looked at my tattoo and wondered if I could cut it off with a knife. I could say I fell and the skin got scraped off. But I was afraid. A couple of years later, my godparents would have the tatoo removed with acid.

I got out of the tub and put on my mismatched pajamas; I wanted to go downstairs and sit on Palm's lap. As I went down the stairs, I heard voices. *La Tamalera* and Padre Luna were in the living room talking to Palm. I became frightened. I looked at them and they stopped.

"*Buenas noches*, Padre," I greeted Padre Luna. I smiled at *La Tamalera* as I took a long look at her. I would never again see her as I had before that afternoon and I would never again call her *Tamalera*. I walked up to her and said, "*Buenas noches*, Señora Olga." I held out my hand.

"*Buenas noches*, Yoya," she answered in a soft voice as she took it.

"Gloria, we have told your father what Eduardo tried to do to you this afternoon," Padre Luna said.

I looked over at Palm who was sitting in the brown chair under the weary Indian. He looked so tired—just the way he looked when my mamacita died. Padre Luna said Eduardo was not well since Luís died because he blamed himself for not being here to save him. I didn't understand what he meant.

"Palm, you have to do something. Gloria is without supervision and she is going to get hurt. This time, she was lucky that Señora

Olga came in when she did," Padre told my father. "You're going to
have to find somewhere where she'll be safe. I talked to Señora Alma
about taking Gloria again, but she feels that she cannot because of
her health. I have talked with the *madres* at the shelter. Sister St.
Agnes María will keep Gloria until you can find a family to care for
her," Padre told Palm.

Palm lowered his head to hide his tears. Padre Luna drew closer to
him and he talked in a quiet voice. "It's too much for you to handle.
No one blames you. They just want to protect Yoya."

I turned to look at Señora Olga who was blotting her eyes with a
handkerchief. Her black dress reminded me of her grief last September.
She looked at me and waved for me to move closer to her. I went to
her without hesitation. This was something I would not have done
the day before.

"Gloria, I'm sorry for what Eduardo did. He is not well. We're sending him back to Monterrey where there is a good doctor. They will take
care of him until he gets better." She looked sadly at me. "We knew
when Juan got injured that he took it too hard. When we lost Luisito,
that was more than Eduardo could handle." She talked to me like she
talked to older people. I stretched myself up to listen to her. "He won't
bother you again," she said softly.

"I guess I shouldn't have come into the apartment. But, Señora Olga,
it was about to rain. Remember?" I explained.

"No, *mi'jita*. It wasn't your fault. Eduardo is not well. This war and
the death of my son has been too much for my family." She appeared to
be talking to herself. "Maybe we should have gone back to Mexico when
the war started."

They stayed for a little while longer. When they left, Palm and I sat in
his brown chair. He held me and we talked about the rain, cups and saucers in the puddles, and how much fun it was playing in the *charcos*. Then
we ate supper and we did our usual routine. That night I asked him if I
could sleep in his bed with him.

"*Sí*, but you better not snore," he joked.

I made snoring sounds all the way upstairs. Palm listened to my
prayers and kissed my forehead. I fell asleep to the sound of his voice
talking to my mother.

The next Monday after Padre Luna and Señora Olga talked to Palm,
I went to the *asilo* to be taken care of by the nuns. At first, the *asilo* seemed

cold and impersonal, even though I had made my first holy communion there a year earlier. First communion meant that I no longer could be excused of misconduct because I was a child. I had found the knowledge a heavy weight I couldn't explain. The morning of the ceremony, when Padre Luna put the holy wafer in my mouth, it felt so large and I was afraid to chew it. I couldn't swallow it. If it was the body of Christ, I couldn't chew it. But the look of love in Padre's eyes made me relax and it didn't matter how I swallowed it. But it was never easy.

The nuns were busy when I got to the *asilo* that Monday. Their daily chores made them unavailable for the countless questions of a seven-year-old girl. Suddenly, and without my consent, I was *la huerfanita*, the orphan. The nuns spoke of me in that way. It was as if I were wearing something new. It hurt my father when I told him my new name at the *asilo*.

The head of the *asilo*, Madre St. Agnes María, was an angel. Her soft, fair face peeked out from her white wimple and black veil. Her large black eyes reflected her Spanish heritage. She explained her lineage to me when I asked her why she spoke differently from the people on my block. Her order had fled Mexico during the revolution; Padre Luna had told the story on many occasions. Madre St. Agnes María was all business during the day; she did not hesitate to use a ruler on me. I was embarrassed when she did, but not when the other nuns did. When all the children were picked up at six, she would talk to me as if she were my mother. But as soon as Palm arrived to pick me up, she was a *madre* again.

One afternoon a week later, I felt sick and very tired. The sisters had gone somewhere and I was to wait in the hall for Palm to come for me. I fell asleep and woke to the concerned looks of Madre and Palm. I was sick with the measles for the next week and I stayed with the nuns.

By the end of my illness, Madre Lourdes María would come and stay with me until I fell asleep. She would tell me stories as she crocheted; she was a wonderful storyteller. When she told me the story of "*Caperucita Roja*, Little Red Riding Hood," I remembered Eduardo and being trapped by him in my apartment. I was relieved when she finished the story and I recalled how Señora Olga had rescued me. Later, I dreamed I was Little Red Riding Hood and the wolf was Eduardo, López was the grandmother, and Madre St. Agnes María was my rescuer!

Soon I was well enough to go back to my apartment with Palm. I missed the attention the nuns had given me, but I was glad to be at

home with my father and our usual routine. Palm was in better spirits
than I had seen him in a long time.

"Apá, why are you so happy? Is it because I'm home?" I loved to hear
him tell me nice things. And, I knew something was different. "Tell me!"
I asked him.

"Ay, Yoya. I am so glad that you are home. I have been very worried
about you even though I know all children get measles. It's just that you
are so thin and small," he answered. The public health nurse who came
to the *asilo* to put a quarantine sign on my door had told Palm that I was
undernourished and small for my age. She was glad there had been no
complications. I knew it hurt Palm to hear criticism of how he cared for
me. He did the best mothering he could.

After a while, Palm said to me, "Yoya, I have met a young woman.
She is from Delicias, but lives in Juárez with her brother. They live on
Mejía across from the bakery that you like." Palm was alarming me with
this information—surely he could see it on my face.

"You mean you have a *novia*, a *huisa*, a girlfriend? Just because I was
sick and not here. Apá . . ." I started to cry. Palm hugged me and tried
to console me.

"Yoya. She's just someone I met. It has nothing to do with my
love for you." He talked fast. "I have been alone for two years. My
children need a mother. Look how you had no one to take care of
you when you were sick."

"A mother! I don't need a mother, I have ten of them at the *asilo*!"
I cried. "And my brothers do not need anyone!"

"I just met her. That's all," he said as he turned up the radio to hear
a song he liked. I sat on his lap and thought of the story of *"Cenicienta,
Cinderella"* that *madre* told me. A *madrasta*, stepmother, was not what
I wanted. We talked about other things. I prayed that night that Palm
would forget the woman or that she would go back to Delicias.

One late afternoon in July, Palm came home with a young woman.
He called all of us home and explained that he had married her in Juárez
that morning. She was here to stay with us.

"This is Carmen. She is from Delicias." He smiled at her and at us.
I didn't care where she came from. I did know what I wanted: *que se vaya
a la porra*, that she go to the devil! No sooner did I think that than I felt
bad. I noticed Palm looked so much younger. Carmen was very young,
skinny, and simple. She looked all one color in the brown dress she was

wearing. I stood up and extended my hand to her. I said the most polite greeting that people use when meeting someone new; I wanted to please my father. His bony chest pushed out as he smiled at me. I was already regretting my introduction. My regrets grew with each passing day as this new wife disrupted the wonderful routine Palm and I had had before she came. She was very quiet and didn't seek me out. I tried to talk to her, but she would only give me short answers. Soon, I only spoke to her when I needed something.

The routine of the summer was what interested me. I played all day with the boys. Our main interests were cowboys and *las calaveras*, a serial with skeleton-costumed men. Each Saturday we went downtown to the Alcázar, the Wigwam, the Ellenay, or the Colón to see the movies. Then we would come home to our jalopy and play the characters we liked. And, because I was always the singing heroine, we would stage cowboy musicals filled with Mexican songs. "Jalisco" was the one we did best. We would sing at the top of our voices and the neighbors would come out to cheer us on. It was the best of summers. Ever since my bout with the measles, I had seen things differently. I didn't know what the difference was, but it was there. I felt more real and things were clearer. Palm said it was because I was getting older.

Two weeks later on August 15, 1945, the war ended. Everyone was yelling outside their apartments. The gaiety was contagious. We all shouted: Viva America! Viva Uncle Sam! Happily we gave up our plays about the war. No more "Johnny got a Zero!" yells. No more stamps to buy with our dimes at school for liberty war bonds. (My book only had five stamps in two years.) No more air raid drills. Later that night, I heard a pistol shot followed by a blood curdling yell proclaiming in vulgar terms how tough Americans are: I was embarrassed.

Palm was hit by the excitement of the end of the war. He became optimistic that business in *ropa usada* was beginning to pick up. He had just survived several years of pain over my mother's death and he had a new wife. He was feeling high, so high that he went out and bought a new car for two hundred dollars. That was a lot of money in 1945. It was a black sedan, big and rounded, with four doors and running boards on each side. I was beside myself because the boys were so impressed. I was proud we had a car, but I soon realized that he had bought it to impress Carmen. López, who hadn't come to the apartment since Palm had married Carmen, came by to see the car.

"That's all the money you have, Palm." López informed his annoyed son-in-law. "*¿Qué estás loco?*" Palm ignored the question because he felt so good with his new life. Having a bride who was impressed made him even happier; she had never known anyone who owned a car.

Palm brought home for Carmen the best of his used clothing. She was pleased and accepted everything he gave her. What she didn't want, she gave to her relatives. They would drop by during the day when Palm wasn't home. Then, she was talkative and cheerful. She and her relatives seem to enjoy some joke and whenever I entered the apartment, they would all be quiet. I sensed something, but I didn't know what. The neighbors talked about Carmen, but they would shut up whenever I tried to listen.

"My mother says that Carmen married your father just so that she could come over to this side," Prieto confided to me. She is just interested in what your father can do for her."

"*Qué te importa*, what business is it of yours?" I defended Palm. "My father is handsome and he has money."

The summer of 1945 came to an end and as September arrived I found myself unhappy with a stepmother whom I didn't know well and resentful that I had to share my beloved father with her. I wanted her to die and then I became afraid that she might because I wished for it. When I went to confession one Saturday with Padre Luna, I confessed my evil thoughts to him. I related all the gossip the boys had told me. He asked me to try to accept Carmen. Then he gave me extra penance for wishing her harm. I accepted the penance with courage because doing it kept me from feeling bad about my thoughts.

The summer brought the end of the war and I was growing up. Maybe I would understand more in the second grade. All I knew was that I didn't have to worry each night about the Japanese attacking the Segundo Barrio while I slept.

5   The Trouble with English

In the Segundo Barrio during the 1940s, people spoke Spanish. They spoke the Spanish they brought with them from their *ranchos*, villages, and cities. They also brought the music of their accents. You could tell by the quality of their speech whether they were country or city people. Spanish in the 1940s in south El Paso was formal and polite. People apologized if they said a word like *estúpido*. I would often wonder why that required an apology. And I would be told that people from rural areas are not open with criticism and do not want to offend with what they consider vulgar language.

When people left the barrio, they began using English more. You still spoke Spanish at home because that was what your family used. Then when you spoke with someone who also spoke both languages, the language evolved to a mixture of English and Spanish that became an art form. Sometimes sentences might be in one language with certain words in the other. Other times whole paragraphs might be in one language and only a few sentences in the other. It was a living language, a musical score that conveyed the optimal sense, meaning, and feeling from both languages that a single language might not achieve. The combination drew criticism from purists and people who did not speak both. They accused the bilingual person of being lazy or undisciplined. But I think it was a love for both languages that made it impossible to be faithful to just one. On the other hand, cussing or profanity were best in English. The words were just words to me. Cussing in Spanish was painful and created emotions that led to guilt. And, it was unacceptable to our parents and priests.

The first time I remember having problems with English was the year before Carmen came to live with us. At least once a week Palm and I would have a talk about why I wasn't learning English. I saw no reason to. I had to experience a need for it, and that is what happened.

43

"You have to learn English, Gloria," Palm would say.

"I don't want to. I don't have to. I don't need it," I would stubbornly refuse.

"I suppose you didn't need it at the border on Saturday when immigration held you after you were in Juárez with López and you couldn't answer their questions?" he said firmly. "I had to leave the store to go and get them to release you. All because you can't carry on a conversation in English."

I had created problems for Palm and myself, but I didn't want to learn English and that was that.

On this particular morning, I waited for Palm to get tired of the topic and to move on to something else. But he didn't. He continued.

"The note the teacher sent home says that you will not speak English. She says that everyone speaks for you. And she says that you talk all the time, but in Spanish! It's been a month since school started and she says you will not cooperate. She says she is going to have to punish you. She wrote to inform me that she is at the end of her patience with you," Palm said.

"So that is what the *mugre*, dirty, note said. I thought she liked me," I said as I thought of how she and I grinned at each other every day. I didn't understand what she was saying and she didn't know what I was saying. She could have been speaking Chinese just like the Chinos near the Cuauhtemoc market in Juárez. I just didn't want to speak English.

"It sounds ugly. And I look stupid speaking it," I admitted when I saw the look on Palm's face.

"It's because you don't use it enough to get used to it," Palm tried to explain.

"My friends and I don't need to speak it. We have our own way of speaking." I continued the argument until I noticed that Palm was frustrated and quiet. I decided to play. I put my left hand on my hip and shook my right index finger menacingly.

"Wo do bo to do ri ra do fo, da mo, meeester!" I said in gibberish. "Ha, no, meeezter?" I raised my eyebrow and looked at Palm. "That's English!"

"*Payasa*. You are very stubborn. You need to learn English." Palm started up again. "My son is coming to visit and he speaks English."

The last remark caught my attention. I turned my eyes to the picture of Palm's son, which was displayed in a large oval frame. He resembled

Palm. I wondered why he was only my half brother. When I was younger, I thought it was because only the upper part of his body was in the picture. Palm corrected me. He told me his son had a different mother and was the only one of his children who stayed in touch with him. He loved Palm very much and would write to him every week. He was the youngest child and had been in college when my father went to Mexico. Palm's son's light eyes seemed to follow me around the room.

Palm was still talking about a visit from his son when I found my voice and said. "*¡Que suave!* When he comes, I'll tell him all about me and the neighborhood." Palm just nodded his head and gave me a strange look.

The next week, when I got home from school, I was frightened because I thought someone was in the apartment. But Palm called to me when I pressed my nose against the screen to look inside.

"*Entra, mi'ja.*" Palm's voice was happy. I pulled the screen door open and entered the living room. A man was with my father. He looked like my father but he wasn't old; he looked familiar. Then, suddenly, my eyes turned to the picture on the wall. I looked at the man and I looked at the picture. They were the same!

"*¡Hola! ¿Cómo estás?*" I yelled with happiness as I ran to hug the stranger. He returned the hug. I was overjoyed. Palm was telling the truth about his son coming to visit. Here he was . . . all of him!

Palm's son opened his mouth and said something to Palm who was telling him something too. They were speaking Chinese!

"Apá, tell him that I speak Spanish," I told my father.

"Yoya, he knows." Palm spoke slowly because he knew how I would react. "He doesn't speak Spanish. He only speaks English. I told you many times."

I was speechless. What a dirty *trampa*, trick!

"Didn't you tell him I didn't speak English? Did you forget?" I questioned my Palm as the other Palm looked on with the biggest and sweetest smile. How could he not speak Spanish? I started to cry, but the other Palm understood as my father told him in Chinese what the problem was. Palm's son laughed as he picked me up and kissed me as he said something to my father. I looked to Palm for a translation.

"He says you're as precious as he knew you would be. He's sorry that he can't speak Spanish. He has never been able to learn," my father said.

I hugged his son and just watched them as they talked. Occasionally, Palm would tell me what they were saying if he thought it might interest me. I just kept looking into our visitor's beautiful face. My little chest was heavy with the weight of my broken heart. I had so wanted to be able to talk with him. I couldn't believe it. And I knew Palm had warned me.

When the sunset, the color of a West Texas sweet potato flesh, began to spread across the barrio, our visitor said he had to leave. We went outside. Palm's son picked me up and kissed me. Palm softly told me what his son was saying to me.

"He says he loves you, Yoya. He hopes that when you meet again, either you'll know English or he'll know Spanish."

I hugged and kissed my favorite visitor back. It would be many years before I would see him again and it would be long after our father's death. But on this evening, my father and I watched him as he walked to Virginia Street where he had parked his car. Palm and I sat on the cement step. As the car pulled off with my half brother, I turned to Palm and said with determination and sadness,

"It's time I learned English, Papí."

"*Sí, corazón*, yes." He understood.

English continued to be a problem for me for the next few years. In September of 1945, after Carmen came to live with us, my friends helped me with a clever solution.

The morning glories in the widow's garden were the true sign that September was here. The little blue-purple flowers were spreading and growing anywhere they could. The roses were also in bloom, which indicated that it was not a hot September in El Paso. The nights were cool and the windows of the two-story apartments were open all day. School started and my English was not as good as it had been when school let out in May. During the summer, I lost some English vocabulary because I didn't use it. I had only been back in school two weeks and the teacher and I had already gone around and around about my speaking Spanish.

"English is spoken in school . . . even when you are speaking to your friends, young lady!" the teacher snapped when she eavesdropped on a conversation I was having in the closet of our classroom. I had just commented to Raquel that I wished I could get a new coat this winter just like the one she had last year. The teacher appeared from nowhere and caught us speaking Spanish. So, Raquel and I had to each stand in a

corner of that stupid closet during recess. You may as well have put me
in front of a firing squad because it hurt just as much to miss recess.
"*Dísparen*, fire!" said the teacher *commendante*, in my fantasy. "Only
English is spoken in school, in El Paso, in Texas and in America,
entiendes, do you understand?"

My pledge of allegiance had already earned me a note home to my
father. In the note, Palm was informed that my version of the pledge was
a mockery. How was it possible that he could not teach me such a small
task? Would he or his wife please teach me the pledge? The note said,
"Gloria enjoys the laughter and disruption she causes each morning."
Palm smiled when he read the part about Carmen teaching me the pledge.

"Gloria, let me hear the pledge." He wanted to hear for himself what
the problem was. Palm listened with interest and smiled a couple of
times. When I was finished he put on a serious face and talked to me
about my presentation.

"You mix the words around . . . you move the words in your pledge."
Then seeing the puzzled look on my face, he said, "You take a word out
and put the wrong one in its place." He struggled to explain. "You don't
know what you are saying. Didn't the teacher explain?"

"I guess that she did . . . but I didn't understand her Chinese."
I replied, trying to be clever. "You explain it to me."

"Stop clowning! And stop calling English Chinese. You're not funny
anymore," he said, annoyed. It took a long time but he tried to explain
what each of the words meant and in what order they went. But each time
I tried to say the pledge I would make new revisions. I couldn't get it right.

"I will give you a *tostón*, a walking Liberty fifty cent piece, if you learn it
by your birthday. That gives you a week. Practice saying it with your friends
and you will get the fifty-cent piece." He knew that I loved the walking lady
silver coin because I loved what it could buy. That would encourage me to
learn the pledge. For that much money, I agreed immediately. I started
thinking of how I would spend the money. My dreams were full of fifty-cent
pieces that night: beautiful silver ladies dancing with silver stars all around.

The next day, I met the boys at the jalopy. I told them what the
teacher had done and what Palm had promised me if I learned the
pledge. They were impressed with the money. We quickly made plans
on how to spend it. It could easily buy us all *raspadas*, ice cones, and some
gum. Or it could pay for all of us to go to the movies on the Saturday
after my birthday. It was endless, what we could do with fifty cents.

Then my brother Carlos, who was the oldest and a fourth grader, reminded me that I had to recite the pledge correctly in order to get the money. We all agreed that it was a problem since I didn't understand the words. So each of them proceeded to recite the pledge slowly and carefully, right in my face. They put a great deal of acting into the words. Still I didn't say it correctly any of the times I tried.

"I guess you want to put me in front of the firing squad just like the teacher would like to," I said, explaining my fantasy to them. They liked the idea and said why didn't we take time to play the scene. They would shoot me down if I didn't learn the words.

Carlos and I went home to get broomsticks and hats. Flaco was to get a handkerchief to put across my eyes. Pelón was to bring back his cowboy holster for Carlos, the *commendante*. We agreed to meet after lunch. I hoped that Carmen had something for us to eat because all the pledging had made me hungry.

After lunch we gathered at the jalopy. Carlos was in charge. The other boys were the soldiers who helped me learn and they were also the members of the firing squad. It was agreed that we would break the pledge into parts. As soon as I learned a part, we would move on to the next part. They were very relieved when they discovered that I had no problem with the first part.

"I pledge allegiance . . . ," I began well. "To the republic . . ."

"No . . . No! To the flag . . . the *bandera*, Yoya! Flaco would yell. "*A la pared*, to the wall." We walked over to the jalopy. I stood in front of it. Prieto put the handkerchief around my eyes and said a prayer for me with his head bowed.

"That is not necessary!" barked Carlos as he yelled for the men to ready themselves. "Shoot! *A toda ametralladora*, like a machine gun."

"We only have rifles, Commander," Flaco yelled sharply.

The rest of the afternoon went like that. Each time I made a mistake, I faced the firing squad. It was a lot of fun. By the time the sky started to turn the color of a Sinaloa mango, I had thoroughly exhausted the group. I didn't want to play any more. Let Palm keep his *tostón*. But the boys said we would try again the next day. Carlos would think about the problem.

"Palm said you have to learn it by your birthday?" asked Flaco. "When is that?"

"In a week, I think," I answered. "It's September the 12th. Pretty soon, no?" Carlos nodded yes.

"Are you having a party?" asked Prieto.

"I have never had a party. Not that I know of," I said.

"Don't you want one? A party with a *piñata*," Carlos added. "We can ask Palm."

"Yes, but I don't think I am going to have one," I said sadly. "It would be nice. Don't people bring gifts?"

"Yes, let's plan a party. We'll make invitations and take them to the neighbors," Flaco said excited by the idea. "Palm will have to give you a party!"

"Yes, *cómo que no?* He got a new wife and a new car. He can give me a party," I said bravely. "And we'll tell everyone to bring a present. No gift . . . don't come!"

The next day we met at the jalopy. No one could find any paper to make the invitations, so we simply went to all the neighbors' houses and invited them in person. Flaco was in charge of telling them to bring a present. I felt it might be *falta de educación*, lacking manners, for me to say it. Then we agreed that I had to tell Palm that evening. I became a little uncomfortable with that idea. But who cares, that's how he told me he had a new wife and a new car.

We got back to the problem of the pledge. Once again, we set up our scene. Carlos encouraged me with whispers and yelled at me when I missed. The rest of them loved it when they had to execute me.

"Young lady, that is not right!" Carlos would imitate his teacher. "Now, say it after me. Indivisible is what you should say, not invisible. Invisible means you can't see it, Yoya!" Then he gave up. "Let me explain it to you in Spanish, but you must say it in English. Spanish will not be right." Soon, we stopped the play and talked about the party until I saw Palm coming home. Carlos and I turned to meet him.

"Tomorrow we'll sing the pledge . . . for sure you'll learn it then," said Pelón. He was inspired by the idea as he went off singing the pledge to play with Flaco in his apartment.

After dinner, Palm and I were sitting in the living room while Carmen was cleaning up the dishes. Palm took out a pack of cigarettes that he had bought at the store. Carmen didn't like the smell of the ones we made so he bought Lucky Strikes just to please her. They were so fat and smooth, unlike our homemade ones. And she didn't let him fix his one drink anymore. He didn't complain. She certainly had changed things.

Palm asked me how my pledge was coming along. I told him about the game the boys and I had made of it. He smiled as he always did when

I would tell him about our plays. He explained the word indivisible with
the box of cigarettes he had just opened. And he explained the word invisible by telling me it was like the ghosts I saw that no one else saw.
I softly hit his arm for saying that, but I finally understood. When he
asked me to recite the pledge to see if I had learned it, I refused. I told
him that I wanted to surprise him on my birthday. And speaking of my
birthday, the boys and I thought it would be nice if I had a party.
We invited the neighbors today. What did he think?

"A party, Yoya! Whose idea was that?" He muttered some nasty words
under his breath. "I don't have the money for a party. Where am I going
to get the money?"

"You had the money for the car. All we need to have is a piñata, candy
for the piñata, a cake and some Velvet ice cream. The big people will
want some *cerveza*. I will ask López to bring some from Juárez. Everyone
will be happy. Especially me." I tried to solve the problem. When Palm
didn't answer, I continued to give him ideas as to where to get the things
for the party. "The cake can be bought at that bakery at the corner from
you. López can bring the piñata from Juárez."

The poor man couldn't answer. Then Carmen came into the living
room. She saw how Palm looked and asked what was the matter. I didn't
really want to tell her, but I didn't know what to do about my father's long
face. So I told her about the party. She started laughing, something I had
never seen her do before. It made her seem real. She told Palm what a
clever child I was. She said that she had always felt bad because she
didn't have a party when she was eight. Her family and some friends
in Juárez could bring the cake. Carmen's excitement lifted my father's
spirits. I was grateful to her for that, but at the same time I was surprised.
He laughed. After a while, he said that since I had already told the neighbors and since Carmen was so happy to give the party, that it would be
all right. He just didn't like parties that he couldn't afford.

"Your birthday is in a week, but we can't have it then because it is a
Wednesday. We'll have to wait until Saturday September 15. That is also
the night before Mexican Independence. You remember how many
people were in the neighborhood last year?" he groaned. "Now for sure
I know I can't afford it."

I started thinking about the year before. The terrible thing that
happened to Luisito in Juárez. I hadn't thought about it in months.
It seemed like it was so long ago that we went to sit with his family.

I wondered if Señora Olga would join us in the backyard. It was ten days until my first birthday party. It seemed like a long time.

The next day at the jalopy, the boys and I tried singing the pledge and making each of the boys represent one of the words that I couldn't get. Pelón had a small flag that his rich cousin had given him when he went to visit him on the 4th of July. The boys formed a line that represented the flag, republic, nation, liberty and justice. The flag was in Pelón's hand and he was also the republic. Flaco was one nation and indivisible. Prieto was liberty and justice. Pelón was the first, then Flaco and then Prieto. All I had to remember was the order of the boys by their age. Carlos, the commander, was in charge and the one who thought of the idea. By the second time, I could say it without any mistakes. I jumped around and fought an invisible boxer just like the Brown Bomber did. Then we started planning how we would spend the money.

On Sunday, the widow came over and talked to Palm. She told him that Eduardo was coming home next week and that the rest of the neighbors wanted to help with my party and get together with the boys home from the war. She said the whole neighborhood wanted to do the midnight cry that begins Mexican Independence. Everyone was going to pitch in with the grownup part of the party after Yoya and the children had their piñata. Palm was relieved and thanked her for her help.

I was so excited for the next couple of days. The teacher was happy that I could recite the pledge and had stopped clowning around. On my birthday that Wednesday, I said the pledge for Palm and he was proud of me. He gave me the fifty cent piece. I also said it for López, who did not speak English. He kissed me and said that I looked pretty saying it. Because I wanted Carmen to make me a good party, I was on my best behavior. Friday afternoon, the boys and I bought *raspadas* and gum with my money. On Friday night, I went to sleep wondering if Señora Olga and Señora Alma would be at the party. The two women detested the war; no medals made up for their losses. Only the widow's son came back without any wounds.

6   A September Party

Let me tell you about the Mexican ethnic heritage as I understand it.
First we were Indians—Aztecs, Mayans, Tarascans, Zapotecs and
Mixtecs. That was the base. Then came Hernán Cortés and Spanish
culture was introduced to the Indian. Later came other European groups
that mixed with the Indian culture. Most of the Mexican population has
some Indian background even if it isn't acknowledged. My grandfather
López used to tell me that before the glorious Revolution of 1910,
people were quiet about their Indian blood. He, for one, never denied
it; his heritage was obvious.

There were three revolutions in Mexico. The first was for independence from Spain, celebrated on September 16. Then due to a lack of
money during the government of Benito Juárez, France took its debt
payment by taking the country. There was a second revolution for
independence. That victory is celebrated on May 5. The third revolution
took place in 1910. The Indian identity emerged like a phoenix and
the rule of modern Mexico rose from the ashes of revolutions.

Mexican-Americans in the barrio in the 1940s usually observed Mexican
national celebrations. With Juárez a stone's throw away, everyone was aware
of patriotic celebrations of the fatherland. They listened to the radio in
Spanish and read the two Spanish newspapers: *El Fronterizo* and *El Continen-
tal*. After all, the only thing that kept the Segundo Barrio and Juárez apart
was a river and a bridge. And for many, they didn't even exist.

The only national celebration we observed on St. Vrain was September 16. To have become independent from Spain was the greatest triumph.
Racial resentment of the invasion of Cortes and the defeat of
Montezuma II ran deep in the Mexican identity on our street. It was
almost rivaled by the resentment that followed the loss of more than half
of Mexico at the hands of that incompetent Antonio López de Santa
Anna, the general at the Alamo. During his administration, Mexico lost

to the United States Arizona, California, Colorado, Nevada, New Mexico, Texas, and Utah. For one hundred and fifty years, Mexicans have tried to return to those states either legally or illegally.

Saturday morning, September 15, 1945, began a long day that would stay with me for the rest of my life. After having some *atole*, I went outside to find the boys. Flaco was at Señora Olga's table having a *pan dulce* with some Mexican chocolate. I licked my lips hoping Señora would offer me some. That didn't happen. Flaco got up and ran outside to greet me. He gave me a bite of his bread and I had to be satisfied with that.

Flaco started to whistle in a telegraphic style that all the boys in the neighborhood seemed to understand. He whistled so loudly that I had to cover my ears. Soon Pelón stuck his face outside his door and whistled in the same fashion. It was almost like talking for them.

"Flaco, now that I have my two front teeth back, I need to learn how to whistle," I said to him. "Then I can talk with the boys like that."

"You have to know how to curl your tongue and tuck your lips. That is all there is to it," he said. "Let me see you curl your tongue."

I tried and was still trying when Carlos came up to us. He saw what I was doing and slapped his forehead.

"Oh, no! It was hard enough to teach her the pledge. I will not teach her how to whistle like us. She can just purse her lips and whistle like girls do," he stated in a firm voice. "Whistling like we do will make you look ugly, Yoya. Do you want that?" My brother was wise. He knew the right question.

"No, I don't want to learn anyway," I conceded. "What are we going to do until the fiesta tonight? Palm doesn't get home until six. López will be here in the afternoon with the piñata. What shall we do until then?"

Prieto arrived with a baseball bat. This was to be the weapon to slay the piñata. The boys acted real *macho*, claiming that their blows would make the piñata rain its goodies to the ground. They stretched and strutted around with the bat, intimidating me because of my size.

"They are really going to need to lower the piñata for you to hit it, *chaparra*, shorty! They're going to have to take it all the way to the ground," Pelón said as his arm made the sweeping motion of a baseball umpire just above the ground. He broke up with laughter. My hands went to my hips and I stood my ground. The boys all laughed at how Pelón *me agarro el chivo*, got my goat.

Just then, we became aware of Señora Olga's loud voice at her back door. The recipient of the aggressive talk was the woman who lived next door. Señora Olga's voice was so loud that we stood frozen, waiting to see what she would do next. Her mourning dress made her very threatening as she waved her arms, but the neighbor seemed determined to stand tall in her argument. The boys and I knew that was pointless— no one outshouted or outtalked Señora Olga.

"Flaco, what is wrong with your mother," I asked.

"I don't know. My father says that it's because it was a year ago that Luisito died. Don't you remember how he sang all night long a year ago today?" he asked sadly and we nodded that we did. "Her *luto* is over today or tomorrow. My father hopes she comes to the fiesta tonight. She has been fighting with everyone. My father says that *ella no puede hallar su lugar*, she can't find her comfortable place."

"Maybe López can go and ask her to come. She seems comfortable with him," I said. "Ever since my mother died and Luisito died, they have valued each other. López says they understand each other's loss."

Señora Olga stopped yelling and we looked over to see what was happening. She was looking across the street at Teresa. Looking very pregnant and intimidated because she sensed Señora Olga's eyes upon her, Teresa was walking by as fast as she could in her advanced condition. Chillo, the pachuco who stole Teresa, had been sent to prison three months before along with five of his gang friends. He never married her and that made it even sadder for those who loved Luisito. He would never have done that to her. Slamming the door, Señora Olga went into the house.

A taxi pulled up at the curb behind our jalopy. Dressed in his army uniform, the real owner of the old convertible stepped out. Ignacio was home! A chill went down our spines as we realized that our jalopy was no longer ours. Ignacio looked across the street at Teresa and waved to her. She waved back and hurried on down the street. He looked puzzled after her. Flaco said that they had dated a couple of times when he was home on leave. That was before Luisito and Chillo. Ignacio had four suitcases and boxes. We ran to help him carry the luggage. He looked at his jalopy and a horrible look spread across his face.

"*Qué le pasó a mi carrucha?*" he gasped. "*Está toda destripada*, it's gutted."

"It has rained and the wind has blown," Carlos tried to explain. "You know how nothing survives the wind and sand." He took a deep breath, "And you have been gone a long time."

"Did you have a tornado?" Ignacio asked sarcastically. "Did a hurricane hit El Paso? Oh, my God!" He shook his head as he picked up the boxes. We rushed to help him and to distract him from the old wreck.

"Carlos, what is going on with Teresa? Did she get married? My mother never wrote me that," Ignacio asked in a disappointed tone. "Is she pregnant? Boy, what else has changed?" He paused, "*No me digas.* I don't want to know."

We walked silently with Ignacio to his apartment. The widow opened the door and started crying. Nacho hugged her and said loving things to her but she was unable to stop crying. We took the things inside and left quickly because we felt uncomfortable.

We decided to go home to see if we could help our families get ready for the fiesta. I felt tired and wanted to be alone a little while so that I could figure out how to break the piñata with one huge blow. I knew a can of spinach would give me the muscles of Popeye and then I could prance around and break the piñata with a little tap. That would show the boys who was tough. But we didn't eat spinach. I didn't even know what it was.

Carmen was busy in the kitchen, so I went upstairs to take a bath. I didn't have any new clothes and everything I had looked dingy. Palm didn't know how to sort clothes well, so everything was washed together before Carmen came. I took out the little dress Palm brought me home on Wednesday. It would do, although it had a big seam where the dress had been repaired. But it was better than nothing. I dressed and went to watch Carmen fix herself up. She rolled her hair into big rolls on each side of her face, as many women in the forties did. She made the rolls bigger with *ratas*, material stuffing.

"Are you a pachuca, Carmen?" I asked. Pachucas used *ratas* to make their rolls bigger.

"What a stupid question," she said in an angry voice.

"Pachucas wear *ratas*," I said innocently.

"That's not true. I am not a pachuca." She ended the talk as she spit into the little red box of mascara. She put the little brush into the groove of mascara and ran it back and forth until she got the amount she wanted. Then looking into the hand mirror, she applied the mascara to her lashes. She had to pick off little balls of mascara that she created when she put too much on the brush. I was surprised by the amount of make-up she was using and the care she was taking to prepare herself for the party. I hadn't thought she was particularly interested in her appearance.

She dusted her face with loose powder that made her look like she had rolled her face in flour. Then she brushed it off. I watched, intrigued by the whole process.

The door opened downstairs and I heard López yelling for me. I ran down the stairs and right into his arms. He hugged and kissed me and sang *las mañanitas*, the birthday song, to me. I loved López to sing to me. He said that he had thought about me all day long on Wednesday, my real birthday. He told me that he couldn't stand Carmen, so he hadn't wanted to come over until today. I told him I understood and that it was all right with me. But I had missed him on Wednesday.

"Tata, the piñata?" I asked quickly. "Did you bring it?"

"Of course," he smiled at me. "It's in the kitchen."

The piñata was on the kitchen table. It was a big white duck with a large yellow bill. It had a big red ribbon around its throat and huge yellow feet. It was exactly what I wanted.

"Oh, thank you Tata, it's beautiful!" I kissed López. Then I examined the bowl inside the duck that would hold the candy. There was no candy inside.

"And the candy?" I asked López.

"Your father said he would stop at El Canton Grocery to buy the candy," López assured me. "Is that your new dress?"

"Oh, Tata, I have never had a new dress. It's the one that Palm brought home for me on Wednesday. Do you like it?" I asked so that he would say something nice about my appearance. "How do I look?"

"*Como una muñeca*, like a doll," he said enthusiastically.

We went outside to look at the clothesline so López could figure out how to suspend the piñata. Then he sent me to Señora Olga's house to borrow the big rope she kept for piñatas. She answered the door and I asked for the rope.

"Señora Olga, are you coming to the fiesta tonight?" I asked. I really wanted to know. "Everyone will be there."

"Yoya, *estoy de luto*, I'm in mourning. You know that," she answered in an annoyed tone.

"Flaco says that today is your last day of *luto*. Please come over to see my piñata and have some cake," I answered.

"We'll see." She smiled at me. I knew then that it might be possible for her to join the fiesta. I didn't push it.

López got everything ready to go with the piñata. The children started arriving. Veronica, the only girl my age on our block, came.

Her mother didn't let her play outside with us because she had asthma. Every time she tried to play with us, she had to go home because she would start wheezing. So I either played with the boys or I didn't play at all.

Palm arrived home with the candy. He became irritable when he saw all the children. He muttered something to López, who let out a loud laugh. Then they put the candy in the piñata and attached the rope. They took it outside to put it on the clothesline but started arguing about how to attach it. They were two little old men fighting like ten-year-olds. Señor Lino walked over and got involved in the argument, and finally the task was done. López and Palm took turns tugging the rope that raised and lowered the piñata. They were a sight. Then López asked for the stick to hit the piñata. Pelón produced the bat and gave it to López.

"*Qué estás loco?* You can't use a bat! The first person to hit it will rip the duck open. No, go get a broom stick or any kind of stick. A bat, can you believe it, Palm! *Se van grande estos chavalos*, they think big, these kids," López laughed.

Prieto went home to get the stick his mother uses to bang the pail when she wants him home. He returned and we were all set. Then López asked for the handkerchief.

"The handkerchief . . . I forgot," I whined. "I forgot that you were blindfolded when you hit the piñata. I don't stand a chance! I'll never be able to find the piñata."

The boys started laughing and strutting around. I felt my blood get hot. I'd figure out something. Then López made everyone get in line to try to hit the piñata. The little children were helped by their parents. The older children were outwitted by the clever rope work by Señor Lino, who took over the job when López and Palm started arguing again. I asked to be last so that I could break the piñata. The boys didn't break it when they took their turns, although they gave it hard blows. Some of the hits should have broken it, but they didn't. When I had my turn, I didn't even hit it but I wasn't about to give up the stick. I insisted that because it was my birthday, I could hit it as much as I wanted. The boys became furious. Pelón tugged at the stick in my hand. We had a tug of war. Palm came over and asked me to give up the stick. I wouldn't. Then he had a tug of war with me over the stick. Finally, he managed to get it out of my hands. I cried and said that it was my piñata and it was mine to break. I ran over and got the bat and ran after the piñata while Señor Lino tried to keep the piñata away from me by raising the piñata

as high as he could. Palm lost his patience. He walked over to me and
asked me for the bat. I wouldn't let it go. He took it from me and gave
me two swift swats on my behind; I was mortified. I ran into the house.
Then Carlos shattered the duck and the candy and pottery came flying
down. All the kids dove into the mess on the ground except me. I was
crying upstairs in my room. Palm had never hit me before. López came
up and told me I had to blow out the candles on my cake. And he told
me that Palm shouldn't have spanked me and that we would stick together. Reluctantly, I went downstairs and the sight of the cake that
Carmen's family brought over from Juárez lifted my spirits again.
I grinned from ear to ear as the children sang *las mañanitas* to me.

By seven, the older people started to arrive. The widow and her son
Eduardo came to the yard with two of his soldier friends. They looked
handsome in their uniforms. Everyone spoke to them and asked them
questions about the war. Señora Alma came with her two daughters and
her husband. She started to cry when she saw the men in uniforms.
Ignacio went over to speak to her. One of her sons killed in the war had
been his best friend. He hugged and held Señora Alma, who was dressed
in a gray dress. Everyone looked at her and was relieved that her *luto*
was over. Carmen's parents and some of her young friends joined the two
uniformed men. Carmen walked over to them and seemed unusually gay.
I saw her and the one they called Chuy smiling shyly at each other. I
wondered.

There was food, beer, and *pisto*, liquor. The radio was playing and
everyone was either talking or dancing on the sidewalk. Don Benito,
Pelón's grandfather, came with his concertina. I hadn't even expected
him to be at the fiesta because he had been ill all summer. Padre Luna
came in regular clothes—khaki pants and a red checkered shirt. He
didn't look normal to me. I was fascinated; I kept wondering if he wasn't
a priest any more. He was talking to Don Benito when I went up to him.

"How are you feeling, Don Benito?" Padre Luna asked him. "What
does the doctor say you have?"

"*¿Cuál doctor*, Padre?" Don Benito exclaimed. "I don't believe in doc-
tors. No, no, I don't trust them. They always find something wrong with
you and send you to the hospital where you die. No doctor, please!
When it's my time, it's my time,*cuando me toca, me toca!*"

"It might help to see one," Padre Luna suggested. He knew it was
useless to try to convince Don Benito, but he also knew he must try.
He took him over to some chairs and helped him with his concertina.

By nine, the party was well underway. Teresa joined Ignacio and Señora Alma. They talked very seriously and Ignacio shook his head many times in disapproval. Señora Olga looked at Teresa many times that night. The boys and I watched. Ignacio's soldier friends chatted with Señora Alma's young women. Carmen and her friends seemed to be having a good time, too, and every so often you would hear a big laugh out of Carmen. Every time she laughed, Palm and I would look her way. We found it unusual. I was still hurt over the two swats Palm had given me and I kept away from him.

At ten, the older people started talking about the significance of September 16. They all knew some of the history and repeated it matter-of-factly. When the talk turned to the Revolution of 1910, the mood became more emotional, the stories more forceful. Many had lived in villages that Villa had raided when he and his men needed supplies. One woman recalled Villa coming to Juárez. Don Benito said that his aunt had made love to Villa. López let out a howl.

"That was a man, Villa!" López said. "I would have followed him into *el infierno. Perdóne me*, forgive me, Padre." He didn't want to offend Padre.

"Don't worry Señor. But I don't feel the way you do. I personally hate the Revolution of 1910. It destroyed my life in Mexico. But I'm not telling you anything you don't know," Padre Luna said sadly.

One of the soldiers with Ignacio looked very interested in what Padre had just said. He walked toward Padre and asked.

"I don't know your story, Padre. Will you tell me and my friend. My parents don't talk much about the revolution, but I know they came over in 1915 to escape the change. They figured that if they had to change, they may as well come to this country to do it."

Padre Luna welcomed a new ear for his story. The boys and I were glad because we didn't know all the details.

"The revolution began when I was an adolescent. My parents had just left me with a Spanish order in a small town near Morelos. The order was an old one and I felt strongly about being there. One night, we could hear firing and shooting all around us. The padre hid me and another novice in the basement. The next morning, we went out and found the padre hanging in the courtyard. The same occurred many places." He paused, overwhelmed by emotion. "They hung them on the telegraph poles. They hung them like criminals."

I didn't have to look at Padre Luna to know what I would see on his face: Padre was crying. He often cried. Padre cried when he gave com-

munion. He started to cry when he kissed the cloth. And when he broke
the bread and drank the wine, the tears rolled down his face. When he
gave the *ostia*, the wafer, the altar boy occasionally tried to blot the tears,
but Padre pushed him away gently. He didn't care if anyone saw his
tears. Sometimes children and adults cried too when they saw this for the
first time.

"It's 10 o'clock. I have to leave," Don Benito said. "Can we do the
grito? It may be my last one. I can't do it, but I'm sure one of you can."

Don Benito always gave the *grito de Dolores*, cry of sorrow, cry of freedom. His illness made him weak and he didn't have the strength to do it.
He looked around at the group and appeared to be giving permission for
someone to do what had always been a duty of love for him.

My grandfather López stepped forward and said, "*Con todo respeto y con
su permiso*, Don Benito, it is I who will give the cry. I am the oldest after
you and the only legitimate Mexican here—the rest of you are transplanted Mexicans." He looked around to see if there were any protests.
There were none.

López took the Mexican flag from Don Benito to begin the ceremony.
He held it in front of him as if offering the flag to the group. He cleared
his throat and said in a loud voice that I will never forget, the cry of freedom. Everyone cheered for the republic, the heroes of the revolutions,
and they cheered for the endurance of Mexico.

"*Viva México! Viva México!*"

The group became very emotional and loud. Some women started
crying. Señora Luz was crying the loudest. I wondered why. Everyone
was quiet and very somber for several minutes. Just then, Padre Luna
grabbed the American flag that Pelón had in his hand. He joined the
three soldiers and he held the flag in front of him just as López had done
with the Mexican flag.

"*Viva* America!" Padre yelled. The crowd was taken by surprise.
The soldiers also yelled *viva!* The group was quiet for a few seconds as
they looked at Padre who once again yelled.

"*Viva* America!" Padre yelled again, inviting the crowd to join him.
This time the whole group yelled: "*Viva* America!" Then they all started
laughing. They grabbed for their drinks and started talking to each
other. Palm called out to the group.

"*Señores y señoras*, may I have your attention. As you know my daughter Gloria is eight years old as of Wednesday. She has had a hard time

learning the pledge to the American flag. I know you will enjoy hearing her recite it for you. Yoya," Palm said.

I was still angry at him for the swats and I wanted to run and hide behind López, but I knew by the look on my father's face that it was something he wanted me to do. The boys all got in line with Carlos and the flag in his hand. They were not taking a chance that I would say it wrong. They looked at me with the pride of a teacher gloating over her favorite pupil.

I stepped forward, put my hand on my heart. I felt funny, but I looked at Don Benito, Padre Luna and the soldiers and I recited the pledge.

> I pledge allegiance
> To the flag of the United States of America
> And to the republic for which it stands
> One nation, indivisible, with liberty
> And justice for all.

(I'm sure you know that "under God" was added in 1954.) Everyone praised me and told how proud they were that I had learned the pledge. I enjoyed the attention. A very tired Don Benito said goodbye and left with Pelón's parents. I found López sitting quietly near the beer.

"Tata, you did good on the *grito*. You added the heroes that were your favorite, *que no?*" I confronted my grandfather because he said the cry different from the way Don Benito usually did.

"Yes. I love the heroes Hidalgo, Morelos, Madero, Zapata and Villa *con toda mi alma*, with all my soul. Those times are gone." He seemed lost in thought as he continued. "Peasant men and women fought side by side for what they believed. Your grandmother was by my side." López drew on the ground and said, "The heroes drew a line on the ground and said to the government: 'Give us some land or here we will both die.'" I could see that he was in his cups and he was feeling sad. I looked at him and remembered what I wanted to ask him.

"Tata, why did the women cry?" I asked. "Señora Luz cried a lot."

"Oh, they cry because they remember that they worked like burros in Mexico and they came here to get away from that. And, they work like burros here, too." He paused as he took a sip of his beer. "They live like chickens in a chicken coop in the projects. They don't own the land beneath them. They wonder why they came." He paused. "And, they don't know the answer!" López spoke in a heavy, slurring way. "Señora Alma lost the best she had to the war, her two sons. Señora Luz lost her youngest son to another pachuco in a gang fight. Either way, they lose their sons."

Just then, Palm made me go inside to bed. The people stayed until all hours of the night. I thought about Señora Alma, Señora Luz, and Padre Luna. I realized that I couldn't take communion the next day because I had not been to confession on Saturday. I guessed I would just watch Padre when he gave communion and understand why he cried. That night I dreamed of flags: Mexican and American flags. Palm, Padre Luna, and López fought invisible beings with the flags just like the three musketeers fight with swords in the movies. As I watched them, I recited the pledge while the boys watched with pride.

7   *Plata*

The silver moment is similar to the one I described to you just before it rains. It's the moment when all the colors in the atmosphere become one single silver color and allow you to see a situation as it really is. In the months that followed my eighth birthday, Señora Olga, Palm, and I would have our silver moments, our turning points.

Don Benito died in early fall. It should have been apparent to everyone at the 16th of September party that the angel of death was close at hand. Don Benito died quietly after a few days of fever and delirium. His kidneys stopped working, and since the family respected his wishes, no doctor was called. They were at the side of the deathbed day and night until he slipped away to join the revolutionary heroes in a place where there is no limit to the amount of land a man can have and no government to tell him what to do with it.

Pelón came to my house Monday evening to tell me about his *abuelito's* death. He was calm and quiet as he described the deathbed. He said everyone took turns going in to say goodbye and to kiss the head of the wise old man. He said his *tata's* skin was cool for the first time in many days. Pelón told me that it did not seem real to him.

The sitting with the family was calm and serene. I stood with Palm for about an hour. He held my hand throughout the whole thing. He felt my anxiety when a family member cried out loud and he gently counted my fingers so as to reassure me of his presence. It was so different from the sitting for Luisito. Padre Luna comforted Pelón's father who sat very still and made no emotional outbursts.

The funeral was set for ten in the morning. López went to represent our family because Palm had to work and we didn't have a way there. Later, when Pelón told me about the burial, I tried to picture it in my mind. He said he had felt as if his body was in the coffin with his grandfather. When the coffin was lowered into the *pozo*, the people went one by one to throw in a handful of the dirt on top of the coffin. It was then, Pelón said, that his father had broken down and the other men had to keep him from throwing himself into the grave. At that moment, Pelón said, he realized that Don Benito had truly died. It was his silver moment.

For me, Don Benito's death reminded me of the loss of my mother and the fear I had of losing Palm. I had been worried about him ever since the party in September. He and Carmen seemed to quarrel every day about money and about her wanting to go to Juárez to see her family. Every afternoon when I came home from school, I noticed that Carmen's eyes were red as if she had been crying. When I asked about it, she would just say that she had a headache. But I wasn't sure about that.

Every morning in October when I awoke as my neighbor went to the *molino*, I would see Pelón's father coming home drunk. It was strange because he didn't drink much even at parties. When I told López about it, he told me that Pelón's father was drowning his sorrow.

"Sometimes men have to drink because they can't cry. The *pisto* gives them relief from the pain. Women are lucky they can cry because they don't choke on their pain." López rubbed his forehead and continued, "When your grandmother died, I didn't see a sober moment for a month. When your sweet mother died, I couldn't drink like that any more. The pain has never left me."

"You seem happy, Tata!" It pained me to think otherwise. "You smile and say funny things. I didn't think you were unhappy."

"You don't think so, *preciosa?* Actually, I look at you and a part of Panchita is still here," he said in a cracking voice. "I have to stay sober to help Palm. That is what your mother would have wanted me to do."

"Carmen seems unhappy, Tata." I wanted to tell him what I was observing. "Her eyes are red every day when I come home from school. What do you think?"

"I think she's too young for Palm," he answered too quickly. "She didn't realize what it would mean at her age to marry an old man with three children. She has to break her pain up into little pieces and eat it every day. That's what women do when they make bad choices."

I thought about what López said about choices whenever I saw Teresa in her ripe condition. Flaco said that from their window, his mother watched Teresa in such a way that concerned his family. Señora Olga's quiet vigilance over Teresa's comings and goings made the family uncomfortable. But, naturally no one dared ask her about it.

On the Day of the Dead on November 2, Pelón invited me to go to
the cemetery with his family. We went in the back of his uncle's truck.
Our job was to keep the flowers steady and the cleaning tools intact.
At the graves, we helped pick up the trash and stood around looking at
all the people in the cemetery. Then Pelón and I went to look at the big
grave markers and tried to figure out why people had died. We returned
to Don Benito's simple metal and plastic marker. After a while, Pelón's
mother pointed to the grave of a sister of Flaco who died right after birth.
We rushed over and stood quietly in front of the grave. We were whispering to each other when Señora Olga and Flaco came up behind us.
I jumped a foot because I was scared; it was my first visit to a cemetery.

"Buenas tardes, Señora Olga." I recovered from my scare and greeted
her in a proper way. She answered softly and busied herself with the
cleaning around the grave. When she started crying, Pelón and I excused
ourselves and went back to Don Benito's grave only to find Pelón's father
in deep despair and crying. It was a difficult afternoon.

The next day, Flaco came by for me to go to school. I found that
unusual because he usually liked to go with the boys. As soon as we
were away from my apartment he slowed down and said he wanted to tell
me what happened the evening before after they returned from the
cemetery. We stopped at the jalopy to talk.

"We were home about fifteen minutes when there was a knock at the
back door." Flaco was very animated. "I went to the door and there was
Señora Luz looking very nervous. She asked me to get my mother, which
I did. My mother greeted her and asked her what she needed. Señora
Luz proceeded to explain in a frantic voice that Teresa was in labor and
they were having a very hard time with her. The baby had turned in the
womb and they were not having any luck turning the baby to the normal
position. My mother just stood there the whole time looking in disbelief
at Señora Luz, who told her that the family could not afford a doctor.
She asked my mother for help since my mother is the most capable *partera*,
midwife, around. In fact, Yoya, she is the best because she is so strong."

My heart stood still. I couldn't imagine Señora Luz asking Señora
Olga to help deliver the woman who had caused her son so much pain.

"My mother just said no and practically threw Señora Luz out." Flaco
continued his story in a very serious voice. "She said something about
the nerve some people have. She slammed the door and Señora Luz left
very embarrassed. About seven, Señora Chole, Teresa's mother, knocked

quietly at the door. This time, my mother answered it. She nearly fainted when she saw Señora Chole standing there. Teresa's mother asked for my mother's compassion and begged her to come and help with the delivery. But my mother slammed the door in her face and said many ugly things under her breath."

Flaco continued in a suspenseful voice that had me hypnotized. "About seven thirty, there was a knock at the door. My mother stood up from the kitchen table in a rage." I could just imagine the Russian bear shimmering all the way to the door. "She was just about to yell at the person at the door when she saw it was Señora Alma. My mother controlled herself because she knew what Señora Alma had lost and asked her what she needed. Señora Alma told my mother that Teresa's family had sent for Padre Luna so that he could give the last rites to Teresa. She said that unless someone who knew what they were doing didn't help soon, both the mother and the baby would die. Then Señora Alma took a big breath and looked my mother straight in the eye and asked her: "How many more children do we have to lose, Olga?" Flaco continued his spellbinding account. "What Señora Alma said shocked my mother. She didn't speak. My father and I went to my mother's side because we were afraid she was going to hit Señora Alma. She didn't. She let out an anguished cry and said, "Vamos, let's go" to Señora Alma and they left together. I ran after them, not wanting to miss a thing."

"Then what happened?" I asked when Flaco stopped for a moment to catch his breath. We were leaning against our old convertible all this time. "Hurry, tell me what happened next."

"My mother is the strongest woman alive. The women said she turned the baby and gently coaxed Teresa through the delivery. By the time Padre Luna arrived with a doctor whom he had talked into coming to the projects, the baby boy had arrived crying as loud as a little pig. I could hear him. Padre baptized the baby there and then just in case."

"And, your mother? What did she do then?"

"Señora Alma told me that my mother took the baby in her arms and cleaned him up. She cleaned Teresa and all the mess that goes with childbirth. She would not let any of the women help her. Then she and I came home. She sat in kitchen and cried for a long time. When she was calmer, I asked her about the baby. She looked at me and smiled and told me the baby was beautiful." Flaco's face was becoming contorted and I braced myself because I knew he was about to cry. "Then it took her two minutes between crying and sobbing to tell me that Teresa named the baby Luís after my brother." Flaco started crying and I did too. We leaned against our jalopy and cried together.

Look at all the countries that speak Spanish and you will understand what Spain was doing at the end of the fifteenth and sixteenth centuries. By the simple use of two pronouns, this romance language shows who is master and who is not. It appears when the Iberian mentality began it knew it would need a language that provided boundaries between master and servant. Spanish was the perfect vehicle.

Usted, formal you, is the pronoun for talking to the master. It is also used when you don't know the person to whom you are speaking, or if you don't want them to get close to you. It is a well-developed device that maintains space and privacy. It is the pronoun you use to talk to the boss, the mayor, the bishop, your favorite teacher, your older neighbor, and an initial pronoun for someone with whom you may eventually develop a love relationship. *Usted* is necessary and comfortable most of the time in ordinary conversation.

Tú, familiar you, on the other hand is many times subordinate to *usted*. The master may call you *tú* if he or she wishes. You don't have the same reciprocal privilege. And *tú* is for loved ones: parents, siblings, lovers, friends, pets, and children. Many people talk to God and the saints as *tú*. I always do.

You would think that learning the difference between *tú* and *usted* would be natural and easy for Mexican children, but it is not that simple. A child's world is immersed in the *tú* mode for the first few years of his or her life. Parents, siblings, pets, and baby Jesus are all *tú*. A child is corrected by adults or poked in the back when she uses the *tú* with people outside the home. Actually, it sounds cute most of the time, but it is tolerated only in the very young.

Sunday December 16, 1945, was joyous in Segundo Barrio. It was cold but sunny and the air was pristinely clear. Everyone on the block was invited to Señora Alma's house for the laying of the Christ child in the manger. Whenever there were parties for children in the barrio, parents also attended. Palm and Carmen were talking that morning about the event when I entered the kitchen.

"*Pues si usted quiere*, if you want to go, we'll go," Carmen whined. "I don't feel good. I have a cold."

I stopped at the entrance to the kitchen because I thought we had company. I looked around to see who the *usted* was. Palm was the only one in the kitchen. I was confused.

"No, *si usted no se siente bien, no vamos*, if you don't feel well, we won't go," Palm answered matter-of-factly. The *corazonadas*, premonitions, I was feeling told me that his use of *usted* meant something. They were talking to each other like strangers or at least not like husband and wife.

"*Buenos días,*" I greeted the two. They replied the same. "Papí, will you be able to go to Señora's Alma's house with me?" I looked at him, trying to understand the shift in pronouns between them.

"No, *mi'ja*. Carmen is coming down with a cold. We don't want Señora Alma or one of the children to get her *gripa*."

Carmen hurried to say. "Sí, Yoya. *Usted*, I mean *tú*, you don't want Señora Alma to catch my cold. She is doing so well now." I listened to Carmen as I felt a cold settling inside to match the cold outside. I shivered and got close to Palm.

"Apá, can you tie my braids with red ribbons? I want to wear all red for the party." I beamed my biggest smile as I visualized myself. Carmen laughed a silly laugh. She seemed alive for a few moments. I watched her eyes and mouth as she talked to me.

"Outside Delicias live some Indians. When the young girls come to town, they all wear red. They look like ripe red jalapeños coming to town," she told me cheerfully. "I always loved *la noche buena*, Christmas Eve in Delicias." She ended with a sad note that annoyed me.

I looked at Palm who got up from the table and walked out the back door. The screen door slammed and a puff of dust escaped from the tiny wire boxes that make up the screen. The bright sun caught the dancing particles. I wondered where he was going.

By three in the afternoon, I was ready for the party. My red dress looked silly with my pink sweater, but I knew Palm would not let me outside without it. He said I could take it off when I was inside, and that is what I did the minute I was inside Señora Alma's apartment.

The boys were already in the living room. They were talking to each other and took no notice of me. I walked *con garbo*, elegantly, past them to the kitchen. They looked at me quite indifferently. In the kitchen were the neighbors I saw every day. Señora Olga was there with Teresa's baby, Luisito, in her arms. She beamed like a formidable *madrina*, godmother. Teresa and her mother stood by waiting for Señora Olga to let them hold the baby. The rest of the group was eating taquitos and tamales and drinking beer. I greeted them and they asked about my father and Carmen. I repeated the excuse Carmen had given me. They exchanged knowing looks and winks. I heard one of them whisper something to Señora Olga, who became annoyed by the comment. She looked very intently at me and asked me if I wanted to hold the baby. I said that I was afraid I would drop him. The remark must have scared her—she didn't ask again.

I became more interested in what was going on in the front room where the boys were. I went back to the living room and walked aloof past Pelón who watched me with a smile on his face.

"*¿Y usted, Señorita?* Are you from here?" He played along with me. "*Usted se ve muy guapa*, you look very attractive," he said as he brushed an imaginary mustache with his right hand.

"*¡Calla de 'usted', menso!* be quiet with that 'formal you' stuff, stupid," I snapped at him.

"*¡Cuidado!* Is that the way we treat each other, Yoya?" He looked at me searching for a reason for my outburst.

"I'm sorry, Pelón. *Dispénsame, por favor.*" I kept looking at the manger as I apologized.

"What is wrong, Yoya," he asked softly.

At first, I didn't want to answer. He didn't tell me what was wrong with him every time he felt hurt. But needing to talk to him, I said, "Palm and Carmen are speaking to each other in *usted*. She almost spoke to me in *usted*!" I confided in him. "What do you think it means? Do your parents speak in *usted* to each other?"

"Sometimes when they are playing around they do," Pelón continued with a very serious look on his face. "My grandfather Benito used to tell me that married people from *ranchos*, the country, sometimes talk to each other that way. He said that they did not know any other way. It seemed natural to the old Indians. They learned Spanish from the their landlords." He looked at me and flicked one of my red ribbon braids.

"Besides, *esá desabrida*, the sour one, is from a rancho outside Delicias. Maybe that is the way she speaks there."

"I don't think so. She isn't happy with us." At last, the truth came out of my mouth. Pelón looked at me without saying a word. I knew by his silence that he understood.

"She's too young for Palm, Yoya." He stopped. "Don't think about it now." He motioned for me to walk with him toward the manger. Señora

Alma brought out the beautiful porcelain baby that her son had sent her
from Europe before he was killed—a pink child with a gold halo attached
behind his little head. It looked like a crown. No one said anything. We just
watched as she laid him in the manger. We all prayed for what seemed to me
a long time. I started to yawn and Pelón gave me a push. Afterward, the children ate sweet tamales and candy and talked about Santa Claus. We all
wanted to go see him downtown at the Popular Dry Goods Store. I was so
excited that I forgot all about Palm, Carmen, and time.

The sun sets at five in December. I loved it and I hated it. I hated
having to stop playing but I loved the coziness of being at home with the
cold darkness outside. I could blow my hot breath on the window and
draw pictures with my fingers on the fogged up pane. The apartment
was dark when I came home from the party. I could see Palm sitting in
his chair surrounded by a cloud of cigarette smoke. The radio was
quietly playing his cowboy music and he was alone. As I approached him,
I could smell a faint odor of alcohol—he was holding a watered
down, sugary drink. He didn't seem aware of my presence.

"Papí, I'm here," I said, nervous that he had not greeted me.
"*Estás solo?* Are you alone?"

"Yes, *mi'jita.* Carmen went to bed." Palm pulled his frail body up from
his big brown chair. "How was the party?"

"I loved it. I always love it. Señora Alma and the other grownups told
us stories of the *posadas,* Christmas celebrations they had when they lived
in Mexico. The food was delicious, *muy sabrosa.*" I talked to a silent
Palm. After a few moments, I found my courage and spoke to him in
a nervous voice.

"Is Carmen unhappy?" I looked at him in the dark room. He smiled a
faint smile when he caught me searching his face.

"She misses her family. It's hard for her not to be with them at Christmas." He sighed deeply and the alcohol on his breath made me back up.
I pushed his hand with the drink slightly and made a sign that I wanted
to sit on his lap. He quickly accommodated me.

"You're getting to be such a big girl. A big and pretty girl whom I love
very much." He hugged me and I felt a wave of forgotten pain that his
hug helped contain in my small body. I felt as if I were going to cry.

"I love you so much, Papí. Don't worry about Carmen. Let her go
to her people. We'll be happy like we were before she came." I secretly
liked the idea that she would leave. "López and Pelón say she is too

young to have a family." Palm looked at me with a surprised look, which told me I was telling him something he didn't know. I must have looked the same way when Carlos told me that there wasn't just one Santa Claus. Feeling a pang of guilt, I quickly added. "She takes good care of me. She makes good flour tortillas." A white lie.

Palm looked at me for a long time. It was becoming hard to see by the faint orange glow of the radio tubes so I went to turn on the stairwell light.

"I told her that we should spend Christmas together. And, the following day, she could go to Juárez to visit her family if she took you along." Palm spoke in the darkness of the room. "I told her you and she could stay until New Year's day."

"And did she like that?" I asked.

"Well, she accepted it and was pleased she could go the next day." Palm added in a low voice, "No, she's not very happy."

We listened to the radio for a while longer. Then I felt myself being gently shaken—I had fallen asleep in my daddy's arms. He asked me if I could walk upstairs to my bed. I nodded and walked crookedly to the stairwell. I turned around and looked back at him. The music was softly playing and his face was in his hands.

"Are you coming, Papí?" I asked the dark figure of an old man. "Papí?"

"In a minute, Yoya." He lifted his face towards me. "I just want to smoke another cigarette."

As I walked upstairs to my bed, I knew that Palm's silver moment had arrived and he wasn't ready for it.

8 Macho

Macho, manly, now has a connotation that I don't think was originally meant. The idea, associated with fighting and defending oneself, goes back to the early Mexican Indians. Because there were many tribes they had animosity and fear toward each other long before Cortez arrived on the shores of Mexico. They fought each other and the fiercest and most belligerent were the Aztecs. When Cortez stepped onto the land with his soldiers, his armor, his horses, and smallpox, a new kind of fighting and defense was defined.

A man's ability to fight and defend himself was a value that meant survival for his family. Perhaps this explains the Mexican's appreciation for bullfighting and the heroes of the bullring. Most Mexicans know the name of those heroes: Lorenzo Garza, Carlos Arruza, Silverio, and Cañitas. My grandfather said the bull was the government or the forces of nature and the bullfighter represented the peasant. Later, a man was considered a *macho* with respect and prestige if he could provide for himself and his family in a hard environment, as Mexico has always been. To be a *macho* meant one had pride and power: it meant self-reliance. Along the same lines, self-defense has always meant that a person protects himself from any type of aggression or hostility. While aggression is not encouraged, defending oneself is considered a necessary value.

School let out for Christmas in 1945 with a lot of excitement. We spent the last days singing Christmas carols and pasting Santa Clauses and Christmas trees on green and red sheets of construction paper. The teacher complained that the paste was being used too rapidly. During recess, we compared how much paste we had eaten. It smelled and tasted so good. Carlos warned me against eating paste when he picked some off my face. He said that I could get *lombrizes*, or worms, if I continued to eat it.

"You may even get *empachada*, clogged up, and López may have to give you a *sobada*," he warned me.

"*¡Nel!*" I said to Carlos, annoyed at his protective pose. "Didn't you eat paste when you were in my grade?" I hurried to justify the habit. "Or were you always an angel?"

"I never said I didn't eat any. I just know from experience that you get sick." He was always so honest. "I just want you to know what can happen"

The Christmas break was always welcomed, even if it became unbearable waiting for the big day. The boys and I roamed the neighborhood in search of places to hang out since we didn't have our jalopy anymore. The week before, a junk dealer had hauled our beloved convertible away. Because it no longer had any tires on it, it had to be taken away on a flatbed truck. The junk man said terrible things about the broken down car as he loaded it up. The boys and I stood at attention and saluted our metal playmate. The jalopy, in return, practically fell apart in the process as if to protest being hauled off. The frustrated junk man yelled some horrible cuss words; I covered my ears up as the boys howled. Then Carlos directed us in our farewell song to the magical car. We sang "*Adiós Mariquita Linda*, Goodbye Lady Bug" and ended with a loud final line of the song.

The jalopy dropped a front fender as if in recognition of the group under the lamp post, a final protest that received a huge scream of "*¡Viva!*" from us.

On Christmas Saturday, we decided to go on an adventure. We planned to go and play on the San Jacinto schoolyard until we had to go to confession. The San Jacinto School was just outside the Alamito Projects. The boys were particularly fond of the school's enclosed cylindrical fire escape. It would be the first time I would explore the fire escape since I had always been afraid to enter it, but now the boys had convinced me it was fun. It would provide a private and cozy place where we could talk. We planned to take our ditto-paper copies of Christmas songs we'd received in class.

At eleven in the morning, we started out on our adventure with our lunches packed. We stopped at a little corner store and bought some Nehi grape and orange sodas. The owner reminded us that we could get a refund if we returned the bottles. We told him to expect us in a few hours. Then we started on our way. At first, we walked four abreast: Carlos, Flaco, Pelón, and me. Then we marched in a single line with Carlos at the head and me at the rear. At different blocks, we added whistles or singing as it pleased us. The cold West Texas December wind and the hot sun gave color to our cheeks and dried our lips. When we reached the fire escape, we went into the spiral walk and sat down comfortably on the its cold sides. The first thing we did was eat our lunch. Everyone took out his or her flour taco, except for Pelón. We had to share with him because his family did not eat flour tortillas. They ate maíz tortillas, which do not make good tacos because they break when they are cold. Flaco complained about sharing his egg and chorizo taco and he told Pelón that his grandmother said corn was only for animals. Pelón laughed as he took a bite of Flaco's lunch. In our house we ate both types of tortillas, depending on the meal. When we finished we began singing our Christmas carols. Everyone asked for their favorite. Mine that year was "Silent Night." Our teacher had allowed us to learn the Spanish version, "*Noche de Paz.*" A sixth grader, Magdalena, came in to teach it to us. After we had sung all the songs we knew a few times, Pelón told us the Christmas story. We all knew it and loved to hear it out loud. By the time he had finished, our bottoms were numb from the cold and we decided that we had had enough. We laughed as we slapped our *nalgas* to wake them up. We decided to head toward church and sang "Jingle Bells" all the way back to the little corner store where we bought some candy with the refund money.

As we approached the church playground, we could see a police car and some people in front of the church. We turned the corner and Carlos, who was in the lead, started telling us what he could see.

"*¡Chotas!* The police! They're in front of the church," he said. We had picked up our trot to a slow run by this time. "There is Padre Luna . . . Señora Petra, Chango's mother . . . Chango's father . . . Chango is in the police car!" Carlos was sizing up the situation as we approached the group in front of the church. We stopped and watched. Other people were coming out of their project apartments, asking what was going on. Someone said Chango was in trouble. We could hear Padre talking to the policeman.

"How do you know it was him?" Padre asked the policeman as he pointed at Chango, who was quietly sitting in the back seat of the police car.

"He had the zip gun in his possession, Padre. The witnesses said that he fired the gun at that gang member over there. The witnesses are not from here . . . they were just driving by when they saw the whole thing. We wouldn't just pick him up for nothing." The policeman was trying to reassure Padre.

Chango's parents drew close to Padre as he turned and told them in Spanish what the officer said. The parents were very upset. Then Padre turned and spoke to the policeman for them. He asked where they were taking Chango and what the family could do. The policeman replied that Chango would be taken to the juvenile detention center. The boys and I looked wide-eyed at each other. We knew that Chango prided himself on his greasy ducktail hairdo. He was constantly grooming himself with a little black comb he kept in his shirt pocket. Whenever anyone was unlucky enough to be taken to the juvenile detention center, he always returned home with his head shaved. It didn't do any good to tell people that you had been ill and that your mother cut your hair as a remedy. No, everyone knew where you had been when they saw you shaven.

The black and white police car left with Chango. We could see him looking at his parents through the back window. We got closer to the group so that we could hear the conversation between Padre and Chango's family. Everyone got closer. In the barrio, everyone minds each other's business.

"*Y usted Padre!* Why didn't you do something?" Señora Petra cried out. "What good are you? Why did you let the police take Chango. You can speak English. You know we can't speak to them. Why didn't you take him from them?"

"Señora Petra, your son has broken the law. He fired at that pachuco over there with his homemade gun," Padre tried to explain. "Chango fired at that *tirilongo* and nearly hit him. You should be grateful he didn't kill him."

"Grateful, Padre! What is there to be grateful about. Certainly not you. You don't have any sons." Señora Petra's anger towards Padre was mounting as her husband kept trying to calm her down.

"Petra! *¡Respeto!* That is Padre Luna you are talking to," Chango's father firmly told his distraught wife, who continued her loud complaints.

"And why didn't they take that pachuco, too. He has been threatening Chango for weeks. Chango couldn't even step out of the house without his brothers or some of his gang friends."

"Chango should not have taken the measures that he took," Padre continued to explain. "The law does not allow people to carry guns, Señora."

"My sons have to defend themselves!" Señora Petra said to Padre. "*Se tienen que defender!* You know that Padre! My children have to defend themselves or they can never walk the streets again!"

"That is not the way it should be, Señora. Your sons should not belong to gangs and shoot other gang members." Padre was angry and tired of explaining to the family and the large group of people that had gathered. "Defending themselves is going to get them in jail."

Señora Petra asked, "What are they supposed to do? When we came to this country ten years ago, we thought we would be safe here. My sons didn't want to become pachucos. But, Padre, they had to! They have no power against the pachuco by themselves. We tried to keep them from becoming gang members but it was no use. They say the only power they have is in the gangs."

"We were going to send them back to Mexico last year. But Padre, they came to this country as little children. They can't make it on a rancho in Mexico. What are we supposed to do?" Chango's father said sadly. "The gang is their *jefe*, their father. They don't listen to us."

"Teach them to defend themselves by getting an education. They have to learn new ways to defend themselves." He repeated what we had heard many times from his pulpit.

Someone in the crowd yelled. "*Sí*, Padre, as if it is that easy! In the streets, books don't save your *pellejo*, your hide." A loud laugh followed the remark. The boys and I covered our mouths so that Padre would not hear us giggle.

"Maybe not, but you can learn other ways. And, you parents, you cannot forget your responsibility for your children. You must find a way to help them. They are not yours. They belong to God. He has only placed them in your lives so that they have care and guidance." Padre ended his sidewalk sermon and turned to go inside the church. He stopped at the door and turned around to tell Chango's mother one more thing.

"*Usted se equivoca*, you are mistaken, Señora Petra. I don't have children of my own but, all these children are also my children. I too have responsibility for their guidance. So do the rest of you," he said to the adults as he pointed to the children in the crowd. Chango's parents got directions to the juvenile detention center and they hurried to catch the streetcar. The boys and I went inside to prepare ourselves for confession.

As I sat in the pew waiting for my turn, I remembered how in September López had explained to me about defending myself. This had happened after I came home with a cut on my cheek that I had received in a fight with a crazy girl from the next block. I had been playing outside the Alamito Projects library when she cornered me. She wanted to fight me, but I was terrified. I couldn't move. She had me backed up against the red brick building as I looked past her at the boys who were watching. I couldn't understand why they didn't do something. The girl tried to hit me but I bent down. The boys yelled at me to defend myself. Frightened to death, I closed my eyes and flung my arms like a windmill at the girl. I managed to hit her and she scratched my cheek. She started crying and ran off. She probably hadn't expected me to fight back. I ran home and López cleaned the scratch and gave me a dose of advice. He said fighting was stupid, but you have to defend yourself if you're attacked. Sometimes all you have to do is look hard at the attacker. Sometimes all you have to do is raise your voice. He showed me how to do both. My grandfather then said other times you have no choice but to fight *mano a mano!* He pranced around like a skinny boxer. I knew my grandfather meant to help me, but I felt bad inside; I was so embarrassed.

Later that evening, the boys and I sang victory songs. They were so proud of me. I told them that I like to pretend to be the Brown Bomber but I don't like to hit a real person. They said that I had to defend myself, because they couldn't hit a girl. They would have defended me if it had been a boy, Carlos assured me. But boys don't hit girls.

As I sat in that pew on Christmas Saturday, I recalled that awful fight in September and said many prayers. I didn't have to confess the fight because I already had in September. Christmas was almost here and I didn't want to feel any shame because I had fought. That night I dreamed I was battling a brown hawk with big claws in the spiraled fire escape. López and the boys shouted hints on how to defend myself against the big bird. Padre Luna kept waving a book at me. My sobbing woke me up. As I tried to fall back to sleep, I wondered how I could defend myself if I met the hawk again in a nightmare.

9   December 1945

Many Mexican Catholics have special saints they turn to for favors.
The saints' pictures appear on the walls of their homes or in some honored
place in the houses and there are usually candles under them to solem-
nize the importance of the saint. People always suggest saints to pray
to for special problems or special requests. Some saints protect certain
groups, like children, the poor, or the sick. The Virgen de Guadalupe is
the patron saint of Mexico. Many people pray to her when they are sick
or when they want a baby. And you pray for help from St. Jude for the
impossible. I loved the Santo Niño de Atocha when I was a child.
I loved the way he looked with his little black hat and frilly collar.

Children are also given a saint's name when they are baptized.
At least one of your given names should be a saint's name. This isn't hard
because there are hundreds of saints—almost every day is a saint day.
Having a saint's name also gets you a kind of second birthday because
people celebrate their saint day with all the people of the same name. So you
get a *pilón* for being a Catholic. My saint day is Holy Saturday, the day
before Easter Sunday. It is called *sábado de gloria*.

December 12 is the day of the Virgen de Guadalupe. This beautiful
morena, dark-skinned, virgin represents our Indian identity in the Catholic
religion. Most often, she is enveloped in bright yellow, green, and red attire.
She appears humble and her demure downcast look speaks to the hearts of
all Mexicans. Her gentle gaze mirrors the value of respect and dignity that
permeates the social consciousness of most Mexicans and Catholics.

The first Sunday of December 1945, which I remember as very cold,
Padre Luna told us that Advent was upon us. We were to prepare our
hearts for the coming of the child. Also, he reminded us of the Feast of
the Virgen de Guadalupe. It was a holy day of obligation for Mexicans.
But since it was on Wednesday, I didn't think about it until one of
Señora Alma's daughters stopped me on the way to school.

78

"Yoya, come in please," María Linda called to me from the door of the apartment. I went in and smiled when I saw the statue of Saint Anthony turned upside down on their praying table. This was done in order to get Saint Anthony to grant marriage to the two single women of this family. When the request was granted, Saint Antony could stand like everyone else. María Linda told me that her mother was ill but that she still planned to have the yearly party for the children when she would lay the baby Jesus in the manger. She asked me to help; I quickly accepted.

At home, Palm and Carmen seemed to be avoiding each other. They spoke to me instead of each other but I wasn't interested in their conversations, and I felt uncomfortable when they talked. I told Palm that I had been asked to help Señora Alma on Wednesday. He said I should take one of the boys with me. I didn't want to, so I pretended not to hear.

The next morning I arrived at Señora Alma's at seven in the morning. I had a roll and some hot chocolate with the whole family. I was very careful to eat with my mouth closed and I finished eating before I spoke. I wanted to show them I was grownup. On the way to church, Señora Alma walked very slowly. I didn't want to rush her. She told me that her heart was in bad shape. The loss of her sons *la había acabado*, had aged her. She asked me to tell the children on our block that she would set out her nativity scene by the window in the living room on Sunday at three. By the time we arrived at the church it was already full of worshipers. Padre Luna met us at the door. He took Señora Alma by the arm and told me to wait until he sat her in the pew. When he returned, he asked me to step outside with him. I was scared—maybe he knew that I had disobeyed Palm. Quickly, I started thinking of an excuse. Outside he asked me how things were going in my house. I told him everything was fine. He asked me if I was getting along with Carmen and I realized that he and Carmen must be talking about our home life. Then he changed the subject.

"Yoya, there is a group of young people in one of the rich churches north of here who want to do something for some children in the projects," Padre said in a gentle voice. "They have collected money and want to take the four young children to buy them some new shoes. What do you think of that? That is you, Pelón, Flaco and Prieto."

"New!" I said in a loud voice as I looked down at my huaraches that were hard as rocks from getting wet. I was delighted. "Do you want me to tell the boys?"

"Yes. Come to the church rectory Saturday at two. The young people will take you to the store," he replied.

"Tell them to take us to the B.B.B. Store on Overland, Padre. I saw some white and black shoes that have laces." I was excited. "I have never had shoes with laces."

"Those shoes are called saddle oxfords, Yoya," Padre smiled. "And, Gloria, you must speak English because the young people do not speak Spanish. And no fooling them, understand?"

On Saturday, I was ready at noon. The time seemed to drag. I wore clean socks that were too small for my feet with my huaraches: my huaraches kept eating them. When the boys and I arrived at the rectory, Padre was standing with a young couple by a car that looked like a small bus made of wood. Padre introduced the boys and me to the young pretty girl with yellow hair and green eyes. I couldn't take my eyes off of her. Inside the car, the boys and I giggled at each other. Pelón spit on his hands and pushed his hair back and rolled his eyes just like Cantinflas does when he likes a woman. Then he threw kisses at the young girl whose back was to us. We giggled and slapped each other.

When we got to the B.B.B. Store, we followed the young couple in and began looking around. Pelón, who was the oldest one, tried to take charge of us but we ignored him. Flaco and I ran and sat down in the row of seats. Then the young woman approached us with the salesman.

"These are poor children who live in the projects," she said as she pointed to the south wall in the direction of the projects. "The young people in my church collected this money to buy them new shoes. These are probably the first new shoes they have ever had." She emphasized "new" and "ever." "We only have this much money." She showed him some green paper in her hand.

Pelón twirled around as fast as a top to look at the young woman. He stared at her with his mouth slightly opened. I happened to look at him because he had turned around so fast. For a moment I thought I saw Don Benito as he had looked the last time I saw him shout the cry of freedom. I grabbed the measuring gray plate out of Flaco's hand and said it was my turn to measure his feet. I sat on the ground oblivious to the fact that my legs were open and my underwear showing.

Pelón moved quickly towards me and said in a firm voice, "Yoya, stand up. Pull your dress down." He sounded like my brother, Carlos. "Sit in the seat." I looked at him and started to say something sharp when I noticed that he was not happy. I sat in the seat next to Flaco, who also looked at Pelón.

"What shoes do you kids want?" the salesman asked.

"I want some Buster Brown shoes," Flaco laughed. "Some Buster Brown shoes with the picture of the boy and the dog inside the shoe so people will see that they are good shoes."

"I want some shoes with laces. Some white and black saddle oxfords," I said as I kicked off my huaraches. I settled back in the seat and waited to be attended to by the salesman.

Prieto said he wanted some black shoes that he saw in the window. He went to show the salesman which ones he meant. Flaco and I looked at Pelón and asked him what was wrong. He didn't answer. Then the young woman asked Pelón which shoes he wanted.

"I don't want any shoes," he answered in a high voice. "I have some new shoes at home. Don't waste your money on me." Flaco and I stared at each other in disbelief.

"Why did you come?" she asked with a confused look. "We told Padre Luna that we had enough for four children."

"I came to look after Yoya. I am the oldest here and her father expects me to watch over her," he said in such a way that stopped me from challenging him. I knew to keep quiet; I had never seen Pelón like this.

"Well, don't get any shoes," she said, annoyed. "There will only be three pairs of shoes," she said to the salesman. She paid for the shoes and we started to leave.

Pelón nudged me and the other boys. "*Se dan las gracias.*" We three who had shoes said thank you. No one spoke on the way home except the young Anglo couple, who chattered cheerfully the whole time. At the church, Padre said goodbye to the two then looked at us and at our new shoes.

"Where are your new shoes?" Padre asked Pelón.

"No, Padre. *Yo no soy limosnero,* I am not a beggar." Pelón continued in a hurt voice, "*Soy pobre pero orgulloso,* I'm poor but I'm proud." He excused himself from Padre and ran off. He turned once to yell at Flaco to make sure that I got home safely. The tears on his cheeks sparkled in the sunlight. Padre looked at the vanishing Pelón and shook his head. Mexican pride is something no one had to explain to him. He waved at Pelón and turned to us.

"I'm late for confessions. Inside children! Get your confessions said." He ran inside and we followed. I wasn't going to get on the wrong side

of the saints so close to Christmas. Besides I already had to thank the
Virgin for the shoes with laces.

After confession, the boys and I headed back to our apartments.
On the way we talked about what happened with Pelón. We understood,
but we were also very happy to have the new shoes. We waited for Pelón
to come join us. He didn't.

In the Segundo Barrio, children took care to reassure their parents
and priest that they were happy because of the real meaning of Christmas. All of us kept secret our wishes for toys. I deeply loved Jesus, but I
also wished for things that I knew Palm could not give me. Nevertheless,
I told Palm that I would love a new dress and some skates. When he
didn't say much at the request I made, I knew that oranges and hard
candy were what I could expect.

Christmas Eve, 1945, was to be a long day, probably the longest day
in the year for the boys and me. When I complained, Palm said with a
smile that he remembered when he was a child that his parents had had
to keep reminding him to behave on Christmas Eve. I looked at my old
father and marveled that anyone had to tell him to behave.

The morning began when I found myself awake with the first hint
of light. I thought for a few minutes and realized it was the day before
Christmas. I went from my small cot to the window to see if anyone was
awake. I heard the milkman drive off and realized it was too early to get
up so I lay in bed thinking of what the day would be like. After a short
time I heard a screen door slam and I ran to the window again. Señora
Luz was off to the molino with her steaming batch of maíz to be ground
for the traditional tamales. Another neighbor emerged from the next
apartment with her pail of maíz and the two women were off. They
would make tamales all day long at Señora Olga's house. I quickly rushed
around in the cold room and went down the stairwell in search of my red
socks and my saddle oxfords. I found both of them neatly waiting for
me in Palm's brown chair. I realized that he had left them there for me
beside the green dress and red sweater that I would wear that day. I smiled
with joy. As I rushed to put my clothes on, I could hear Carmen coughing in the kitchen as she was preparing breakfast. My nose lifted as I
caught a whiff of the coffee that was boiling on the stove. I thought how
good it was that I was the first one up and that there would be no one to
fight with me over the biggest coffee cup. When I entered the kitchen,

Carmen was pouring the coffee. I was so pleased as I reached for the biggest cup. Carmen looked at me in a strange way as I took it but then shrugged her shoulders as she handed me the canned milk and brown Juárez sugar to put in the coffee.

"*Al que madruga, Dios le ayuda,* God helps early risers," Carmen muttered. I smiled in agreement. Then, embarrassed, I realized that she had poured the cup for herself. I told her to take the cup, but she said that she could get another. Oh, the joy I felt with every drop of coffee that wonderful day. Coffee, I thought, was surely a gift of love from God. I rushed because I was anxious to start the good day of the good night.

Outside my apartment I decided my first move. I ran to Flaco's apartment and knocked on his door. I knew Señora Olga did not let anyone sleep late in her house. As I rapped on the screen door, it bounced back and forth because the hook was loose. In a few seconds, Flaco jumped out of his house and sang in a loud screeching voice:

"Caldonia! Caldonia! What make your big head so hot!"

In those days, everyone listened to the radio. There was a radio playing all the time. There was music for everyone, from Mexico, from the United States, for every age. Palm listened to a radio Station we called C-L-I-N-T. The radio was the only entertainment at home at that time. And everyone seemed to love music. People sang as they worked and many couldn't work unless there was a radio playing. Pelón could not study unless the radio was on and Flaco could not fall asleep without it. And we all got stuck on songs to the point someone would tell us to stop. Flaco was currently stuck on "Caldonia." I was stuck on a song called "Till the End of Time" and Palm constantly had to correct what I thought the words to the song were. Frankly, I didn't understand either song: I just loved music! Flaco would screech in a funny way when he sang "Caldonia."

"*¡Deja!* Leave me alone!" I yelled at Flaco who was by this time singing the song right in my face.

"Caldonia! Caldonia! What make your big head so hot!" he continued with great animation as I pushed him away.

"Let's go get the other boys," I suggested. "Everyone must be up. It is *nochebuena* tonight!" I told Flaco as he sang.

We walked across the breezeway to Pelón's house. Carlos joined us. I walked briskly as Flaco followed dancing and singing. By the time

I knocked at Pelón's screen door, we were of a single purpose—to make this a busy and happy day.

Pelón yawned as he emerged from his apartment. His hair was sticking up on the top of his head and his mouth was framed by a coffee-milk mustache. Carlos made a face when he saw Pelón.

"Pelón, please wash your face and clean your eyes," Carlos told him laughingly so as not to offend him. Pelón looked wide-eyed at us as if waking from a sleepwalking trance. He ran back into his house. After several minutes, he came out, his face shining in the morning light and his hair separated into neatly combed wet rows. He smiled and sat down on the cement with us.

"We have to plan the day. First, we'll go by Prieto's apartment and look at his mother's jars. She's already left for El Canton to buy groceries. Then, we'll decide how we will do our usual *nochebuena* day." Carlos assumed his leadership role, as he always did. Since we had no complaints, we went to Prieto's house. Pelón and Flaco whistled their signals and Prieto answered with two sharp whistles from inside his apartment. I satisfied myself with a regular pursed-lips whistle, even though I could not hear it over the boys' whistles.

Prieto opened the door and invited us in. He slapped Pelón on the arm and said something about how tired he looked. Pelón replied that he had a hard time sleeping because his mother had cried all night—his father was on a binge. We all looked at him but didn't ask any questions.

Getting back to our business at Prieto's house, we walked upstairs, pushing each other as we went up the stairwell. We went to the bathroom and gathered around the toilet. On top of the toilet tank was a spare roll of toilet paper and the two jars that were the object of our visit. One jar contained Prieto's tonsils in alcohol. He had them removed in the spring after a long winter of tonsillitis. Before then, all we could see when we looked into his mouth was a small slit of black with two red-and-white-spotted tonsils. We all kept an eye on them. We would tell him to open his mouth and holding our noses with our fingers, we would check his progress. Prieto wanted his tonsils out because he knew that they let you eat all the ice cream you wanted after the operation. That was all right, except, no one told him how sick he would get. Not even the ice cream made him feel well. Each of us had a turn helping him eat the ice cream.

"My mother says that I can keep them in the jar until *el día de los tres magos*, Epiphany. Then she said we should throw them out." Prieto lifted the jar and we inspected the tonsils closely. Then he picked up the other jar. This jar held Prieto's father's gall stones. Just the gall stones, no alcohol. The stones were different sizes and some were very round and colorful. This is what I had come to see.

"They would make great marbles," I suggested as the boys laughed and we nearly dropped the jar into the open toilet. Prieto laughed the hardest. We stayed a while longer because there was no one to throw us out. Then, when we became bored, we left.

Carlos decided that Flaco's apartment should be our next stop. All the women would spend the day there. They would follow a process as old as the Mexican Indian to make the tamales. Señora Olga was in charge. She had the reputation of being able to beat so much air into the masa that when a ball of it was dropped into water it would float almost instantly. She did all this to the admiration and watchful eyes of the other women. Of course, it took a long time to get the masa that fluffy when you did it by hand and you had to be very strong. Señora Olga had the strength and patience not to test the masa until it was ready. She was the best tamale maker on St. Vrain Street.

The women's voices could be heard the minute we stepped into the living room. We did not go in by the back door because Señora Olga did not want any dust or sudden burst of wind to come in uninvited. Also, the kitchen was set up with many chairs all around the table ready for the participants in the *tamalada*. We approached the arena slowly because we knew that the job of washing and cleaning the *ojas*, corn husks, was ours: it was a dirty job! The corn husks contained bright reddish-brown hairs along with a great deal of other junk. It was a small adventure to open a stack of corn husks and discover what had got into them while they dried and waited for the day to become useful again. Señora Olga bought her *ojas* from Juárez. They were the hardest to clean but she like the price.

The best part of the *tamalada* was the talk of the women. If they were talking about religion or someone dying, they were respectful and serious. But if the talk was about the problems of people or human nature, they were funny and loud. They competed in rhyming and making puns, each trying to be more clever than the other. They spared no one with their tongues.

As the boys and I approached, I could hear the high voice of Señora Luz. From the pitch of her voice, the boys and I knew *que le estaba sacando la garra a alguien,* she was gossiping about someone. López would say this about her: *Cara de angel, unas de gato,* face of an angel, nails of a cat. The boys and I looked at each other and grinned. I wondered who the poor victim was.

"Yes, you all know what happens. *Gato viejo, raton tierno,* old men like young girls." Señora Luz's *dicho* froze me in my steps.

"*Calla* Luz, be quiet!" Señora Olga looked at us as we entered the kitchen. "The children are here. Come in welcomed guests. We have been waiting for you."

Noticing me behind the boys, Señora Alma called out to me. I looked at her and smiled. She waved to me to come give her a kiss. As I kissed her hot cheek, I noticed how pale she looked.

"Do you feel good Señora Alma?" I quickly asked her. "You feel as if you have *calentura.*"

"Ay, *corazón.* You are becoming such a big girl. So considerate," Señora Alma said as the boys turned to hide their laughter. "No, it is just hot in the kitchen with the meat cooking and the hot tongues of the women."

The boys and I went to the pan where the husks were soaking in water. This would make them soft and pliable when the masa was spread on them. By lunchtime, the masa was still not ready. The meat for the tamales was cooling on the stove.

By two in the afternoon, we all gathered around the table to make the tamales. I either got too much masa on the husk or not enough. Everyone took turns telling me how to do it. By the time the boys and women had made hundreds of tamales, I had only made ten. I was so unhappy.

"Well, Señora Olga, I'd rather eat them than make them," I reasoned as she assured me that she had made my share too. Once again, she saved the day for me.

The women talked about their families. Señora Rita sadly told how her son Salvador could not come because he was in Chicago. Señora Luz made a crude pun on the word "Chicago" that concerned toilet behavior. She was obnoxious.

The boys and I tired of the conversation. We asked Señora Olga if there was anything else she needed us to do. She said that the cooking was up to the stove and that we were free to go, although we were to come back to get the tamales for our families when it was dinner time. The long time spent without playing had made Flaco restless. He jumped up and started singing his "Caldonia" to the annoyance of his mother.

"Caldonia! Caldonia!" he sang in a high voice. Señora Olga pushed him outside.

"That is not a Christmas song, *chavalo. Lárgese*, get out of here!" Señora Olga tried to say it louder than Flaco's singing. Outside Carlos told Flaco that he would give him a dime if he would just wait until Christmas was over to sing the song. Flaco thought for a moment, sighed deeply, and reluctantly agreed.

By dinnertime, all the children of the block were inside waiting for the evening to end. Dinner was tamales and coffee. Carmen made some *buñuelos*, a fried pastry. My father and my brothers praised her cooking efforts. I personally wished I could be eating Señora Olga's *buñuelos*.

When I went upstairs to bed, I left a silent Carmen and Palm sitting opposite each other in the living room. My bed was a welcome sight because I was tired from my busy day. I thought about Christmas and I prayed again for some skates.

10 Sayings and Secrets

A *dicho* is a folk saying, a harmless way of making a comment. The most effective *dichos* are short, visual, and clever. Children like *dichos* that use animals to make a point. Many *dichos* make observations about human nature or life. Some can be long. If a *dicho* is too long, the person looks silly saying it. A short, sharp, and saucy *dicho* can vitalize, energize, and teach in a respectful and non-offensive manner. By the time a person becomes a parent, the value of the *dicho* is clear. Middle-aged and elderly people have the greatest facility with the *dicho*. For this age group, the *dicho* is a jewel that can shed light on the many dilemmas and woes of humans. Older people have a bag of *dichos* to salt and pepper their conversations. Most Spanish-speaking people enjoy the *dicho*; they appreciate the intent of the message. Everyone knows that the speaker is not the author of the *dicho*, he or she is merely the messenger of the culture. I loved the *dicho* when I was a child and my grandfather was a walking treasury of them. He would listen carefully to a conversation and with the same diagnostic skill that he used to select herbs for his clients, he came up with the appropriate *dicho* every time. He could frame the message in such a way that you were informed without losing your integrity.

My apartment was still dark when I awoke on Christmas Day, 1945. I waited for what seemed the longest while until I heard Palm tip-toe quietly down the hall. He went downstairs and I heard the closet door open. Then I heard Carmen follow him.

When I went downstairs, I saw some boxes on kitchen chairs, which had been placed in the middle of the living room. The radio was playing Christmas music and Carmen was rustling around in the kitchen. Hanging on the rung of the chair were some net stockings full of candies, pecans, walnuts, apples, and oranges. There was a card on each one that read: "Merry Christmas to a sweet child from the Church of Jesus."

I went into the kitchen and rushed into my father's arms.

"*Feliz Navidad.*" I hugged my smiling father hard. He wished me a merry Christmas and kissed my forehead. Then I hugged Carmen and wished her a *Feliz Navidad*. Her eyes were red and swollen. I politely tried not to notice because I knew she would be embarrassed.

Palm and the rest of the family gathered in the living room after everyone had eaten. I gave Palm and Carmen a picture we had made in school. Then they gave me a box that I could tell was a shoe box. I felt myself sadden because I didn't need any shoes; Padre Luna had seen to that. I smiled as I unwrapped the box and to my surprise there were a pair of silver skates with a shiny silver skate key. I wondered why it had not occurred to me that the skates would come in a shoe box. I was given a dress from my father's store, as well. This Christmas there were the usual bananas and oranges, as well as the yearly gift of fig preserves that Palm's sister in South Texas would send him. He looked at one of the jars of figs for a long time. He must have remembered Christmas with his family.

Around nine, I had put on my new dress and my saddle oxfords. They were the only shoes to which the metal skates could be attached. I practiced tightening and loosening my skates, shiny, silver wings of freedom. I was lost in my imagination when I saw Pelón coming from mass with his mother. He waved to me as they went into their apartment. After a while, he came outside and sat on the step with me while I was getting acquainted with my silver wings.

I got up and wobbled on the skates. As I started to fall, Pelón caught me and we both laughed as he steadied me. I looked up at the bedroom window where Palm and Carmen were watching me. I took a big breath of the cool Christmas day air and felt that I was the happiest child in El Paso. But I looked again at that upstairs window and was surprised to see the two apparently quarreling. Pelón pulled at me and we went down the walk. It was a free ride for me until we arrived at our lamp post. Pelón propped himself against our mulberry tree that was pathetically naked and dry. He encouraged me to try to skate without assistance. We did this for a long time until Flaco came running out of Señora Alma's apartment. Looking very serious, he ran across to his apartment. Pelón and I became nervous. I quickly sat down on the ground and we got my skates off. Pelón buckled the two straps of the skates together and put them across his shoulder. We started walking toward Flaco's apartment as Señora Olga and Flaco rushed out the kitchen door. They ran across the street towards Señora Alma's back door. Something was wrong.

"Flaco . . . Flaco!" Pelón called out. "*Qué pasa*, what is going on?"
Flaco didn't stop but he said the words that sent fear through my body.

"Señora Alma cannot be revived." He rushed into the apartment with
his mother. Pelón and I sat outside the door. We knew we just had to
wait until Flaco came out. After a long time, Flaco came out and leaned
against the red brick wall of Señora Alma's apartment.

"She's dead, Yoya," he said in a quiet voice. Taking a deep breath
he said, "They say she sat by the manger ever since she came home
from mass this morning. About a hour ago, someone noticed that she
was asleep. Then when they were ready to serve lunch, someone went
to her and realized that she wasn't asleep. She had her sons' picture
on her lap. My mother tried to revive her, but she had been dead for
some time." As Flaco finished, I cried quietly. I had known she was
sick the day before.

After a while, Padre Luna came up the walk. He went inside the
apartment and as he opened the door, I could hear Señora Alma's daughters crying. I walked back to my apartment to tell my father. I was feeling
bad and I wanted to tell him. I wanted the knot in my chest to go and I
needed comforting.

In the apartment, I could hear Palm and Carmen talking. When I
entered the kitchen, I saw that Carmen's eyes were red. She's been
crying again, I thought. How would she feel if she had lost someone who
had taken care of her for as long as she could remember? I told Palm
about Señora Alma. He stretched his arms and I went to him. My father
understood that I was sad. After several minutes, he reminded me that the
next day I would go with Carmen to visit her family. I softly protested that
I would miss Señora Alma's funeral. He said he was sorry, but Carmen
was planning to visit her family.

The boys and I spent the rest of Christmas sitting under our mulberry
tree. We talked about the nice things Señora Alma had done all our lives
for us. I reminded them of the day that President Roosevelt died and she
was so upset. We all remembered the party she had for us on the Virgen
de Guadalupe day. Christmas turned out to be so sad for us. The sitting
with the family would not be until the next day, and that night I kept
turning and turning in my bed. Carmen came in and asked me if I
wanted her to put some mentholatum on my eyelids. I remembered
how Señora Alma would do the same so that I couldn't open them and
would have to fall asleep. I agreed because I was so tired.

The next day I prepared to go to Juárez with Carmen. My grandfather came to attend the *velorio*, wake, for Señora Alma. He comforted me when I told him how sad I was.

"Yoya, *para todo hay remedio menos la muerte*, for everything there is a remedy except for death"—an appropriate *dicho*. "I had no herb for what made Alma's heart sad," López said softly as he braided my hair.

López took me and Carmen to the streetcar stop and waited there with us. When the streetcar was a couple of blocks away, he leaned down and kissed me and wished me a happy new year.

"*Amor, salud, y plata, mi mocosita*, love, health and money, my darling." He took my hand and put three silver pennies in it. I looked down at them in delight.

"Oh, Tata. Three 1943 pennies *de plata*. Now that makes 16 that I have." I thanked him especially because he rarely had American money. My grandfather reminded me that they were not made of silver. "They are made of steel. You need to know the difference," he cautioned me as he put me on the streetcar with Carmen. I rushed to a window so that I could wave to him. He waved back with the brown felt hat Palm had given him from the store. It matched the color of his skin.

That was the last time I saw my Tata. I suppose I didn't see him ever again because he was busy with his old wife or because he was ill or because my life changed. I just don't know why. That day he slipped out of my life and became a memory forever in my mind.

There were always secrets in my neighborhood. I thought grown-ups had a lot of secrets and that they knew something about death that I didn't. It wasn't until Don Benito died that I realized that there was no secret. Death was death.

Secrets were something private like when I had the tattoo or when Eduardo tried to rape me. The boys and I had many secrets—hiding places, secret words, and information. They had secret whistles and gestures. A secret was a special kind of glue between us. It meant being trusted with information you were even afraid to say aloud. López sometimes seemed to stop his stories just short of what seemed a secret, either his or someone else's.

The boys and I once tried to figure out who knew the most secrets. We all agreed that Padre Luna knew more secrets than we would ever know in our lives. In the dark confessional booth, Padre heard the best secrets. Flaco figured that by the time Padre died he would have heard one million secrets.

The women in our block all knew each other's secrets. They knew whose husband got drunk, which one threw a kiss at another woman, or which husband had a girlfriend in Juárez. Some women knew who was pregnant and who stopped being pregnant after a Saturday visit to Juárez. Then, Padre Luna was told after the fact. Many secrets were about who was illegal or who had something to hide. The pachucos had a whole organization based on secrecy.

In 1945 people seemed to know secrets about my family that I couldn't see. I knew they did because they would stop talking when they saw me coming. The boys would be very quiet if I asked what the *huirihuiri* was about. They would say that it was probably some *chismes*, or gossip. Pelón told me not to listen to busybodies.

Carmen and I sat in the streetcar until we got to Mejía Street in Juárez. She was so jumpy. I had never seen her like this before. During the ride, she chattered all about what foods she could hardly wait to eat. She promised to get me some *cajeta de membrillo*, quince candy. That cheered me up briefly. I would rather be on St. Vrain Street eating my hard Christmas candy.

We got off the streetcar and I was annoyed that I had to carry the *bolsa de red* full of clothing Palm had given Carmen to give to her family and friends. It was heavy and I dragged it more than I carried it. Carmen didn't seem to mind. In the third block off Lerdo, we were met by Carmen's oldest brother. He took the bag from me. This delighted me because I could spend my time looking at the stores and the different beggars who used Mejía as a thoroughfare between Lerdo and Avenida Juárez. They would catch the tourists as they entered on Lerdo or as they would exit on Avenida Juárez.

Once in the apartment of Carmen's family, her mother treated me like an honored guest. I soon forgot what I had left behind. At the appropriate time I thanked her for the meal and asked if I could walk around outside with Carmen's cousin. We returned when the sun was setting.

There was a single kerosene glass lamp lit when we came home. All the objects in the room cast big shadows on the plaster wall. I wished I could be in my own apartment. I had visited Carmen's family many times before, but I had never spent the night. Carmen became concerned that I would not be able to sleep on the quilts arranged for me next to the bed that she shared with her two sisters. I made her swear to me that there were no roaches or mice. She assured me there were none. She suggested putting some mentholatum on my eyelids again. I complained, but knowing that I would not be able to sleep for worrying about roaches, I agreed. I fell asleep with no problem.

The next day, the family had *pan dulce*, and some fresh milk someone brought to the apartment. The bread and the milk were so sweet and smelled so delicious that I ate more than I should have and became ill. They agreed that I wasn't used to raw milk. I wasn't used to milk, period. The next two days I spent inside the apartment and didn't miss being outside because, as usual, the weather became bad as soon as Christmas was over. In the morning when I woke up, I heard Carmen's mother crying in the kitchen. I could hear her scolding Carmen who cried in turn. I tried to listen, but I couldn't hear anything because a radio was playing. Still the sounds made me realize something secret was happening. I decided to stay alert.

That night, Carmen again said I should get a lot of sleep because I had been ill. I agreed and submitted myself to the mentholatum treatment. As soon as she left for the kitchen, I wiped the ointment off and quietly sang to myself so as to stay awake. I was just about to fall asleep when I heard the kitchen door open. I looked around and saw that everyone was in bed except Carmen. I got up, went to the kitchen, and peeked around the doorway curtain that was pulled at night. In the kitchen, Carmen's body made a long spooky shadow that almost sent me back to the quilts. Then I heard a deep voice and I could hear Carmen talking to a man. She moved and the lamp light revealed the boyish face of the man they called Chuy; he had come to our September 16 party. Heaviness overtook my body as I realized my silver moment. They got close but I couldn't see because Carmen blocked my view. I knew she was kissing Chuy. I went to the quilts and thought about what I had seen. I thought about Palm and I became angry. I knew I had to do something. The next two nights, the same thing happened again. Each day, I would behave as if nothing had happened. I didn't talk much and no one expected me to because I had been ill. I ignored the pained look on Carmen's mother's face. Apparently, she was the only one who knew the secret: Carmen was in love with Chuy. I managed to busy myself and I counted the hours before I could leave.

On New Year's Eve, some of Carmen's friends, including Chuy, came to visit. They planned to walk to the strip on Avenida Juárez to see all

the people celebrating the end of 1945. She said I could go if I promised
to go to sleep immediately after the excursion. I agreed and grabbed her
hand. Once when I looked at Chuy he smiled at me but he quickly
turned his eyes. I thought to myself: you just wait until I tell Palm.

Avenida Juárez was packed with New Year's Eve celebrants, mostly
Americans. Carmen said they were American soldiers. When I saw a
group of them singing and shouting out their home state names, I
wanted to call on them to help me beat up the *gavilán pollero*, chicken
hawk—Chuy. In front of the Tivoli Bar, a group of soldiers sang a New
Year's song that I didn't know. Then they counted the numbers down
and they all yelled, blew on horns, tossed hats up in the air, and wished
each other and everyone on the street, Happy 1946! Then all the people
I was with hugged and kissed each other. I felt as if I had a chicken bone
stuck in my throat.

The next day we left. The streetcar was full because people were
going to the New Year's parade in El Paso. All I could think about on the
way home was how to tell Palm. Would I tell him in a sad voice or would
my voice be matter of fact? Should I be angry or sad. How could I tell
him? It never occurred to me that I shouldn't tell him. I was so angry.

When we arrived at the Virginia approach, I stopped for a minute in
front of the Price's Velvet Ice Cream sign at the corner. I realized as I looked
at the projects what I had not known before, the secret all the neighbors
knew and the boys knew. I finally understood what they had been whispering about all this time. The anger grew inside me. I thought of all the
remarks I had overheard and I couldn't believe that I had not guessed that
Carmen was unfaithful to my father. Carmen turned around and asked why
I had stopped. This Carmen was not the Carmen in Juárez, gay and happy.
This Carmen was the sour and unhappy woman who lived with us.

"I have a pebble in my shoe," I said. "I'll catch up in a minute."

She walked ahead of me to the apartment. I wondered where the boys
were and I was silently rehearsing my words when Pelón came out of his
apartment. He waved at me and rushed over.

"*Hola, Yoya. ¡Feliz año nuevo!*" He grabbed and hugged me. I was stiff
and unresponsive.

"Oh, *qué nos pasa?*" he asked immediately as he looked at my downcast
eyes. "Didn't you have a good time with your *madrasta?*"

"No, Judas! Why didn't you tell me about Carmen? And don't make
out to be so innocent," I answered. "You knew what she was doing,

didn't you? You and all the *viejas*! *Se burlaban de me*, you laughed at me! All those times you said they were just gossiping, you knew they were gossiping about Palm. You knew that Carmen *le estaba haciendo los tamales de chivo a mi padre, que no?*" I was angry and spitting the words out.

"I didn't know if you knew about things like that . . . about men and women. *¡Perdóname!* I thought you were too young," Pelón said.

I thought to myself that yes, I did know about men and women, ever since Eduardo took me into the bedroom. That secret between men and women was something I had almost learned. And Sister St. Agnes María told me the other secret about men and women the week after the attack—how babies got in a woman's body. I was not happy to learn the secrets but the truth is the truth!

"Well, you could have told me!" I told him as we walked to his yard. "I didn't know there were secrets between us," I said sadly. "*Tú eres mi cuate*, you are my buddy."

"Yoya, there are always secrets. There are things that you can't always tell anyone. I didn't want to hurt you. And I thought the *desabrida*, the sour one, would leave anyway. What happened?" Pelón asked.

I explained to him what I had seen in Juárez. He sympathized and then asked me what I was going to do.

"I'm going to tell Palm," I said simply.

"Are you sure you should, Yoya?" Pelón looked very concerned. "Do you want to hurt your father? Maybe Carmen will tell him herself." Pelón tried to change my mind. "My grandfather Benito always said: *la verdad amarga*, truth embitters."

"*¡Calla!* I can't have that secret and not tell my father. He will smell it on me," I started my justification. "He'll know I have a secret. I don't want to hurt him, but, *nadie se burla de mi padre*, no one laughs at my father."

"*Bueno*. Do as you wish." Pelón answered sadly. Then he told me all about Señora Alma's funeral. I tried to listen but all I could think about was Carmen and Palm. After he finished telling me, I said I needed to go put my things in the apartment. I told him I would return in a while.

In the apartment, Carmen was sitting in Palm's brown chair listening to some *ranchera*, country music, on the radio. She was absorbed by her own thoughts and she didn't seem to want to talk, which was all right with me. I went upstairs and lay down on the cot with my beloved skates. I thought about what I was going to do as I made my silver skates go up and down in the air. That I was going to tell Palm was no question. Just

how and when was the problem. I must have fallen asleep because the
next thing I knew my father was waking me up.

"*Mi'ja*, are you feeling all right? Carmen said you were ill in Juárez."
My father was smiling at me.

"Yes, father. I'm fine." I sat up and grabbed his neck and kissed him
many times.

"Oh, my goodness. Maybe we should take vacations from each other
more often. I don't think I have ever seen you so glad to see me," he
asked, "Is everything okay with you?" By the time he finished what he
was saying, I could see that he was becoming concerned. "Yoya, is something wrong?"

"No, Papí," I rushed to tell him as I looked toward the window.
He looked at me and smiled.

"Aren't you going outside to skate. You have a couple of hours of
sunlight. Pelón just came by for you. I told him you would go over to his
place as soon as you awoke," Palm said as he started to walk out the door.

"Apá! There is something wrong." I knew I had to tell him now or
never. He turned around and looked lovingly at me. He waited. "Papí,
Carmen and Chuy kissed. They were together after I was asleep," I said
hurriedly. He just stood and after a while he nodded his head.

"It's all right, Yoya. I'll take care of it. You go outside and play,"
he said as he turned around and left the room. I jumped out of bed and
grabbed my skates and went downstairs. I could hear Palm and Carmen
talking quietly in the kitchen. I left and closed the door hard so they
would know I was gone.

I met Pelón and we talked for a little while. I told him what I had said
to my father. He just shook his head and said he hoped I had done the
right thing.

"*Palabras y piedras sueltas no tienen vueltas*, loose words and stones can't
be taken back," he said in a serious voice.

"*Ay sí, abuelito!*" I pushed him as I felt fear enter my body. Still, I knew
I had had to tell Palm.

It was beginning to get dark when Pelón and I noticed some black
smoke down past St. Vrain. Carlos ran past us saying that there was a fire
below the projects. He yelled to us to come along. Flaco ran out of his
apartment as a fire engine came down the street. It clanged and whined
as it passed us. We decided to chase the engine to the end of the block.
The fire and smoke were getting bigger. I told them to come with me to

ask Palm if I could go and watch the fire. As we got to the apartment, Carmen was coming out. She had two big bags and her eyes were red from crying. She walked past me; my father was walking behind her. I asked him if I could go with the boys to see the fire. Because he was so preoccupied he said I could but not to get too close. Pelón told him that he and the boys would take care of me. That made me angry. But if I got to go, what difference did it make, I thought. As we ran past the lamp post, I turned around to look back at Carmen and my father. Pelón came up to me and said softly so that only I could hear: she's leaving. Then we ran off to see the fire. We stood a long way from it. The police and firemen were having a hard time keeping the people at a distance. I coughed and complained to Pelón that I was scared. It wasn't only the fire that had me frightened. We stood quietly watching. After a while, I turned around and my father was right behind me. The street light and the fire made his face very visible. There were tears rolling down his face.

"Papá!" I gasped as I saw his face.

"*Mi'ja*. It's nothing. Smoke always bothers me," he said as he wiped his face with his handkerchief. I knew better. I remembered what López would say with one of his *dichos: Amores, dolores y dinero, no se pueden estar secretos*, love, grief and money, can not be kept secret. And, for a moment I wished I had never told Palm my news.

That night Palm gave me a laxative that came in a small chocolate bar. It didn't taste bad. Then he put some alum on the blister inside my mouth and in front of my teeth. Every time I got sick, this would happen to me. My father cured me in his way. López would have cured me with herbs and rubs. I didn't care because I was just glad to be home. What I didn't realize was that Carmen's departure was the beginning of the end of my life with my father on St. Vrain Street.

11 Hijo Natural

In the l940s, a child born to a woman who didn't have a husband was called *un hijo natural*. That didn't mean children born to a married couple were not natural. It meant that the child was born in a natural way, a product of person's *naturaleza*, or basic drive. Children weren't called illegitimate, unwanted, or born out of wedlock. When such a birth occurred, it was accepted as a natural consequence of a strong drive. It was a way to handle an unexpected blessing.

López explained that natural children have been happening in the world ever since Adam and Eve. He argued that Jesus was a natural child whom Joseph was willing to claim as his own. Furthermore, my grandfather would tell the parents of an unwed pregnant girl, when they consulted him, that she was not the first one nor would she be the last one. Señora Alma would say that the child was a gift from heaven while Señora Luz, on the other hand, wasn't as kind.

It sometimes happened that some young girl would go on an extended visit to the *rancho* the family came from. When she returned, there was a new foundling that the family said had been abandoned. No one questioned such an occurrence out loud. Besides, the child was usually a source of joy for the family and neighbors.

Some *hijos naturales* were raised by grandparents who were young themselves. Other such children were raised by their uncles or aunts and were sometimes called *arrimados*, protected ones. Then there were the homeless children. These *hijos* were abandoned and had to go from one family to another until one of the families let them stay permanently. These children were sort of community charges. Everyone *les llamaban la atención* if they were misbehaving. Padre Luna encouraged people to care for these unfortunate children. If a child had nowhere to go, Padre would see that he or she was placed in a Catholic orphanage. He preferred that the child stayed in the community.

The day after New Year's Day, Palm woke me up early and told me to dress myself quickly because I had to go to his store with him. I obeyed and later in the kitchen asked him why I had to go. He told me in a very cool voice that because I had been sick, he didn't want me to go to school for the rest of the week. He sent a note to the school with Carlos. I didn't care because I wanted to be with him anyway.

It was cold outside when we left for the store. We had to walk because Palm didn't have his car any longer. He had sold it a couple of months before, when his money ran out. Once we came to the bakery on Stanton Street, we turned right and were at the store. It was cold and dark inside. Palm pulled a string and turned on the light. I slapped my arms and body to warm up. There was a wood stove in the middle of the room and a small, metal kerosene heater that Palm didn't use in order to save money. I went to the wood stove and looked around for paper or cardboard to burn. There was none. When Palm from the back, he was carrying a bucket filled to the top with old shoes.

"Apá, what are we going to burn?" I asked him.

"This," he answered as he put the bucket of shoes down next to the wood stove.

These were the boxes of old shoes that Palm had bought for a cheap price a few months back. They were the fuel for this winter. Actually, I had a lot of fun. Learning to judge how well each type of shoe would burn became an adventure for me that day. The light and cheap women's shoes burned the best. The men's shoes with heavy soles were the worst. I had to fish out the heavy shoes with long pliers when they wouldn't burn or if they smelled too bad. I was thoroughly entertained for the major part of the day. I kept wondering what kind of person had worn each pair of shoes.

In the afternoon, I went into the back part of the store where there were boxes stacked up against one wall. On the other side were drifts of clothes waiting to go to the tables in the front. I dropped down on a big stack of clothes and fell asleep for a while until Palm and a woman came back to where I was. I sat up and startled Palm who had some problems seeing in the dark room. He introduced me to the woman.

"Madama, this is my daughter Gloria." Palm used that strange word "madama". I don't know anyone who ever used the word. He knew the word from somewhere.

"This is Señora Dolores and her son, Ponchito." My father made the introduction. I could see Señora Dolores, but I saw no son. I opened my eyes wider. Perhaps he was in the other room.

"I am pleased to meet you," I greeted the woman.

"Luís Alfonso! Ponchito!" Señora Dolores shouted. I looked towards the curtained doorway. Then suddenly, a small boy about my size appeared from behind her skirt.

"This shy boy doesn't know how to talk," she said.

I took her to mean that he couldn't speak. So, when he softly said, "*Buenas tardes*," I was surprised.

"*¡Quiubole*, hello!" I answered as I looked at the small boy, who had coarse black hair, dark skin, and pox scars on his face. His big, dark eyes stared back at me with interest.

Palm and Señora Dolores were busy looking at the different stacks of clothes and they eventually went to the front. I looked at the boy.

"In this country, you have to talk!" I told him in a very official way. "And I have found it pays to speak English. Where are you from?"

"Coyote," he answered.

"Where is that?" I asked him.

"It's a village near Torreón," he reluctantly answered, hoping that I would stop asking questions. But, noticing his discomfort, I naughtily decided to continue.

"Are those small pox scars?" I asked him as I remembered that López had said there was so much small pox in Mexico that when Mexicans got their passports in the thirties and forties, it was noted if they had no small pox as an identifying feature.

"No! Chicken pox!" he replied politely. I was suddenly embarrassed that I had been so rude and I said, "Forgive me, Ponchito. *Fué falta de educación*, it was impolite!" I apologized for being nosy.

"Oh, don't worry," he quickly added, but since I had been so impolite, he decided to ask me a question. "What are those dots on your face?" he asked, pointing.

"Dots? Oh, *pecas*, freckles." I had a mental picture of polka dots on my face. I smiled that he had the nerve to ask me.

I invited Ponchito to join me in selecting shoes for the wood stove. He wasn't surprised that we were burning shoes but he would only pick them up with two fingers. After we were through, he asked where he could wash his hands. I pointed to the bathroom and was surprised that he wanted to wash his hands. It wasn't as if he had mud on them. He returned and watched me toss in the shoes, explaining which ones burned better. I offered to let him pick the shoes and put them in the fire. He said no, he'd rather watch me do it. I knew he didn't want to touch them.

My father talked to Señora Dolores for a long time. She agreed to help him straighten up his stock in exchange for clothing to take back to Coyote to sell the following week. Palm was pleased with the arrangement so they smiled and nodded at each other. The next few days, they worked together. Once, I heard him tell her that he didn't know what he was going to do about me. He said he needed someone to care for me. I resented that he told her about our situation. But it didn't bother me when I told Ponchito about Carmen. He and I got an RC Cola and a bag of Fritos and sat on the street curb outside the store to exchange stories.

"¿Y tu Papá?" What about your father?" I asked him.

"Soy hijo natural," he answered. I wanted to know more, but it was too soon to ask.

"¿Y tu mamá?" he asked me because I had asked him a question.

"¡En el cielo con Tata Chuy! In heaven with Daddy Jesus" I laughed. Ponchito was surprised by my answer. He laughed for the first time. His Fritos flew out of his mouth.

"¿Cuando murió?" he asked quietly.

"Oh, a long time ago. When I was little," I answered.

"How old are you?" Ponchito had a puzzled look on his face.

"Eight years old," I replied, taking in a deep breath just like my Tata López. "It has been a hard life. How old are you?"

"Seven. On March 13, I'll be eight." He answered as he counted on his fingers when I told him that September 12 was my birthday. He said, "You are six months older than me." It made me happy that he knew I was older. I was used to being the youngest.

The street car passed on its way to Juárez. Ponchito and I waved at two little girls who were waving at us. We talked about where we lived and he told me that they were *arrimados*, living temporarily with a relative of his mother.

"What's your relative's name?" I don't know why I asked.

"María." He answered. "María, *la fiera*, the wild one."

I was about to ask why she had such a nickname when his mother came out of the store. She waved at him to follow and she said goodbye to me. I went back into the store. It was colder inside than outside. Palm was sitting in front of the wood stove smoking a cigarette. I told him

about my findings on the best shoes to burn. He smiled at me. He took
me in his arms and we sat in front of the fire. No one came to shop and
we left at five.

"Apá, are they coming back tomorrow?" I asked him. I enjoyed
Ponchito's company. It wasn't the same as with the boys, but it was nice
being the older one.

"No, I think they'll come to visit us at the apartment Sunday," he
answered as we walked home. It was becoming dark and we hurried.
We didn't talk anymore because we were tired and it was cold.

When Carmen was with us, I was unhappy. It wasn't that she did things
to upset me, she just didn't make me feel as if I mattered. Her body was in
our house, but her heart was in Juárez. Now that she was gone, I didn't miss
her at all. But I missed something—a woman in the house.

At first, I worked hard at helping Palm when we came home from
the store. By Friday I was tired of chores and I just wanted to play.
My enthusiasm for helping left just as Carmen did. Even the bad feeling
I had after telling my father about her and Chuy was less by the end of
the week. Yet there was a void in the apartment.

Palm was very quiet and I had to force him to talk. He tried hard to
be interested in my chattering, but loss once again drained him. Every
evening he sat in front of the radio listening to his music as he smoked
his cigarettes and drank his one drink. He seemed just a phantom of a
man sitting in his brown chair—an empty cicada shell.

On Saturday, I played with the boys. We visited the neighbors and
just by standing around in their kitchens we learned how everyone was
doing. In Señora Olga's kitchen we found out that Ignacio and Teresa
were very serious. He had given her a ring on Christmas Day. Señora
Olga was happy that Teresa's *hijo natural* was going to have a father; she
said all children should have a mother and father. I felt uncomfortable
when she said that because I didn't have a mother. In Señora Luz's yard,
we learned what the pachucos were doing. She had kept an eye on all of
them ever since El Pajaro Prieto killed her son. Whenever she knew
accurate information about the gang, she passed the information to the
police or the rival gang. She never worried about what she was doing
because she knew that the gang members didn't hurt women or children.
Flaco whispered to us that there is always a first time.

On Saturday afternoon, we went to confession. I had the unpleasant
task of telling Padre Luna about Carmen and Chuy. I also confessed how

bad I felt that I had told my father. Padre said that he knew I meant no harm and that it was natural that I wanted him to know. He said Carmen would have left eventually—*con el tiempo maduran las brevas*, everything comes out in due time. Then I knew that he too had known Carmen's secret. I felt better that Padre didn't scold me. That evening, I helped my father and I also laid out my wool dress and shined my shoes ready for mass the next day. The boys and I were going together.

That night I dreamed that I was alone in the Concordia Cemetery, running from tombstone to tombstone in search of my mother's grave. I could read the names on some of the gravestones but in others the letters would fly off as I approached them. I found Don Benito's metal marker but still I couldn't find my mother's. When I found Señora Alma's grave, it made me so happy because I hadn't gone to the funeral. Round and round I ran in the cemetery but I couldn't find Panchita's grave. Nor could I find my way out of the cemetery. I cried and cried and called out for my father. But he didn't come. When I awoke, I thought about the dream. *¡Tonta!* I said to myself: Mamásita is buried in Juárez, not in the Concordia Cemetery. I let out a sigh and got out of bed.

Downstairs in the kitchen, I had a cup of coffee with Palm. He and I had a lifeless conversation until I told him about my nightmare. And, once again, he said that he should have taken me to the funeral. He said that someday we'd go and find the grave together.

"Then, you won't have such terrible *pesadillas*," he said confidently.

"I don't want a *pesadilla*, but I'll take a *quesadilla*," I said with an open mouth and lifted eyebrow.

"*Payasa*," Palm said as he laughed. It was the first time he had called me that in a long time. He chuckled as he repeated the words, *quesadilla no pesadilla*. He looked at me with a big smile on his face; he liked my cleverness.

When the boys came by for me, I left my father sitting in front of the radio listening to some hallelujah preacher. That was his religion. I didn't enjoy the man's yelling. When I asked Palm why the preacher was so angry, he just laughed. I preferred the quiet of the Mass and the low buzz of the prayers. The Mass always seemed to me like a beautiful dance with soft words and bells. I loved the sound the echo of someone coughing created in the cold church. Padre Luna was emotional enough for me. When he went to the cubby hole where the chalice was stored, I watched with great attention as he pulled the little curtain. Until I

turned eight, I believed that God was in that cubby hole. I was certain
that Padre stored God in there each time after communion.

After mass, we returned to our block. Flaco invited us to his house
for something to eat and Señora Olga served us all a big bowl of *menudo*,
with a *birote*, a small roll. The chili in the dish was too hot, but I ate it
anyway. Señora Olga said my stomach was weak from my recent illness.

Around three, I went home because it was cold and I wanted to see my
father. I fell asleep on the living room floor and awoke when I heard several
people enter the apartment. I opened my eyes and looked into Ponchito's
face in front of me. Dazed, I looked around and came back to Ponchito's
face. He whispered that his mother and María, *la fiera*, were there.

I stood up and looked at the two women talking to my father. The
three were engrossed in their conversation and it gave me a chance to
look at the new woman Ponchito called *la fiera*. She was almost as tall as
Palm. The light from the windows revealed a stocky, broad shouldered,
strong but not fat woman. As I drew closer, I could see that her skin was
the color of a copper penny. Her face was large and somewhat flat with
ruddy cheeks. Her coarse black hair was combed straight back and braided
into a single thick braid. She wore silver earrings made of tiny silver Mexican money. But her most impressive feature was her large, almond-shaped
black eyes that sparkled with life. Her mouth was small and she held it in a
serious pose as she spoke with my father. Years later, I would see a picture of
Indian women and think of María. As I approached, she looked at me and
gave me a faint smile before she turned back to Palm and Señora Dolores.
She certainly was a strong woman, but not a *fiera*. I drew up next to my
father who was discussing how to sell used clothing with them.

"Madama, this is *mi hija*, Gloria." Palm looked down at me. "Gloria,
this is Señora María, a relative of Señora Dolores."

"*Mucho gusto*, Señora María," I replied shyly because I was embarrassed that I had stared so hard at her. I knew she was aware of it.

"*Qué linda*," she said. I felt the warmth of the compliment, but not
for long. "*¿Créo que tienes seís años, no?*"

"*No, señora. Tengo ocho años y pico;* I am eight and more years old,"
I replied, offended.

"She is very small for her age." My father rushed to soothe my
feelings and justify María's error.

"I'm sorry *mi amor.* I haven't had a little girl in so many years that I
have forgotten how to judge age." She answered in such a sweet voice

that I felt a wave of emotion go through my small body. It was like music from an unexpected source.

"*Pierda cuidado*, it's alright, Señora." I wondered about this woman who wore a dress with small flowers on it and who smelled like freshly washed clothes. Who are you, I thought to myself as I stood very close to her.

"My two daughters are young women and it's been a long time since we have had a little girl in the house," Señora María said to me as we went into the kitchen to drink a soda. María motioned to me to sit down next to her. I did so willingly and was pleased to have the attention.

Palm and the women talked for a long time. I didn't leave as I normally would have with other visitors. As I watched María talk, she would look at me and smile a soft smile. Señora Dolores and Ponchito said goodbye because they had to go to Juárez to leave for Coyote. Ponchito told me he would see me in a week. He always had to come to El Paso with his mother because immigration didn't bother his mother if he was along. After all, no one takes their child to work with them.

"Señor Palm, *quien le cuida su hija?* Who takes care of your daughter? I know you are alone and that you work," María asked Palm, who seemed very interested in her question.

"It's a problem, Madama. I can't leave her here while I work because she is not safe." Palm opened up to her. "I am going to ask the *madres* for some help. They like Yoya and they will see that she learns how to be a little girl. Here, she runs around with boys and has no proper training."

María and Palm discussed how difficult it is to be a parent by themselves. They had different problems but they understood each other. I loved listening to them as they told stories about difficult times. As they talked, I stood up and went to María. She put her arm around me and her eyes became somewhat red. My body ached and at the time I didn't understand why. She was a mother looking for a child and I was a child in need of a mother.

My father watched us with delight. He continued to talk to María, but I could tell he wasn't concentrating. María kept the conversation going but she seemed to be enjoying me more.

"Señor Palm, if you would allow it and if Gloria wants to, I would like to take care of her," María said to my father in a soft voice. "We are poor, but my daughters and I can manage. *Me hace falta una niña que cuidar*, I need a child to take care of." And, I thought to myself, I need someone to take care of me.

My father smiled and was clearly moved. He looked at me and asked. "What do you think, Yoya?" He asked in a happy way that told me he liked the idea. "Do you want to stay with Señora María and her daughters?"

"How old are your daughters Señora María?" I asked, taking my time so that Palm would not notice how much I wanted to go with this *fiera*.

"*Señoritas*. Eighteen and twenty-two years old," she replied.
What luck! Three women to care for me.

"Oh, Papí. I want to go with her." I answered my father's question with lowered eyes because I was worried I might hurt him.

"It's all right, *mi'ja*. I know you need to be taken care of. And I am so old and tired. I don't do a good job," he answered sadly as I rushed into his arms and hugged him.

"I love you Papí," I answered between sighs. "And you are a good father."

It was agreed that I would go home with María. I put my clothes in a *bolsa de red*. I told Carlos where I was going. He wasn't satisfied with my directions as to where María lived, so he asked María. She gave him the address and instructions how to get there. He didn't appear too happy.

Outside, he was frank. "Yoya, she lives in a tenement two blocks from the river. *Te vas de Guatemala a Guatepeor*, you are going from bad to worse." After a while, he added. "Maybe I can talk to Father to see if I can take care of you." He paused, "*¡Caramba!* I can take care of you."

"Carlos, I appreciate it, but I like María. I like how she is." I tried to make him feel comfortable. "And you can come visit me and we'll go to the store. I have to show you how to burn shoes." I had told him about the shoes and the wood stove.

"If you are not happy, Yoya, I'll bring you back," Carlos told me in a reassuring voice. "If you're unhappy, scratch your head many times so that I'll know," he said in case we were not alone when we visited.

When the sky was turning red-orange, María and I left my apartment. As we walked together and talked, I felt as if I had always known her. When I asked her what kind of work she did she answered, "Oh, lots of things, *mi amor*! I do a lot of things, you'll see." I wondered what she meant. We walked quickly and in silence toward my new place.

PART II

THE TENEMENTS

12 Poverty and Work

In 1940 El Paso, it was possible to be poor and not be aware of just how poor. When everyone around you is poor, poverty seems normal. Adults knew the invisible trap poverty masked and they tried to escape it through hard work. My grandfather López used to say: *El pobre es contento aunque se encuentre apurado y apretado hasta las clavijas*, the poor are happy even though they find themselves worried and squeezed up to their teeth. Perhaps poverty teaches you how to rise above it.

Although I know some immigrants came to the United States after the Revolution of 1912 to escape real or unreal persecution in Mexico, the majority of Mexican immigrants came to find economic opportunity. These immigrants came to the United States to stop being poor. Since they didn't speak English, had minimal education, if any, and for the most part had no money, they took the jobs in fields, kitchens, factories, and yards. They did so for several generations. In truth, many of the immigrants of the 1930s and 1940s benefited minimally from the move from Mexico because of the depression in the United States and the war. They had dreams of making enough money to return to Mexico to buy land; some dreamed of making enough money to buy back the land they once historically owned in this country. For many, they were just dreams.

Poverty had a positive side. It made you appreciate food, clothes, or a home when you had them. Poverty helped you appreciate people who were kind. It made you cling to the message of religion on cold winter Sunday—the promise that someday you would get more than you received on earth. Poverty also helped you develop resources within yourself and helped you to see the possibilities others more fortunate didn't notice. And poverty, in all its manifestations, gave birth to the pachuco.

María and I reached the corner of Kansas and Seventh. She pointed out Aoy Elementary School to me. It was a red building just like my old school. Palm was going to see the principal the next day about my start-

ing there. Down Kansas, just past Aoy, we came to a fence that was a
barrier for fiercely running water. "What is that?" I asked, frightened by
the sight and the smell of the water.

"A canal. Have you never seen it before?" María asked me. "It's all
right, *mi amor*, the fence won't let you fall in."

We rushed past the canal and I was beginning to think that Carlos was
right. Maybe I was going from *Guatemala a Guatapeor*. A familiar feeling
of discomfort was rising. We walked down a dirt street to the tenement
where María lived. The red-brick, one-story building was flanked by
other tenements and they all looked the same. The building was made
up of two parallel sets of apartments that began at the street and went
back to the alley, from west to east. There was a small breezeway that
gave access to the five apartments; a single toilet for the ten apartments
was at the junction in the alley. Each apartment had two doors to the
outside, shotgun style. This made it easy to cool off the apartment in
summer. María's place was the third apartment from the front of the
street. I made a quick mental note because it was hard to distinguish one
from the other. María told me that she also had the opposite apartment
directly across the breezeway. I was impressed until I was inside the
north apartment and saw how it was. María and her daughters used it
as sleeping quarters. The south apartment had the eating and kitchen
area—four very small rooms. The sleeping rooms were filled with their
belongings: boxes, some trunks, a dresser, and two big beds. María
turned on the light on an electrical cord that hung down from the ceiling. As it swung from side to side, I could see many pictures on the wall
and other decorations, all from Mexico. María's parents were in a big
picture that showed them from the shoulders up, sitting side by side,
with somber faces as if they had been forced to pose. The dresser and the
tables were crowded with small and big figurines, mementos, and little
bottles. There didn't appear to be a single space unoccupied by some
possession. María took my things into the adjoining room. She told me
that Caridad and Paloma, her daughters, shared one bedroom and that
she and I would share the other. I liked the arrangement.

We were in the north apartment when María's daughters joined us.
Paloma was the oldest and very fair considering María's coloring. She
had light brown hair and eyes, was thin and small and she was pretty
and very sweet. It was easy to tell that she was a very serious young lady.
Caridad, on the other hand, was a striking *morena* with shapely legs and

a voluptuous body. She had the style of the actress María Felix. I said to myself, this is what I want to look like when I am that old. And she had her mother's almond shaped eyes. One of her eyes had what María called a *nube*, a cloud, or a cataract. María told me later that she was always looking for something to remove it. She maintained that Caridad's cataract was the result of *alguien le hizo ojo*, someone's hexing her when she was an infant. María was very fearful of the evil eye. She would become nervous when people said nice things to me. Once when a woman admired my braids and gave me some compliments, María asked her to touch me just in case she accidently *me hiso ojo*. María said *hacer ojo* was the consequence of coveting and the harm was done to the child coveted. She always warned me about it when I would pay too much attention to an infant and she would make me touch the child just to be safe. The only person who could remove the *ojo* was the person who did it. That is what she said happened to Caridad. Another thing María taught me was the custom of giving an object admired by a person to the person. Whenever I had something another child admired, María would make me give it to the child, even if he or she did not ask for it. María said you had to give it to the person because the object had made the person envious. The only cure was handing over the envied item. I did not like that.

María and her daughters took me into the kitchen and eating area. There was a table with chairs and a slender cabinet containing their dishes and glasses. On a small table was a brightly painted Mexican clay pitcher filled with water and covered with a clay cup to protect the water from dirt and bugs as well as to drink from. The importance of protecting the water was something I would soon learn. In the kitchen was a brown wooden ice box—which I had never seen before—and a kerosene stove like those I had only seen in Juárez. The kerosene was in a glass container that fed the individual burners. I was fascinated by the ice box. I asked María if I could look inside and she said I could. I looked at all the compartments and was curious about the one that held the ice. I asked what happen when the ice melted. María said it went into a pan below. She would show me when she emptied the pan. In my father's apartment, we had had an electric ice box and a gas stove.

María heated some tortillas and served cheese and coffee. It smelled good and tasted delicious. María asked me if I was enjoying the food.

"It tastes good!" I said to her smiling face.

"*Para la hambre no hay pan duro*, hunger is not picky." María smiled and raised her left eyebrow, a gesture I would see often when she was requesting agreement. She and her daughters talked. It felt so natural watching them. In my home, Palm and I usually ate in silence. I did all the talking if there was talking at all. The three talked about their plans for the week. Paloma worked downtown in a pawn shop on El Paso Street, below San Francisco Street. She knew a little English, but it didn't matter because the customers were Mexicans. Caridad did not know any English, so she worked in the fields and in people's houses. There was no field work in January. Later that night, María and I talked further. I was very curious about her daughters.

"María, Paloma and Caridad are different." I was very curious because one was so dark and the other was fair.

"It's because they had different fathers," María answered sharply. "*Son hijas naturales*," she added as if she knew that I was about to ask about the fathers.

"Forgive me if I am too *preguntona*," I rushed to say because I did not want to offend Maria.

"No, *mi amor*. It is natural for you to be curious," she answered in an understanding voice. "Everyone is curious!" She didn't say anything for what seemed an hour to my growing curiosity. But I waited quietly until she was ready to talk.

"My daughters were children of love. My Paloma was the daughter of the son of the Spaniards I worked for in Torreón. I was only sixteen when I had her. And, I was all alone because my family had moved to Chihuahua." She paused. "Caridad was the daughter born of an *engaño*, deception. Her father was already married. I was twenty years old and she was born in Chihuahua." She looked at me and something in my look made her quickly add. "He just forgot to tell me that he was married." She let out a big laugh.

"Oh, María, *que vida!*" I tried to sound grown-up. I realized it sounded funny and I prepared myself for being laughed at by María. But, she didn't. I knew she respected me.

"Now it is time for *mímis*, sleep." María said to me. "Are you ready, *mi amor?*"

"Just sing a song to me," I asked. I knew Maria had a good voice because I had heard her sing quietly to herself. She sang the popular songs "*Mócosita*" and "*Cachito*" to me as I went to sleep that first night.

Each night at sunset for the rest of the winter, we would clean up the kitchen and retire to the bedroom, where it was warmer. In the bedroom, María and I would sing songs and she would tell me stories about when she lived in Mexico and about the people she knew. The world outside was very cold, but inside María kept me warm and secure. I was to share her home for one year.

The following day, María gently woke me to a dark room. She urged me to hurry and dress for my first day at my new school. I had a cup of coffee and a flour tortilla and was ready when Palm came by for me.

"Are you happy, *mi'ja?*" he asked. He looked hard at me. I supposed that he wanted some assurance that he had done the right thing. My poor father, I thought. I explained that I was not used to being in the tenement. But, I quickly added, I was happy. I told him that I loved being with the women. After all, there were only men on St. Vrain. He smiled, convinced that everything was fine.

On our way to school, we came to the canal that was just south of the school. I held Palm's hand as I looked at the ugly brown water. I hated it then and would always hate the Franklin canal. It was so big and deep, like a twisting and swirling huge brown rope that scraped dirt and scavenged things discarded or forgotten. It moved quietly, like a hyena, doing what it wanted without asking permission. This was my first glimpse of it in daylight. When María and I saw it before, it was too big a shock for me to really look at it. The things I would learn about the canal would terrify me more. I didn't realize then that the water was a victim of the canal. It was the restraint of cement that made it the way it was. Once in the valley, the freed water found its purpose.

The principal called my father and me into her office. She heard Palm's explanation that he was a widower and that he needed to place me with a family near the school. They talked for a while and everything was set. Next, Palm took me to the nurse's office. She weighed and measured me.

"Mr. Palm your granddaughter weighs only forty pounds and she is way below height for eight years old. She is undernourished," the white lady told my father.

"He's my father! My grandfather is López!" I said in a very angry voice that made the nurse knit her eyebrows and look at me as if I had spat on the floor.

"I'm sorry, my daughter is sensitive about my age," Palm hurried to apologize to the nurse. "She is small, just like her mother." I listened to his words. My mother was small, I thought.

My father dropped me off at my class. The white teacher greeted me in a sweet way while my father was present. Inside the classroom she was cold. She told the children who I was and that I had transferred from Alamo Elementary. No one said anything and I was embarrassed. The teacher took me to my desk and I smiled at the little girl next to me. She nodded her head at me. I looked around at the others. They all looked like Juareños. They looked that way because they were poorer than the Alamo School children. Later I found out that many still didn't speak English. That was why they were singing songs that we sang in the first and second grade at Alamo School. But because they were older when they moved to this side of the river, they put them in the class as close to their age as possible. Others were children who were held back year after year because they didn't speak English or didn't learn like the others. The teacher took out a pitch pipe and asked the class to sing their favorite song for the new student. I waited with curiosity. It was a song about being clean. The children all pretended to wash their faces, brush their hair and brush their teeth. I thought it was a clever way to tell the children what they had to do. López always said one must not offend people—telling them in song was good. I looked around and noticed that many didn't wash their faces or brush their hair. Forget the teeth—most of them had rotten teeth! I had a big cavity myself. All the children lived in the tenements surrounding Aoy. They didn't wash in cold water that was available in tenements in January.

I made friends with a little *greñuda chivata*, a tangled-haired, mischievous kid named Lupita who lived in Juárez on the weekends. She told me that she was an American because her mother had been in El Paso on the day her pains started. By the time she was about to *dar luz* she was near the county hospital and they couldn't turn her away.

"My mother is a very clever woman. Now I am an American and I can go to school at Aoy. My birth certificate proves it." Lupita told me that her mother rented a room in one of the tenements. She worked as a maid and Lupita went to school. On the weekends, they went to Juárez with their family. I enjoyed Lupita's stories until she told me about the canal. She told me that bodies were found in it, as well as very strange junk.

"The fence is supposed to keep people out, but it doesn't. If you fall in, you're as good as dead because the current is so fast." Lupita sensed my growing fear and proceeded to tell me the story that terrorized me the whole time I lived in the tenements. She told me the real story of *la Llorona*, the weeping woman.

"Then the woman got angry at her children and threw them into the canal," she concluded the story in a hollow voice. "She regrets what she has done, so she searches for her children up and down the canal all night long. Crying, howling, and weeping, she searches but can't find them." She looked at me to see how I was reacting. "They say she is not particular. She would probably take any child." She enjoyed the horror she saw on my face. Then she added, "Especially a *güerinche con pecas*, a fair one with freckles." I thought I was going to faint. I started crying. Then she took pity and said that she made up the *güerinche* part. The rest of the day I walked around in a trance. This was truly *Guatapeor*!

Every day I would rush past the canal. Sometimes, if I was with someone, I would look at the running brown serpent and try to figure out what was in it before it rapidly moved out of my sight. The smell would linger in my lungs during school and then again when I arrived at María's place.

The knowledge of *la Llorona*, dictated some of the night ritual María and I had. After we sang songs and she told me a story about Mexico, she would take out some awful stuff that was for her asthma. She would pile some of the powder on a metal plate and then set it on fire with a match. Then, as it burned, it would smoke and she would inhale it. It was a dreadful smell, but she said it worked. She knew because she was the expert on herbs. She was almost as good as my grandfather, but I always told her that she was the best. After the herb smoke, I would make María stand in front of every wall and bless the house. Each wall had a picture of a saint. She would make a sign of the cross on one wall and then move to the next wall until all four walls were blessed. There was no way she could escape the duty because I wouldn't go to sleep until she protected me. She would tell me that no one could take me away from her, not even *la Llorona*. She would fight to the death for me. That made me feel so safe. I would tell her that I had no fear with her at my side, but just in case she didn't hear *la Llorona* enter through the door when someone opened it, Tata Chuy, God, had to be on our side. Once, when I was especially fearful, María used some holy water from Sacred Heart Church to bless the walls. She always understood my fears and never made fun of them. She didn't complain if I had to sleep right up against her back even if it was hot. She would tell me that someday I wouldn't need all the protection I needed then. They would leave the light on until I fell asleep. If I awoke at night because I had to go to the toilet, there was a chamber pot. It smelled terrible, but who would go outside when it was so cold and *la Llorona* was on the prowl?

En la miseria is a good description of life in the tenements. The atmosphere was many times like a carnival because there was always a great deal going on. That first week I learned from María the rules about living there. First of all, I wasn't to go into anyone's apartment without her.

"What if they tell me to come in and help them," I innocently asked, trying to find out how far the rules applied.

"*A mi no me importa un cacahuate la razón*, do not go into anyone's place. If any one phrase was typical of María, it was the one about *un cacahuate*, a peanut, said in a high humming voice. The peanut stood for the smallest amount she could care. She told me a story about someone disappearing into some apartment and never being seen again. She looked at me to see my reaction.

"*¡No te creo!*" I laughed.

That first week I told María all my secrets, fears, and happy moments. One night I told her about my tattoo and Eduardo while we cuddled around the metal standing kerosene heater in the bedroom. She said that one couldn't have confidence in people by their looks. I had to watch out for myself. That was a piece of advice that I had to learn and relearn as I grew up.

"*El diablo sabe como esconder los cuernos y la cola*. The devil knows how to hide his horns and his tail. You remember that, *mi vida*," she would say.

On the first warm Sunday in February, we went into the kitchen to fix the *comida fuerte*, the big meal of the day. María asked me if I wanted to see her empty the water under the ice box. I answered that I did and as a matter of fact I had wanted to see that for a long time. María had been reluctant or too busy when I was around. She went to the ice box and pulled the white pan from underneath. I went up to her and looked at the pan. The water was black. I quickly became aware of why. The entire surface was a mass of big, dead cockroaches. I looked at María in horror.

"That is why I haven't shown it to you," she snapped. "I knew it would disgust you." She quickly went outside with the pan and walked to the alley. She emptied the pan and returned; I was still standing there, shocked by the sight of the bugs.

"They come in looking for a cool drink of water," María explained. "They don't think: I wonder if this will disgust Gloria. And when they realize that it will, they drown themselves." She started laughing and I did too. I never approached the ice box without realizing what was in the white pan and wondering how many roaches there were.

María prepared the masa for the tortillas She made the *testales*, small individual tortillas balls, and covered then with a white cloth to let them rest. She worked on other foods for the meal. She rinsed the tomatoes and green chilies and put them on the table. Once she had the platter to cut the vegetables for the chili, she called me over.

"*Andele mi amor*, come and watch me make the *salsa*. One learns by watching and then you have to do it to really learn it," María said in a firm voice. I pulled the chair up to the table and drew my legs up under me on the seat. This way I could see the preparation.

"Palm makes *salsa* on a food grinder and I help him turn the handle," I told María so that she wouldn't think I had never made salsa before.

"Yes, that is how *Norteamericanos* make it," she answered. "I usually make it on my *molcajete*. But this is *pico de gallo*. What's wrong Gloria?" She noticed a puzzled look on my face.

"*¿Gabacho?* A non-Mexican? Palm?" I answered, puzzled. I had just learned the street word for a white person. "Palm is a *gabacho* like Señor John that Paloma works for?" I asked.

"*Seguro.* What did you think your father was?" she asked, surprised. "And don't use that word, it is disrespectful."

"*Pos, chicas patas*, Mexican, like us," I answered as she let out a big *carcajada*. I laughed too.

Then María started to make the *pico*. She chopped all the green chilies, then the onion and the red tomatoes. Then she lined up the chilies in a square shape group. Then she did the same to the onion and also the tomatoes. Then she looked at me and said pointing to the chili-onion-tomato squares, "*Bueno, mi amor*, look at this. What is it?" she asked.

"It is chilies, onion, and tomato. It is *pico*," I replied, intrigued by the questions. I looked at her and she kissed me on the forehead and said, "no!"

"But what else is it?" she asked, seeing my confused expression. "What does it remind you of?"

I looked at the *pico* and felt it was something I should know, but I couldn't get it. I drew my face up to her bent face and I kissed her on the cheek and whispered to her:

"*Díme, preciosa india*, what is it?" I wanted to know what she saw.
She smiled coyly.

"The Mexican flag!" she answered in a big, official voice pointing to
the red, white, and green. "*Nuestro Señor*, God, gave us the colors of our
flag in the best sauce in the world," she added smiling. "And the *picoso*,
hot, of the *pico* is the *águila y serpiente*, of the flag." She hugged me and
began singing a song as she twirled me around. I hugged her neck and
breathed in the wonderful smell of *pico*. She sang "*Negra Consentida*,
Beloved Dark One." We sang and danced around the table and then she
told me to wash my hands so that I could make the tortillas. I said I didn't
know how to and I didn't want to make tortillas. Needless to say, she replied
with *a mi no me importa un cacahuate*, and put a *testal* in my hand and one in
her hand too. She patted the ball and started making a tortilla. She told me
to do the same but I said I couldn't do it right. She didn't care.

"*Andele, sin mas acá, ni mas allá*. Without complaining," she answered
sharply as she told me to do as she did. I struggled and made an ugly
shaped tortilla. Then María turned the water bucket upside down for me
to stand on and put it in front the stove.

"Now, put it on the *comal*, iron griddle," she commanded.

As I started to put it on the *comal*, a piece of masa fell on the ground.
I saw it and started to cry. I put the rest of the tortilla on the *comal* and
continued crying.

"¡*Basta! No me chille*, don't you cry!" she yelled at me. "You cry about
cada tarugada, each insignificant thing, *mi amor*. You have to stop that!
Save your tears! The time will come when there is not enough tears for
the pain of the world." She looked at me frustrated. Then, taking a big
breath she said, "Just try to do the best you can." And she rushed to hug me.

That night when we were in the kitchen getting ready to bathe me,
María and I talked about doing things when one doesn't want to. I felt
bad because I did so want to please her.

"Forgive me, I didn't mean to act like an *malagradecida*. I cry when
I can't do something."

"There is nothing to forgive, *mi amor*. We all have to learn." She
kissed my forehead and smiled. Then she took the big metal *tina* down
from the hook on the wall and put it in the middle of the floor. She
poured water into pots and pans and set them on the stove to heat.
When the water boiled, she poured it into the tub and added cold water.
She kept me covered with a towel until it was time for me to step into

the tub. Then she took an *estropajo*, a straw pad, and rubbed it on the big bar of yellow-white soap from Juárez that made no bubbles, was odorless and was used for all cleaning. With the *estropajo* she scrubbed my back and insisted on scrubbing the *roña*, big shapes of dirt crusts, on my ankles and feet. She didn't trust me to clean up well. And since I bathed only once a week in the winter because it was so difficult and because there was always the fear of catching cold, I was very dirty each time. She sang "*Negra Consentida*, Beloved Dark One" again during my bath except that she substituted *Gloria* for *negra*. It delighted me!

Uno trabaja para vivir, one works in order to live, was a reality in the barrio. Work was the most unpredictable thing in the 1940s. People didn't seem to have an occupation—it depended on what kind of work was available at the time. Most of it was manual and menial. Skilled work and clerical work required English and reading and writing. Most Mexicans had no education or very little. One or two could pride themselves in having achieved the sixth grade in Mexico, the last year of elementary education.

In Mexico many of the Mexicans had worked on *ranchos* doing field work. When they came to this country, it was logical to seek work on the cotton farms or vegetable farms. Unfortunately, it was seasonal work. Many men left their families and went to other places where there was a crop to gather. This was hard on families because they had no telephones and communication was sometimes difficult if the persons were illiterate. This was one of the little jobs Paloma and Caridad could get. For a couple of pennies, they would write letters for wives who were left at home. Both Paloma and Caridad had finished the sixth grade in Chihuahua. María, on the other hand, wrote poorly. Nevertheless, she was very resourceful.

Many of the classified ads of the forties and fifties in El Paso stated that Anglos or Americans only should apply. The public reason was that English was required for the job. If an educated immigrant didn't speak English well, he or she could only get work in the shops south of San Francisco Street. But the chances of getting a good job really depended on how light-skinned you were. In fairness, the ads also required Anglo women to be attractive and charming.

María was a working marvel. It was then that I learned how she got her nickname of *la fiera*. It came from the expression *trabajar como una fiera*, to work like a demon. María could do whatever needed to be done, even if she had never done it before. She just wouldn't let on that it was the first time.

"It doesn't pay to be timid," she would tell me as she went off to work, although she did many things at home, too. She read cards for one thing. For ten to fifteen cents, women would come and ask her to read the cards for them. It was a regular deck of cards, but in María's hands, it was truly a divining rod. María would never let me stay with her while she read the cards to the women. María said it was just knowing what women wanted and needed that made the reading easy. If they were having problems with their husbands or children, María would try to be positive.

"María, you know it is against the Church to read cards, don't you?" I asked timidly one afternoon after a well-dressed woman from uptown had come to have her cards read. Apparently, she was the girlfriend of a very rich man. "Padre Luna says that card reading is the work of the devil."

"So what, Padre Luna doesn't pay my rent," she snapped. "The Church doesn't put beans in your stomach. Anyway, you can put a penny for the poor next time to make up for it or confess it for me." She let out a big *carcajada*. She didn't have to tell me, I had already made a mental note to do so.

María cleaned houses, took care of sick people in their homes, made tortillas to sell, and, of course, went to the fields when there was work. She promised me to take me cotton picking after the Day of the Dead in November. She also bought herbs in Juárez and sold them to whoever needed them: *herba buena*, mint; *chuchupaste*, smelly medicine for the stomach; and *polvo de vivora*, dry snake powder. She would consult with her customer and prescribe an herb or a *sobada*, massage. She had very strong hands.

March entered like a lion bringing in all the tumbleweeds from the desert. That first Sunday, Palm came by to see me. He told me that Carlos and Pelón wanted me to come spend *el día de cenizas*, Ash Wednesday, with them. Palm said I could miss school and come help him at the store. I told him that María was busy taking care of an elderly woman in the projects and that Ponchito and I could go with her in the morning. In the afternoon, Carlos, Pelón, Ponchito, and I would go down to the store and help him pack so that he could go to his new store on South El Paso Street. Palm had lost his lease on Stanton because he could no longer pay the rent. He was happy to have the help.

The next day when María, Ponchito, and I arrived on St. Vrain Street, Pelón and Carlos were waiting for us. María went off to her *chamba*, work, and the four of us went off to church. When we went up front to receive ashes from Padre Luna, we wanted as big a mark as possible on our foreheads. Padre smiled at me and as if he read my mind, he put a nice thick cross on my forehead. The rest of the day we walked around proudly with the silver-gray ash on our foreheads so that everyone could see.

After church, we sat in front of Pelón's apartment in the sun. Ponchito was very shy in front of the two older boys because he did not know them. He just listened quietly while we talked. Carlos had a million questions about what I had been doing the last two months. I told him how I lived and he shook his head and let out a big sigh.

"I knew you should have stayed with us," he said in a low voice full of regret. I quickly became angry that he thought he knew what was best for me. But since I knew he was just concerned, I proceeded to tell him why I enjoyed being with María.

"I know it is a hard life, Carlos. But it is very nice being with María and her daughters. And the neighbors are interesting too. Let me tell you about them. Then, when we go this afternoon, I'll show you where each one lives."

"*Bueno*, but don't exaggerate. I don't need to worry any more about you," my brother warned me. I told him about the large family, the five women who work as maids and live in one apartment, and about the man who lives in the apartment next to María's. "He is Maestro De la Barca. He teaches music and plays in some bars. *Es cien por cien español*, a one-hundred-percent Spaniard from Mexico, D.F., and he speaks with an accent. María says he talks *chiple*, baby talk, like a Spaniard." I laughed as I told them. Pelón was annoyed and quickly replied, "That is not his fault, all Spanish people have that funny way of talking. They say that a king once spoke that way and so not to make him uncomfortable, all the people started talking that way. My grandfather Benito told me that. He said that it should be the main idea of polite people . . . not to make someone feel uncomfortable," Pelón said, smiling. I knew he was remembering his grandfather who was part Spanish but denied it to the grave.

"*Bueno, lo que sea*, María hates Spaniards. She spits every time anyone mentions them. Paloma's father was a Spaniard." I hurried to tell him the rest of my story. "Maestro De la Barca is a tiny man who always wears a suit that smells of moth balls, and a tie. He has a small mustache. María says he has a *ciempiés*, centipede, on top of his mouth." Carlos smiled and I continued my story. "Maestro came here in 1922. He has no family and he doesn't speak English. María says he is very educated and considers

himself an *hidalgo*, a noble. He plays all kinds of musical instruments.
At night, if he is at home, you can hear him playing his Spanish guitar;
it is wonderful. He never lets anybody into his apartment. When he goes
to work in the evenings and I happen to meet him outside, he always says
to me, '*arriba los corazones*, chin up, Gloria.' He is so polite. Paloma told
me that even though María makes fun of Maestro, last year some pachucos
were out in the front of the apartments on Kansas Street. When they
saw Maestro, they started making fun of him. When one of them pushed
him because he was ignoring them, María *les llamó la atención*, called them
on it. Later she told Paloma that no one picks on that Spaniard except her."
Carlos laughed and shook his head. "Maestro knows all there is to know
about music and he has a *tocadiscos*, a phonograph, that he takes outside
in the summer. You know, the one with the dog looking into the *trompeta?*"

We went to the store on Seventh Street and bought some drinks and
Fritos. When we returned, we sat in front of our lamppost. There I
finished telling them about the neighbors.

"Then there is a woman *que le falta un tornillo*, has a screw loose,"
I said to Pelón, who looked at me sternly. "All right, she is *loca*. Her name is
Estrella." I tried to change what I had said, but still he wasn't pleased.

"Just say *perdio el juicio*, lost her mind," Pelón said. I didn't want to
argue with him, so I agreed.

"Estrella lives across the toilet and next to the alley. She is about
thirty years old and she walks around with a blanket completely wrapped
around her so as to hide herself from others. She doesn't want anything
to enter her body. María says that her family put her there years before
she moved in. When I said to María that I thought her family should
take care of her, she told me that the woman doesn't want to live with
anyone. María watches over her for the family." I continued the story.
"Last week, I bumped into her and scared her to death. María says that
when the moon is full, she becomes completely frightened. She knocks
on María's door and tells her that the moon is following her. María talks
to her and tries to quiet her down. She fixes her some tea and takes her
back to her apartment." I was enjoying being the storyteller.

"The last one I want to tell you about is the *fichera*, prostitute."
I started my story but Carlos shouted at me.

"Yoya! Where did you learn that word?" he asked angrily.

"María! That is what she says the woman used to be," I quickly
answered. "I didn't know what that meant until María told me. She said

that Alicia, that's her name, worked on Mariscal Street in Juárez. She
said they had a lot of red lights for decoration. Alicia met her husband
when he visited her at her house. They fell in love and he married her
and brought her to this side. They live in the other front apartment.
Eliseo, her husband, works out of town and she is left alone for a week
sometimes. When he is home, she dresses very plain and wears no lipstick.
When he leaves, she dresses like a *coqueta* with make-up and low cut dresses
and stockings with black flowers on them. When he returns, he has an idea
that she has been up to no good. At night, he steps outside of his apartment
and he howls in pain, like an animal. María says that he loves her and he
hates her for what she is. María says that she'll never change."

I dusted my hands off. The boys loved my stories. Carlos said he
could hardly wait to go and see for himself. Then I asked Pelón to tell
me what was going on in our block on St. Vrain.

"There isn't much new. Señora Olga has been very busy taking care
of Teresa's baby, Luisito. He is a sickly baby. They say it is because Chillo
beat her up at the beginning of her pregnancy before he was sent to
prison. Ignacio wants to marry her soon, but they don't have any money. He
stopped talking because he could see María coming up the street. When she
arrived, we all left for her place. It was a good thing I had told them about
the neighbors, because there were none to be found. We left for my father's
store on Stanton Street, stopping at the Colón on the way to take in all the
advertisements for the films that were playing and that were coming.

All this time, Pelón, Carlos and I walked together because Ponchito
had to watch where he stepped. He avoided all the cracks in the sidewalk
and if he accidentally stepped on one, he had to do it three times over.
Pelón was very annoyed and asked me what was wrong with him.
I replied that I didn't know, but that he constantly washed his hands.

"He is afraid of germs," I told them.

When we got to Palm's store, Ponchito didn't want to go inside.
I asked him why. He said God only knows what the people died of who
wore the clothes. We looked at him and asked him what made him think
that the people had died. He argued that some of them may have had
tuberculosis or some other contagious disease. We just shook our heads
and went inside. Ponchito followed. Once I looked at him and noticed
that he was taking in big breaths and holding them. Since Palm had little
for us to do, I showed Pelón the few shoes left from the cold winter
when Palm had heated the store with them.

"It's a good thing that winter is over because there are few shoes to burn. At least I don't have to move them," Palm said softly. "If you just finish putting the rest of those clothes in these boxes, we are all set. I don't have much to move."

Carlos and I worked quickly. We were hoping to go farther uptown when we finished. Suddenly we heard a thump. We looked around and saw Ponchito lying on the floor. We rushed over and tried to figure out what had happened. My father came and looked Ponchito over. He patted him on the face and told me to get a wet towel.

When I returned with the towel, my father said that he had noticed Ponchito holding his breath. He had fainted because he held it too long. He was so afraid to breathe in the germs he thought were in the clothes that he fainted. Palm said that Ponchito's mother had told him about his germ problem. When he recovered we left the store.

We decided to go to the yellow pawn shop where Paloma worked. There we walked up and down the aisles that had a million items for sale, things people pawned when they ran out of money. It was something. There were things stacked from the ground up to the ceiling—guitars, banjos, horns, swords, radios, all types of jewelry. Carlos and I agreed that someday it would be nice to work there. Paloma was waiting on a customer who spoke English. She was self-conscious because we were watching her. Carlos pushed me out of the store to spare her any more embarrassment. We went across the street to the Ellanay to see what was playing. They were showing an Abbott and Costello film. We loved them, but knew it would be wrong to go to the movies on the first day of Lent. Next, we went to the Plaza Theater and looked at the beautiful pictures there.

"Ponchito, this theater looks like a castle inside. It has balconies, trees, and a silver star-studded sky. You feel rich when you watch the movies. They only have movies in English and not many movies for children," I told him, acting like the city mouse with a country mouse visitor.

We ran across Oregon Street and went to the *Plaza de los Lagartos*, alligator park. This park was like a market place because so much went on in plain sight. We watched the alligators sun themselves and sleep for a long time. Ponchito thought they were the ugliest things he had ever seen. They were! Then we went across to the Kress store where we annoyed a toy clerk. We decided to leave by the Oregon Street entrance and stopped to look at the pictures of the movies at the Wigwam before we headed back to the tenement. The picture that was playing at the Wigwam was about the Dead End Kids and their lives in New York.

"These *chavos*, boys, are the Derem Kis," I told Ponchito. Pelón laughed and whispered in my ear:

"Yoya, Dead End Kids." He said it very clearly.

"What are they?" Ponchito asked.

"They are pachucos . . . *gabachos!*" I answered as Carlos laughed. "They live far from El Paso, on the other side of Ysleta," I added knowledgeably. The boys didn't say anything, but I could tell by the look on their faces that they were amused. They knew how far away New York was.

For a few minutes we considered going in to see the movie, but again, we felt too guilty about Lent. Besides, Ponchito told us that he didn't like to go to movies because he didn't like to breathe in other people's breath. We decided it was time to leave downtown. Ponchito never visited me again. Strangely, he grew up to become one of the bravest bullfighters in Juárez. He was gored in 1959 and survived.

13   Sábado de Gloria

The lesson of obligation was best exemplified in the observance of Lent, which begins with Ash Wednesday and lasts for six weeks. We ate traditional foods and avoided others, particularly on "amber days." Meat was not eaten on Fridays in the barrio, even if there was an exemption from that obligation because of a lack of seafood in the desert. Often, when it was available, it was too expensive anyway. But some delicious dishes, such as lentils; *chacales*, dry corn with red chili; *torrejitos*, powdered shrimp omelettes in red chili; and *capriotada*, bread pudding, were cooked. For many people, the deprivation of Lent was not harsh because their usual meals were just as meager.

Holy Week intensified from Thursday, the crucifixion, to Easter Sunday, the resurrection. Holy Saturday, or *Sábado de Gloria*, was the day that belongs to all persons named Gloria. My saint day in 1946 was to be an unusual one.

Every Saturday, as long as I lived with María, we went shopping in Juárez. The night before, I would argue with María about going because it was a very tiring chore. She would bribe me with a promise of something delicious from the street vendors in Juárez or the women in the Sixteenth of September Street market. And her promise hooked me every Saturday.

María and I would leave the house by nine in the morning, carrying only the empty *bolsa de red*. Since we lived so close to the border, we walked all the way down Lerdo until we reach *Septiembre* Street. By the time we reached the city market, I was beginning to regret the trip. But, immediately, María would take me over to the *tortilleras* who were lined up in the center of the market selling food they prepared there. She would buy me *nopalitos con chile y cebolla*, thinly sliced cooked cactus with green chili and onions, served on a tortilla right off the grill. I was happy again. We would buy what we needed and then head for the other market south of the cathedral off the same street. Even though María would

126

be the only one with a full bag, I complained about the walk. When
we reached the Cuauhtemoc market, which is the old market, I became
stimulated by the shops again and cooperated with María. In the summer
I hated the stench of the market with its meats and decaying foodstuff.
This April was pleasant and not too hot. I enjoyed it when María got into an
argument with the *Chinos* over the prices of things. Back and forth they bar-
tered in such a contrast of sounds! Soon they agreed in a friendly manner.
One of the *Chinos* reminded María that this was the *cuaresma*, Lent, and that
it was unseemly for her to be arguing. She asked them if they were Catholic.
When they replied that they weren't, she grumbled something under her
breath. I didn't even want to hear it. In Mexico during Holy Week, very
little serious business was conducted. One was supposed to be in a spiritual
state, not to be spoiled by the baseness of business.

Outside the market, there was a man with a big *tina*, and I knew what
it contained. I pulled on María's skirt and pointed to the tub. She knew;
she had promised me white corn with red chili that they served nowhere
else in the world like they did in the streets of Juárez. She walked over to
the man and asked his price. When she told him what she would pay,
he agreed but pulled out his smallest corn. María complained and said a
larger corn was what she paid for. I was never so happy to hear her bargain,
even if it was Lent. He offered up another—a larger one with big white
teeth. The man sprinkled it with red chili powder and handed it to me on
a sheet of brown paper. I walked away and was lost in my repast until I suddenly found myself alone. I looked for María and couldn't find her. I imagined that she had gone back into the *Chinos'* coffee shop. I waited, eating my
corn and worrying about the juice and chili that dropped onto my dress.

From around the corner came a surprise: two beautiful deep brown
young Indians, a man and a woman, dressed in red costumes. I dropped
my corn and bent to pick it up. I had no idea what kind of Indians they
were. I ran up to the corn man and asked him.

"They are Tarahumara Indians who live outside Chihuahua in the
Barrancas de Cobre. Once in a while they come to Juárez and they dress
up when they do," the old man explained to me. "In Chihuahua, all
Tarahumara Indians must be out of the city by sunset. I don't know
what the rule is in Juárez."

I stared at the Indians, forgetting my manners. I didn't care if I was rude;
I had never seen such beautiful Indians. My eyes followed them until they
were out of sight. And then I started worrying again about my situation.

Where was María? Maybe I should go to the *Chinos* and see if she is there. No, I better wait here where she left me. Maybe she is arguing with the *Chinos* and has forgotten the time. I decided to walk back to the *Chinos* and look around for her on the way. When I spoke to the young Chinese man who waited on María, he just answered me very quickly that she was not there. I knew she wasn't there right then, but had she come back? No, he replied. I walked as quickly as I could to the place where I had last seen María. Nothing. Maybe she had abandoned me? No! She would never do that: Not my precious Indian. Maybe she went back to El Paso because I kept asking for things to eat. No, I was just lost.

I started feeling panic inside my chest. I decided to walk over to the park where the *quiosco* is in front of the cathedral. There were many people around the pavillion and an effigy of Judas hanging from a pole. I looked at it and wondered about it. I walked around the park and some silly older boys threw kisses at me and said hello. I was very annoyed. I walked around once more and came up to the Judas figure again. I turned my back to it and kept looking down the street to see if I could find María. Then all of a sudden, popping noises went off as loud as you can imagine. I was terrified. I turned around and the figure of Judas was being blown up. The firecrackers kept going off and I started crying and sobbing. Maybe this was what María was talking about when she said the time for all my tears would come. I don't know how long I stood there. My body was shaking and my legs were like lead. People gathered around me. Some women rushed to ask me what was wrong. I couldn't answer because I was sobbing so deeply that I couldn't catch my breath.

"Yoya! Yoya!" I heard someone calling from behind the woman who was looking into my face. "Please let me see her," the voice insisted. "She is my friend."

"Pelón!" I sobbed and stammered his name. I couldn't believe my eyes.

"*Calla mi vida*, there, there!" Pelón had a most pained look on his face. "*¡Qué demonios haces aquí!* What the devil are you doing here?" Pelón said. An elderly woman frowned at his language. She reminded him that this was *Sábado de Gloria*. He apologized.

"What are you doing here?" I answered his question with a question. Seeing his disapproval, I sobbed out an answer. "I came with María. She has abandoned me!" I cried.

"No, she hasn't. She would not abandon you," he assured me. "Did you get separated from her?"

"No, she got separated from me!" I replied. "What are you doing here?" I asked again as I noticed Padre Luna a short distance from us. "Is that Padre?" I asked. "Thank the Blessed Mother, you and Padre are here."

"Yes, Padre and I came to bring some things for the poor in the cathedral. He is to meet some of his family there. They have come here because they can't cross to El Paso," he told me as he led me to Padre, who was dressed in street clothes. Padre hugged me and ask me what was wrong. I told him how I had lost María and that the stupid Judas had scared me out of my mind.

"Yoya, they blow up Judas every *Sábado de Gloria*. That is how they let out some of the anger they have towards him," Padre explained to me.

"Well, I don't think it is a good custom to do on my saint day." I tried to get some sympathy from Padre. He was becoming impatient with me and Pelón.

"You come with us. We'll take you back to El Paso." Padre started towards the church.

"Padre, I need to go back to the man that sold me the corn and tell him where I am in case María goes back to look for me," I said. He nodded.

"Pelón, meet us at that restaurant across over there next to the theater." Padre walked quickly toward the cathedral. Pelón and I rushed back to the corn man and asked him if he had seen María. He said that he had not but if he did, he would tell her where I was.

We went across September Street to the restaurant where we were to meet Padre. He arrived soon after with a man and a woman who strongly resembled each other. Padre introduced Pelón and me to the two relatives. They were his brother and sister: Manuel and Soledad. They were here to visit with Padre and had to leave the next day. We all went inside and ordered sodas. A phonograph began playing behind the curtain that separated the kitchen from the serving room The beautiful music of the *Danzón Juárez*, a famous dance song, came flowing out above the curtain. Someone in the kitchen kept playing it over and over the whole time we were there. I loved the *Danzón Juárez*, and it made me forget for a moment my situation. It was the first music I had heard since the beginning of Holy Week. No one played the radio because the adults would scold anyone having a good time. When I complained to María, she just said I should be grateful that I lived in modern times. When she was a child, life during Holy Week was truly a trial.

Padre and his sister and brother were having a very serious conversation. They asked him to return to Mexico. Manuel said it was his obligation. Soledad reminded him what the government had done to the church during the revolution. Padre just listened.

Pelón and I pretended to be flies on the wall. Facing each other in our chairs, we played with his baseball cards. We knew not to speak or interrupt when adults were talking. In fact, they were oblivious to the fact we were there. The three adults looked at each other very intently as we played and listened.

"I can't go back . . . not permanently," Padre answered as he looked into his sister's eyes. "Sol, I can't go back!" he repeated to her as her eyes filled up with tears. Padre quickly looked down at his soda trying to avoid the painful look in his sister's face.

"It's your duty as the eldest of the family," Manuel looked sternly at Padre. His jaw was tense as he fixed his eyes on our priest. "One doesn't choose his duty: one is born to it."

"No Manuel," Padre said his brother's name in a soft voice. "It isn't that simple. I chose the religious life as the life for me. I haven't always been happy about the choice, but it is what I want." Padre returned the hard look to his brother. "My vocation is my life. I became a priest because I believed in the Church and I felt a part of it. I can no more go back to Mexico than I could will myself to be born again." He paused and took a sip of his soda. "My life experiences have shown me that I made the right choice. I love all of you very much but I can't turn back the clock and even if I could, I wouldn't make any other choice other than the one I did." Padre tried to console his brother and sister.

"What the government did to the Church in Mexico only reaffirms for me the power of religion for our people. And, if I can't serve God in Mexico, I am most happy to do it in El Paso." Padre was animated by his thoughts. "I almost lost my faith when they lynched my brothers-in-Christ. I felt evil had triumphed. But I held on to my love of Christ like a child does to his parent. I lost the innocence of faith in systems, but I learned true compassion for the difficult road most humans must travel." He rubbed his forehead with rapid movements. "I have found my work with Mexicans living in America. Theirs is a difficult road to travel and I am a fellow traveler. They leave all they know for a life that brings them more difficulties than they looked for. Hopefully, their children will find their place in their new country."

Just then, I saw María looking in the window of the restaurant. It was the most wonderful feeling I had had inside my heart in a long time. She saw me and waved an angry wave at me. I became a little afraid. She bolted through the door. She looked terrible and I became concerned for her.

"Gloria, where have you been?" she barked at me. Her voice was so strange that I didn't answer. Then I looked at her face and saw tears in her eyes.

"*Pos, preciosa india,* I have gone crazy looking for you," I quickly said to her. "I thought you abandoned me!"

"I told you that I was going to the herb store. I waited and waited. I didn't go looking for you because I was afraid that if I left, I would miss you. Where were you?" she asked again.

"Right where you left me!" I answered, frustrated. "Eating that delicious corn you bought me."

"*Andale!*" María answered in tone that suggested she thought I was trying to sweeten her up. I grabbed her hand and led her over to Padre's table. I introduced her and Padre addressed her in a very nice voice. I liked that because María meant so much to me. He told her how happy he was that she was taking care of me. He said, *Dios se lo pague,* God reward you. She smiled self-consciously. I knew it was because she hadn't been in a church in a long time. When I would ask her why she didn't go with me, she would reply that she didn't live up to the morals of the Church. I refused to believe it.

María and I thanked Padre and we said our goodbyes to the others. Pelón and I talked about getting together soon. As we left, I turned around and saw that the conversation between Padre and his brother and sister had started again. Pelón sat listening. The *Danzón Juárez* followed us out the door.

María and I arrived at the tenement with a bright golden sunset to our backs. That night we talked about the day and the pain it had caused both of us. We pledged never to let it happen again. I told her that I didn't want to go shopping anymore on *Sábado de Gloria.* That is no way to celebrate one's saint day. *Gracias a Dios* I did have a birthday. María said that where she was from, no one really celebrated the day you were born, but a saint day was special because you shared it with so many people.

In my dreams that night, I was chased by a black papier-mâché
Judas with a Mexican flag in his hands. I screamed for María and instead,
a young Tarahumara Indian dressed in red came on a black and white
paint horse around a corner in the Cuauhtemoc Market to save me from
Judas. We rode off on the horse towards the fire-red setting sun. I could
see María, Pelón, and Padre on horses behind me, trying to catch up.
I could hear them shouting to me: Happy saint day, Gloria!

14   Life with María

The one thing I can say about the summer of 1946 is that I learned the idea of ripeness. Everything around me looked ripe, and by July, everything was too ripe. The midday Segundo Barrio sky was almost white because it was bleached by the hot bright sun.

Life in the tenement became almost unbearable. During the day, the heat inside was suffocating and at night, the brick walls would stay hot until dawn, when they would start heating up the moment the sun came out. We would leave the doors open until there were too many flies inside with us. At night, there were other kinds of bugs to contend with.

By two in the afternoon people sat indoors and fanned themselves with broad paddle shaped cardboard fans with pictures on them. Everyone wanted a fan and sometimes there weren't enough to go around or they got broken by overheated people, or when someone sat on one.

In this ripe season, the ice man would come more often. The children knew the sound of the truck and the minute he stopped at the front of the apartments, I would run to the kitchen and grab an ice pick. While the man was delivering the big chunks of ice, we would descend on the truck and try to chip off some pieces. When no one had an ice pick, we would fight for any pieces that chipped off. The ice man was good humored and chased us off his truck without becoming angry. And with all the water when the ice melted, you can imagine how thick with thirsty roaches the white pan was.

Drinking, rather than eating, was a priority during the hot day. María, like the other women in the tenements, was very creative in making *agua frescas*, fruit drinks. She would buy fruits and fix the punch in a huge glass container that she had brought from Mexico. Her *agua frescas*, and her *horchatas*, also a fruit or grain drink, made the hot summer days comfortable.

The evenings were spent outside in the breezeway between the two rows of apartments. The narrow space between them made it seem like dry arroyo. And, it really wasn't comfortable there until ten at night. Then, all the neighbors would take out their kitchen chairs and enjoy the evening breeze, looking up at the stars. Maestro de la Barca would either bring out his phonograph or his guitar. María preferred it when he played his guitar because he would play popular songs to please the listeners. If he played his phonograph it was usually what María would call the *musica de los ricos*, the rich people's music. If you wanted him to play a tune, all you had to do was to hum it and he would have it immediately. It was magic! When I hummed the "Till the End of Time" to him, he smiled very big. He said that it was a classical piece and it was called the Polonaise by Chopin and that it didn't have words. I told him it did because I heard it on the radio. He would play the song for me at least once an evening as long as I called it by its proper name.

Every Sunday afternoon, there were dances in Juárez in different *salones*. There young women and men could meet. The women would go as a group because most of them were shy. They danced with different men under socially acceptable conditions. At the most, they might have a soda with someone. It was all quite innocent. María would repeat a litany of rules that started with the phrase: *una decente señorita* . . . a respectable young woman! Caridad and Paloma, her daughters, would say what they knew she wanted to hear. María took great care with her young ladies. She wanted them to marry properly and certainly didn't want them to have *hijos naturales* because that meant such a hard life. She didn't regret having her daughters, but she would tell them they didn't have to have a life like hers. She expected them to remain *señoritas* until they married. At least that was the topic of their late night conversations when they thought I had fallen asleep. When they were out at the dances, María would be a little nervous. She always worried that someone might run off with them. But they always returned by eleven and would join the neighbors in the breezeway.

"*¡Andavete de aquí!* Get out, *mitotera*, wild one! We are getting dressed and you are just in the way," Caridad yelled at me one afternoon as I ran into their room. I loved watching her get dressed. She was putting on her *zapatos de pulsera*, high-heeled shoes with a buckle at the ankle. *¡Era tan guapa la morena!* She was so pretty! "Besides, you smell like a wet animal . . . you smell like a wet dog!" Caridad said. "You smell like the canal."

They would say things like that to me all summer because I would sweat and get so filthy running around the dirt streets. They would force me to take a bath every night. Since it was so hot, I didn't mind. María would bathe me the hour before sitting outside with the neighbors.

I left the sleeping areas and went into the kitchen to find María. She was busy working in the kitchen. As I entered I could smell a cantaloupe in the house. In the warm weather, the perfume of the melon permeated the whole room. It was such a delicious smell.

"¡Melón! I looked around for it. María, are you going to make *horchata* with the seeds?"

"Of course, I know it is your favorite!" María answered.

"María, the girls say I smell like a dog or the canal. They made me leave," I whined. "Can I take the bath now?"

"¡Sí, mi amor! Let's get the water ready." Caridad and Paloma came in after a few minutes and said they were leaving. María asked them to be careful and not to come home too late. They waved goodbye to me. María and I began singing a little song that I liked and then she asked me a riddle.

"What am I?" María asked.

Por la mañana	In the morning
No me pueden ver	No one can see me
Dado el sol plano . . .	In plain sight . . .
En la tarde	In the afternoon
Aunque quiera	Even if I wanted to
No me puedo esconder	I can't hide
¿Qué soy?	What am I?

I knew the answer right away but, I took my time, finally answering when she was scrubbing my feet with the *estropajo*.

"My shadow. That is a good one, María!" I said to her as she smiled.

Then something caught my attention at the door, which was wide open to let the breeze in. The setting sun was streaming in and I narrowed my eyes to make out what was there. Then I saw! Estrella, *la loca*, was creeping in.

"*Qué quiere la loca*. What does the crazy one want?" I said quietly to María who looked bewildered at me.

"What kind of riddle is that?" she asked.

"No, María, Estrella is at the door," I whispered in her face. "Look, she is sneaking through the doorway."

María turned around, hesitated, and then got up very quickly. As she did, she said to me:

"Hurry, *mi'ja*, get out by yourself." She rushed over to the door.
I reached to get the bucket full of clean water to rinse myself off.
Normally, I would have hesitated to do so because it was heavy. But I
wanted to get out of the tub. I poured the bucket of water starting at my
head. The water ran over my body and some flowed out onto the cement
floor. I stepped out of the tub and grabbed the towel from the chair.
I wrapped it around me and turned around to look at the two women.

"¿Estrella, *qué te pasa*?" María asked almost as if she were sure of the
answer because she turned to look at my progress. Then she turned to
Estrella once again.

"¿Estrella . . . ?" María asked gently.

"¡*El diablo!* The devil is in my apartment!" she said to María and I
gasped. I approached María carefully. I didn't get too close because I was
afraid. I looked at Estrella and saw that she was wide-eyed and frightened. She had on a dirty house dress and she was barefoot. Her hair was
dirty and oily and plastered around her head. Her words came out of a
very dry mouth.

"Don't be afraid, Estrella. You are safe here. Gloria is here with me
too." María repeated it twice to reassure her.

"María, the devil is in my apartment and I can't get him out,"
Estrella said quickly. "I am so tired! He won't let me sleep."

"Gloria, are you through? Get dressed as soon as you can."
María turned to me. "Gloria . . . ?"

"I'm dressed. I don't have any shoes on," I answered. I had slipped on
my dress a moment before.

"Estrella, sit down here on this chair," María said as she pulled a kitchen
chair over. "Sit down, it's all right. You are safe with me and Gloria."

"Gloria . . . ," asked Estrella. "Who is Gloria?"

"She is the little girl who lives with me and my daughters.
You have seen her, I am sure." María looked at Estrella.

"Yes, the little one with freckles," Estrella nodded.

"Gloria, come over here," María said in a firm voice.
She looked at me and I didn't answer or move. "¡Gloria, *ven!*"

"I'm afraid!" I said as I inched toward her.
"Please don't make me come over there, María."

"Gloria! Come!" She meant it. I drew up to her and hugged her waist.
She stroked my head and looked at me straight in the face. "Gloria, I
have to go call Estrella's family."

"No, María . . . don't call my sister!" Estrella started getting alarmed. "They'll take me away!"

"Estrella, sit down and calm yourself. Your sister needs to come and see you. It'll be all right." María tried to calm Estrella. "You talk to Gloria while I go out for a little while." As María spoke I felt as if the earth was about to open up and swallow me. I looked at María and she at me. "Gloria, I must go and use a telephone. You will take care of Estrella! Do you understand?"

"No, *preciosa india*, I am afraid of her," I whispered on María's cheek. "I won't stay with her alone." I started jumping up and down. "Please don't ask me. You know I would walk through fire for you, but I'm afraid of her."

"*Mi amor*, you must help me." María looked at me and I knew I couldn't turn her down. She pulled me away from her and nodded her head to calm me down. She ran to the cabinet and drew some money from a cup then she went to the door and turned around.

"Estrella, I'll be right back. Gloria will stay with you."

I blessed myself and tried to smile at Estrella. As I looked at her, I realized how frightened she was. She was trembling like a wet puppy. I felt a twinge of compassion. I pulled up another chair and sat a small distance from her. She was talking quietly to herself and shaking her head occasionally.

"Gloria, the devil is in my apartment." Estrella said the words I didn't want to hear. "Did you see him?"

"No, I didn't." I didn't know what to say. "How do you know it is the devil. Maybe it is a *ratero*, a thief."

"It's the devil. I have seen him other times," she answered very firmly. "He is red and has horns and he showed me his teeth."

"Don't worry, Estrella, María will take care of everything. She always takes care of what bothers me," I answered as I prayed silently to the Blessed Mother. Estrella looked so helpless that I began to feel less frightened. I pulled my chair a little closer to make her feel more comfortable. I noticed how dry her mouth was and I asked. "Estrella, would you like some water?" She shook her head, no.

"They say that the water is poisoned," Estrella answered. "They say that the food is poisoned too. They say I can't eat or drink. I haven't eaten in so long," she said in a low voice. "I am hungry and thirsty."

"Who says that the water is poisoned?" I asked her.

"They say!" she answered. "They say."

"Who are they?" I asked and not getting an answer, I got up and poured a glass of water for myself. I drank a little.

"See, it isn't poisoned." I showed her the glass and offered it to her. She looked for a long time and then she reached out and took it from me. She drank it quickly and asked for more.

"Little children are angels; they don't lie," she said.

We sat for a while without doing anything. María was taking too long and I didn't want Estrella to become upset. I saw the cards that María used for fortune telling in the cabinet and I was inspired to entertain Estrella. I took them out and spread them face down. I told her I would try to see if I could guess what number was on the other side. The game went well at first until I turned over the Joker dressed in a red outfit and a hat. That scared her and I quickly turned it over and put the cards away.

"Don't be afraid, Estrella. I'll say a prayer for us and nothing will hurt us." I tried to calm her down again. "María always prays with me when I am afraid."

Hail Mary, full of Grace
Pray for us sinners,
Now and at the hour
Of our death.

I motioned to her to bless herself as I did. She did. She was like the child and I was the adult. I sat and tried to talk to her. I told her about my school and the time passed by. Soon María came in and sat down. The way she looked at me I could tell that she was proud of me. After a hour Estrella's family arrived and they took her to a sanitorium in Juárez.

"Will they bring her back tomorrow, María," I asked.

"No, usually it is weeks before she returns," she replied as she prepared our dinner. "Her sister told me that at first when Estrella began having problems, they thought she was *embrujada*. But they went to a good doctor and he said that she wasn't hexed. She had an illness." María looked at me. "I hope she didn't scare you too much, *mi amor*. Sometimes, we have to do things that are not pleasant. You did very well."

"I did better once I realized how frightened she was. Then, I stopped being frightened. I tried to do what I thought you would do," I told María. "I forgot all about my fear. I think it is best to sit on your fears instead of having your fears sit on you."

María laughed and reached over and hugged me. We ate some flour tortillas with some white cheese and red chili. Then she sliced a big piece of cantaloupe for each of us. I felt very different inside although I didn't know exactly why. I felt so alive and the melon with its perfume made me appreciate my life.

When September came to the tenement with its cooler evening temperatures, we continued to sit outside and enjoy the last part of the season. All summer long we had shared *agua frescas* and once in a while a ripe red watermelon brought by some young man who came over to play guitar with Maestro de la Barca. People chatted and told *bromas*, jokes, and stories about when they lived in Mexico. The way they spoke about their *patria* I wondered why they had come at all. Jorge Negrete's *"México Lindo"* expressed their sentiments. The song is about dying while away from Mexico. It always made someone cry. Usually, it was an old man.

Maestro De la Barca and one or two other men would play all the old songs that everybody loved. The older people would get a faraway look in their eyes and the women blotted their eyes with their handkerchiefs. Some of the young men who came to play surely came to see María's black-eyed *palomas:* Caridad and Paloma. María knew it and watched her *pichoncitas*, little pigeons, even more. But the young men used their heads and showed respect. They would dedicate songs to María and as they played looked at her daughters. Plus, they always picked a song with the name María. That wasn't hard to do because there are so many.

The first Sunday in September, Carlos came to visit. He brought a can of Spam and flour tortillas for María. I loved Spam so María fried some and we made tacos out of it. We hurried so that we could go off by ourselves and talk.

We walked around the tenements and found a shady wall. I asked him how my father was. I was happy to hear that Palm was the same as always. I had not seen him in about two weeks. I had wanted to go and visit, but I told Carlos that I found the tenement more interesting.

"Yoya, I have some bad news," he said with a sad look. I felt a rush of fear in my chest and I tried to harden my body for the news. "No, don't worry, it isn't Palm."

"Tell me, hurry!" I interrupted him. "What is it?"

"Yoya, *se murió* Luisito," he said quietly.

"*¡Válgame Dios!*" I replied as I realized that he was talking about the
child Teresa had with Chillo and whom she had named after Luís,
Señora Olga's son. "What happened?"

"He became ill and it became pneumonia. Señora Olga kept trying to
cure him with herbs but it didn't do any good. When they got him to the
hospital, he died only twenty minutes later," Carlos continued. "Teresa
was wild with grief. At the funeral, she clung to Ignacio and Señora Olga."

"And Señora Olga?" I asked. "How did she take it?"

"Oh, she took it hard. They couldn't get her to leave the cemetery.
Padre Luna had to stay with her and he finally convinced her to leave."
Carlos sighed deeply as he recalled the funeral. "The days following the
funeral, she walked and walked around St. Vrain and she wouldn't talk.
Imagine, she wouldn't talk!" Carlos pushed his hair back. "I talked to
Flaco yesterday and he says that she is better, but not much. He said
that she blames herself for his death because they didn't take him to the
doctor in time."

"I'm so sorry." I didn't know what to say. "And, Teresa and Ignacio,
how are they doing?"

"They are better. They were going to get married in October, but
now they will wait until January. She wants to grieve longer, but Padre
Luna told her that January was long enough."

"That's long enough." I said firmly, knowing how hard *luto* was for
women. "So she and Ignacio are getting married. Good!"

"Oh, they have problems. Ignacio is very jealous and he lives in fear
that Chillo may return and that Teresa might go with him again,"
said Carlos. "He watches her all the time. He is so afraid of losing her.
Now that the baby has died, he seems even more nervous."

Realizing he had to get home, Carlos said he couldn't come to see me
for my birthday. It fell on a weekday and he had to help out at school.
He hugged me and wished me a happy birthday and then left.

My ninth birthday was the following Thursday. María, her daughters,
and Señor De la Barca and his guitar came into the bedroom and woke
me up with *las mañanitas*, the birthday song. I was so happy and as soon
as they left I jumped up and slapped myself nine times on alternating
sides on my bottom. That was for good luck. I felt through and through
my soul that I had been born lucky!

I went to the kitchen and found that María had fixed *camotes con
piloncillo*, sweet potatoes with brown sugar. It was my favorite breakfast

and my *preciosa india* loved to please me or my stomach. The kitchen was cool and the cement floor felt good on my bare feet. A chili on the *comal* was whistling loudly and before I could warn María: it exploded like a fire-cracker sending the seeds flying. Naturally, I knew its outburst was for me.

After a few minutes, there was a knock on the screen door and I ran to open it. I knew it would be my father. I wasn't disappointed; there stood my old Palm. He took off his hat and held his arms open for me. I jumped the stair and embraced him. The scent of tobacco and the stale smell of life on him overwhelmed me for a few minutes. I pulled back and looked at him.

"Happy Birthday, *mi'jita*," my father said with a big smile. "Your grandfather López sent a note with someone to the store. He said to wish you a very happy birthday."

"Where is my grandfather? *No se da ver*, he doesn't allow himself to be seen." I smiled at my father. I felt guilty because I was so busy with my life that I hadn't thought about López.

"It seems he lost his passport and he is having a bad time with immigration. I have to go and vouch for him," my father sadly remarked. "It'll be a while before he has a new one."

Palm and I visited a while in the kitchen. María served him a cup of coffee and they talked about business. Then noting the time, he suggested that we should walk together to school. I was so occupied by telling him about life in the tenements that I didn't even notice when we came to the canal. We kissed goodbye and he left for his store on El Paso Street, which was very close by.

On Sunday the 15th we celebrated my birthday officially. Once again it was a double occasion—my birthday and the 16 *de septiembre*. María said it was the celebration of two magnificent events—Gloria's birth and the birth of the Republic. Everyone in the our tenement was happy because we would be able to celebrate the cry of freedom before we went to bed. Maestro said that a group of musicians would come by in the evening to play all the beautiful songs of the Republic.

In the morning, María gave me a gift from herself, Caridad, and Paloma. It was a beautiful pair of black castanets. I put them on my index finger and tried to make a sound. They were wound up too tightly so I loosened the ribbon holding the two black sides together. Then I tried playing them. It was slow. Maestro De la Barca came by to see me. He had a gift for me in a brown bag. Inside was a phonograph record.

I pulled it out and sounded out the title just below the picture of the dog
and the phonograph—Polonaise by Chopin. I couldn't believe my luck.
Outside, Maestro set up his phonograph player. He let me wind it up
and then he put the heavy arm with the needle gently on the record.
The needle moved on the record, which rocked up and down like moving
water in a bucket. I watched and listened as the beautiful music played
through once. I thanked Maestro and I shook his hand because I didn't
feel right hugging him. I showed him my castanets, which delighted him.
He adjusted them for me and he showed me how to use them. Then he
put them on his hands and played them as if he had been born with
them. His thin and flexible body moved with the castanets as he danced
in the breezeway for me. He gave them back. I felt truly lucky to have
someone to teach me.

About seven in the evening, the musicians arrived. There were four
young men and Maestro. They picked at their guitars, violin, and a
trumpet. María said that Maestro didn't have to get such talented men to
play but she guessed he wanted it to be a special occasion. It surprised
her because Maestro was a Spaniard even if he was born in the Republic.
Everyone in the tenement brought out kitchen chairs.

The musicians began playing a sweet melody. I stood by María and
Caridad and Paloma. A table was filled with the food, *cerveza*, and *pisto*
that everyone had brought. Then Maestro welcomed everyone and said
in his Spanish that it was a wonderful evening to be celebrating my
birthday and the independence of the Republic. He motioned to the
men and to my delight the first song was *las mañanitas*. Everyone sang
and looked at me. I felt as if I were going to *reventar*, burst. They all
clapped and yelled *mucha suerte*, Gloria! And, I said to myself, yes I am
lucky! They continued playing and looking at the women, who laughed
like bells in the wind. The men were together talking and laughing like
horns in the night. The children ran around and I joined them after I
got tired of listening to the women talk.

Then one of the young musicians said he would like to dedicate the
song "*María Elena*" to Señora María. Needless to say, he wanted to
please Caridad and Paloma. While the men played, Maestro, who had a
voice very similar to the popular singer Augustín Lara, sang. It pleased
María and the girls. When it was finished I was by her side. She smiled
at the men and she hugged me. I looked up at the stars and took in a big
breath and felt very good inside.

That night María and I talked about the wonderful party. She said that it was a good party and everyone had seemed happy and respectful; no one had picked a fight. If there was a fight, it was usually about *celos*, jealousy.

When I got into bed, I closed my eyes as María did her breathing routine. I smiled as I heard her talking to herself and went to sleep thinking of all the songs about María!

When November came around, María had been working in the cotton fields in the valley. She said I could go with her on November 2, the Day of the Dead, adding that it was better to spend the day working in the fields than at the cemetery. María and I planned how we would use the money we earned. I was sure I would make a few dollars.

"We need to save money so that when we go to Chihuahua next month we can enjoy ourselves," María explained one night as we were preparing for bed. By now I could accept that she turned off the light at night, but she still had to bless all the walls so that the *la Llorona* could not get me.

When the Day of the Dead arrived, María and I were up at four in the morning. She fixed breakfast and lunch at the same time. She made flour tacos of beans, cheese, and chili. She put into the sack some bread of the dead that she had bought on Saturday in Juárez. It was a big adventure for me. I had never seen cotton balls except in pictures at school.

A big army-looking truck with a green canvas cover came for us at five thirty. It was dark outside and very cold. When we got into the truck it had long benches and there were already some people sitting on them. María and I sat close together for warmth and privacy. The long ride rocked us and once when the driver made a quick stop, I fell onto the floor of the truck. A man picked me up because María was busy collecting our things that had scattered. I thanked him and he smiled at me.

At the cotton fields, I couldn't see very much because the sun had not arrived yet. A rooster sang his song, *Quiquiriquiqui!* Someone collected twigs and branches and started a fire. Then the sky began to lighten up. First it was a gray and then started to gather color. I looked around and was surprised to see dead plants in front of us—brown, dead plants with white balls on them. I had not expected them to look like that. A big gringo came up to us and told us in *español mocho*, choppy Spanish, what he needed us to do. He gave us huge cloth sacks. My friends on St. Vrain Street and I could have fit into one of them. He made clear what the pay

would be as well as where we could take care of our toilet needs. All who
had come to *pizcar*, grabbed a sack and were off. I just followed María.
She placed me in the row across from her.

Of course cotton picking turned out to be a disaster for me. I cut and
scratched myself unmercifully. I complained and María shouted at me.
Being out in the country was the best part of the work. I would stop and
look around at the people working and it made me feel happy. It seemed
like decent work; I just wasn't good at it. María and I sang songs and
chatted once in a while. By eleven, the sun had become hot. I had to peel
off clothes and wrap them around my waist. Big drops of salty perspira-
tion would fall into my eyes and I had yet another reason to complain to
María. She just laughed and gestured to me to get busy. When lunchtime
came around, the big gringo provided water and sold us some sodas.
The flour tacos and the sodas were the best I had ever tasted. We didn't
take too long to eat because we had to work. After an hour of my
complaining, María told me to lie down on my sack and rest a while.
She continued to work and the next thing I knew she was waking me up.
I had missed the afternoon. At three we left and all I had to show for
the day's work was fifty cents and a sunburn. María made about ten
dollars and she was exhausted. That night, her asthma was the worst
I had ever seen. I comforted her and told her stories and sang and
danced for her. I did her favorite imitation of Cantinflas for her, the
one where he kisses the woman's arm from the tips of the fingers to
the shoulder. I used María's arm.

For about two weeks before Christmas Eve, transplanted Mexicans
made their exodus from the United States to Mexico. They could endure
the long separation from their homes as long as they had Christmas with
their families to look forward to. Christmas at home in their *ranchos* was
their dearest wish. They saved money and bought presents to take home.
All the employers of the maids who lived in our tenement were aware
that the women went home for the holidays; it wasn't negotiable. Home
for Christmas! There were also those who might not be able to return
after Christmas because of problems getting back across the river.
So for some, going home meant losing their jobs.

María and I got up at dawn on Saturday morning. We rushed around
and gathered all the things María had bought to take to her family, as
well as clothes from Palm to sell in Chihuahua. We crossed the river and

argued with the customs agents over our packages. Custom officers at this holy time made big money from *mordidas*, bribes, from the returning natives who paid them not to confiscate presents. María's things were of no consequence to them. They were looking for appliances or things of more value. María was nice to their faces but made an ugly gesture as soon as we left them. I laughed at her hypocrisy. She said that was the way things got done with *rateros*, thieves.

At the bus station, there was another surprise. The number of people with all their *chivas*, things, was more than I thought possible for one place, although the arguing and pushing was funny. Luckily, María already had our tickets. When we went to the *camión*, I was still eager. Once aboard I knew it was going to be a long trip and it was not going to smell very good. The old rickety bus traveled at a good speed but not fast enough for me. There were babies and kids crying and screaming from the time we got on until the end of the ride. María and I couldn't even talk because of the noise. The many odors and the movement of the bus made me nauseous. María tried to make me comfortable, but it was pointless. When we stopped at Villa Ahumada, a small town south of Juárez, I perked up because I had heard about it. I looked around and was happy I could now say I had been there. The locals were selling sandwiches through the windows of the bus.

We arrived in Chihuahua at three in the afternoon. It was a tranquil town with no big buildings, which is not what I had expected. The biggest building was the church. As we got off the bus, a band was playing "*Jesusita en Chihuahua*." I loved it. Now it was *Gloria en Chihuahua*. When I said that to María she laughed a big laugh. I didn't hear her laugh that heartily again the whole visit.

We walked down to a little restaurant and went inside for a fruit drink. The place was spotless. The radio played "*La Adelita*", an old song, as María and I made our departure for the *rancho*. The visit in Chihuahua was a learning experience for María and me. María realized that home was nice to visit, but that she lived a very different life than her family in Chihuahua. She told me that, at her age, it was hard for her to be a child in her parents' house.

The trip added more to my identity: I was a traveler. I realized that Christmas might not be the same everywhere. The holiday in 1946 had found me in a *rancho* outside Chihuahua and I was probably the only child unhappy that day. No one had told me that in Mexico, Christmas Day was strictly a religious holiday and no gifts were given until Epiphany on January 6! I missed Christmas because I had gone to Mexico, and I wondered how Palm and the boys were. Mexico was nice to visit, but El Paso was my home. On the way back, I thought to myself that even if I were to return to Chihuahua, it would never be at Christmas.

15   Adiós

Adiós was probably the most common theme of Mexican songs and stories of the 1940s. Many of the *rancheras*, country songs, and *boleros*, popular romantic songs, were about fears of being left, leaving without saying goodbye, and leaving never to be seen again. It was the most painful event glorified, full of emotion and sentiment.

Many Mexicans went to the United States. Some were never seen again. Saying goodbye was a formality that was sometimes avoided, denied, or was not possible because someone had got lost somewhere in the Bermuda-like-triangle, of Mexico, New Mexico, and Texas. A formal goodbye was more painful than simply leaving. Leaving children and families without saying goodbye was abandonment.

On Epiphany 1947, I was with my father and my friends after school. The reunion was joyful and they were sorry that I hadn't realized that Christmas in Mexico was not the same as in the Second Ward. My father gave me a purse and some barrettes as well as a doll. I couldn't imagine why he got me a doll. I never played with dolls. The boys and I usually operated on any doll and took out her crying mechanism to play with. I knew what this doll's destiny would be as soon as we could get away with it.

Flaco and Pelón told me that Teresa and Ignacio were to be married on Saturday, February 8th. Padre was to start announcing their approaching marriage each Sunday to the members of the church. Ignacio seemed calm and ready to marry Teresa. Everyone was looking forward to the wedding because the reception was going to be held in a hall. Padre Luna was going to marry them in a small private service. Ignacio would buy Teresa's dress and pay for most of the expenses of the wedding, as was the custom. She would wear a yellow dress because she knew it would not be appropriate to wear white. Only a señorita could wear white. Ignacio's friends were renting the hall and giving a big party. A band of boys who went to Bowie was to play. My family was invited and Palm said that we would go together to the reception. I went back to María's in the late afternoon as the guayaba colored sky began to deepen.

A cold winter had come to the tenements and it was hard on everyone. María had no work, so she stayed home and worried a lot. She
would be happy to see me after school even though I came home for
lunch every day. But because she wasn't working, the afternoons seemed
long to her. We took long walks when I got home because it was warmer
outside than inside the apartment. She made delicious soups from scraps
from the butchers in Juárez. Palm gave her some extra money to help
her get through January even though he was having a hard time also.
By the end of January, she managed to find a cleaning job in a store on
Stanton Street. You would have thought she had been elected president
of the United States by the feeling of importance that job gave her.

The tenement was during the winter. Señor De La Barca suspended
his musical gatherings. Estrella seemed calmer and she only had the
usual moon problem in January. Paloma and Caridad had new boyfriends. I only saw them from a distance because they were not allowed to
bring men home unless they were serious boyfriends. María just kept an eye
on them and insisted they go out together with their *novios*. María tried to
teach me to read the cards. She said I had a genuine understanding of people
and I told her if I did, I had learned it from her. That pleased her.

On Friday February 7, Palm came by to take me home for the week-
end and I kissed my *preciosa india* goodbye. It would be the last time.
I have often wondered whether, had I known that I would never return,
I would have left her at all. I didn't say goodbye forever and it is one of many
I was not able to say in my childhood. I didn't say goodbye to my mother,
my grandfather, and María. Not having said goodbye caused me much pain.

Ignacio's and Teresa's wedding ceremony was simple and only the
immediate families attended. The party, on the other, hand was typical.
Everyone was happy: they talked, drank, and danced. I danced with my
father, Carlos, and Ignacio, who let me stand on his feet while he danced
me around. The band played all the songs of the different regions of
Mexico, and everyone toasted the couple. Carlos and I hit our soda
glasses together in their honor.

The food was a dream. Everyone brought a favorite wedding dish
from their region in Mexico. There were many types of moles including
my favorite, *mole poblano con guajolote*, red mole with turkey. The cake
was made by Señora Olga, who stood by her masterpiece moving her
rosary in her hand the whole time.

Padre Luna stayed with Ignacio's mother most of the night. He didn't dance but did have a drink or two. He went around and checked on everyone. When he talked to me, I told him about my trip to Chihuahua, leaving out the part of how disappointed I was that it was only a religious holiday. Padre always enjoyed the status of honored guest whenever there was a party. This wedding was no exception. People sought him out.

Palm and I left the party at seven. Carlos stayed with Pelón. It seemed strange to me to be spending the night at home. We went into our regular routine except for the sugar drink. Palm had had that drink at the party. In front of the old radio, I sat in my father's lap as he smoked a cigarette. I talked him into blowing smoke rings for me and tried to put my finger through them. We smiled, enjoying the closeness that had been absent during the year. I had a whole life with María that I did not talk about to my father. It didn't seem important this evening. We listened to cowboy music for a long while and then Palm looked at me seriously.

"*Mi'ja*, your *padrinos* came here Christmas Eve. They were very disappointed that they didn't get to see you. They left you some gifts," he said as he got up to go to the closet. He retrieved two packages and brought them over to me. "Your *madrina* told me to tell you that they hoped that you had a nice Christmas." Palm smiled as if recalling that I had not had a good Christmas.

"A ring!" I yelled as I opened an over-wrapped box. "A ring with such a pretty pink stone." I was thrilled. I passed the ring to Palm as I opened the other gift. It was a book of fairy tales. "Why didn't you give me the gifts yesterday? I thought that my godparents had forgotten me this Christmas. It didn't seem like them."

"I didn't give them to you yesterday because I wanted to talk to you about my conversation with your godparents. I wasn't ready yesterday." Palm spoke to me in a strange voice. I wondered what was wrong. "Your godparents and I had a long talk about you."

"About me? Why?" I was becoming a little uneasy.

"Apparently, your godmother talked to Carlos for a long time while they were waiting for me to come home. I worked late Christmas Eve because there were people still coming in to buy," he said in a soft voice. "Didn't Carlos tell you?" I shook my head no and was confused. "He told them that you were living in the tenement. It upset them; they had no idea that you were living with María."

No, *el Judas* didn't mention it. What a dirty trick! I was angry because I knew how Carlos felt about my life with María. I knew he had turned me in. "What did they say, Papí?" I asked, fearful of the answer.

"They didn't say much because they were too upset," he said. "They wondered why I let you go. I told them that too many things were happening to you here. I couldn't watch you as well after Carmen left." Oh, Carmen. I had forgotten all about her. That seemed so long ago.

"Is that all?" I asked him when he stopped talking for a while. He seemed to be thinking about something.

"No! No, that is not all," he answered quickly. "They left Christmas Eve but they returned Christmas Day."

"Did you tell them I was going to be here?" I asked even though I knew that wasn't true. I didn't understand.

"No, they came back to talk about you," my father said in a deep voice. "They told me they were very worried about you. They had no idea I was willing to let you go live with anyone. They said that they took being your godparents very seriously. They knew their obligation. They felt as if they failed your mother by not knowing where you were this past year."

"They are so good," I said to my father, hoping that the conversation would soon stop. I had a feeling there was more to this matter and I was nervous.

"I am not through, Yoya." My father sensed my nervousness. He looked straight into my face. "*Mi'ja*, they said that they want to fulfill the obligation if I agree to it. They want you to go and live with them." He said the words I knew were coming. I didn't want to believe my ears.

"No, Papá!" I said quickly. "I am very happy with María. She takes very good care of me. And I love her with all my soul." I looked at him to see if he understood.

"I know you do, Yoya," he said. "I know you are very attached to her, but you can't stay there forever. That is not a life I want for you. María is so poor and taking care of you takes away from her. She was so worried that she couldn't provide for you when she didn't have work. I felt bad that I didn't have much to give her."

"But, Papá, she has a job now," I added with much animation. "Now we can make it."

"Gloria, you have to try to understand," my father looked at me, his pale blue eyes shining. "I want the best for you. I can't provide it for you and neither can María. Your godparents have more money than I will ever have. He is retired and she is at home all the time. I couldn't ask for more."

"I know, Papá, but why did they wait until now? Why didn't they come for me last year when I needed them? Now I have María and I want to stay with her," I said as I bowed my head so that my father would not think I was being disrespectful by expressing my desires.

"Let's not talk anymore, *mi'ja*," my father said in a very tired voice. "Tomorrow, we'll talk again. I want you to know that I want you to go with them. That is best for you."

I went upstairs with my gifts in my hands. I put the ring on and I lay in bed thinking about the nice things my godparents could give me. Maybe they could get me a bicycle. I did so want one. Then, I looked through the fairy tale book that they gave me. It had few pictures and many, many words. I tried to read the Cinderella story but it had too many words. I knew the story, so I just looked at the pictures.

Sunday morning I awoke with the first pale light. I remembered my conversation with my father and knew it was going to be a hard day. The first thing I did was to wake Carlos and ask him to meet me downstairs. I dressed and ran to the kitchen. My father was already having a cup of coffee. I joined him.

"Yoya, your *ninos*, godparents, are coming this afternoon," Palm said quietly. "They will probably be here around three after they go to Juárez to eat lunch at the Cafe Central. They will want you to go with them today."

I finished my coffee and told my father that Carlos and I were going to Pelón's apartment. He nodded at me. When Carlos came down, we went outside. He knew I was angry. He hesitated at the door and I glared at him.

"Come out here *chismecalliente*, gossip!" I yelled at him. "Come out *traicionero*, traitor," I said with a fist held up for him to see.

"*Calmate! Por el amor de Dios!* What's wrong with you, Yoya?" He looked at me angrily and confused. "*Te pátina el coco?* Are you crazy?" he asked as he walked outside. I shook my hand at him. We walked to our lamp post. He looked at me and seemed to be trying to figure out what to say.

"So you talked to my *ninos* about how I live with María?" I asked him. "Why Carlos? Why did you tell them about her?"

"Yoya, I know you won't believe me, but I never meant to hurt you. I felt I had to let them know your living conditions. It is their obligation as godparents," he said in a firm voice. "I talked to Padre after I had talked to them. He said I did right. He said that when people care, they try to help. I just wanted to get you out of there. You know that."

"I know you meant well. But now Palm wants me to go with them," I answered, realizing that he was just being the protective brother I had always known. "I don't want to leave María. A year ago, I would have gone with them gladly. Now, I want to stay with her," I said as I started crying. Carlos put his arm around me and didn't say anything. He knew there wasn't anything he could say.

"They are coming for me this afternoon. I have to go with them. It is what my father wants," I cried into my brother's chest. "Carlos, I didn't even say goodbye to her. She'll never understand." I stopped to think about María and a wave of pain went through my body. "I don't understand." We sat down on the curb and talked for a long time. He tried to tell me that it was the best thing for me to do. I wasn't convinced.

"Let's go to talk to Padre." Carlos stood up. "He cares for you very much." I stood up to go with him, but knew that Padre Luna and his favorite altar boy had already decided my life. I was proven right. Padre reminded me of all the terrible things that had happened to me and told me that I must obey my father. Nothing he said helped my sadness.

At four, my godparents pulled up at the Virginia approach. They were dressed up because they had been in Juárez for lunch. As usual, my godmother wore a beautiful dress and hat. She always wore a hat when she went out. The black one she had on this day had a small veil that just covered her nose. My godfather was in a brown suit and he always wore a hat, too. From a distance I realized how much he looked like President Truman. When I kissed him, he smelled like Bay Rum lotion. He was very happy to see me. I was glad too because I had not seen them in a year. We went inside to talk. My godmother said she and my godfather wanted to take care of me. When she asked me if I would go with them, I looked at my father and I said yes. My heart was broken but I knew I could not show it.

When it was almost five, we got ready to leave. I had a few things to take with me. I took a dress made out of a flowered flour sack that María had made for me and a little flannel multicolored checkered coat. She had made that for me, too. I still have the flannel coat after all these decades.

When we got to the car, a 1938 green coupe Oldsmobile, my father and I said goodbye. I asked my father in a whisper to go and tell María what happened. I waved goodbye to a sad Carlos.

"Apá, please tell her how much I love her," I said softly. "And, I love you." I held my tears in and I got into the car between my godparents. At that moment, I didn't understand completely that my life with my father and María was at an end. All I could hear in my head was the song "*La Barca de Oro*," "The Golden Ship". The words I was hearing were: "goodbye forever, goodbye."

As we drove towards my godparents' home, I kept thinking about the Second Ward. My godfather was listening to a radio program with a man named Jack Benny on KROD. He would laugh and laugh and I didn't understand what was so funny.

PART III

THE STOREFRONT

16 Alameda Street

Many people agree that Spain's contribution of language and religion to the "New World" was impressive. There also were many useful products—horses, farm animals, and chickens—that the Spaniard brought to the Americas. I personally think that *compradazgo* tops of the list of best contributions. *Compadrazgo* is the relationship between a child's parents and the godparents. This was a special, religious relationship. It usually started when the parents of the child asked a couple to baptize the baby. Participation in the baptism was not entered into without serious consideration of the attendant responsibilities and obligations. For most people, it was almost always a formal and close relationship that seldom resulted in any of the serious implications of being a godparent, namely, the supreme obligation of becoming a parent to the godchild should the parent die or become unable to care for the child. In 1947 my godparents found themselves in such a position. No one asked them, but they recognized their responsibility and wanted to honor it. Taking me out of the Second Ward was the first step.

The *compadrazgo* of my parents with my godparents was an unusual one. Fred, my godfather, was a first generation German-American married to a Mexican woman thirty years his junior. In other words, both my father and my godfather were married to young Mexican women and in 1947 the men were seventy-five and sixty-five, my father being the older one. Martha, my godmother, was thirty-five. Both men were transplants from other parts of the United States but they spoke fluent Spanish, Palm better than Fred. And, it seemed almost as if the hand of destiny provided for me to have identical cultural diversity in my godparents as in my parents. Because both men were businessmen, I suppose they met in that arena and found they had similar marriage situations. I don't remember really ever hearing how they met. My godfather was financially better off than my father and that made my godmother somewhat reluctant to be friends with my parents. She never said it in just those terms, but I sensed it. However, the very fact that they were better off than my parents made them very desirable as godparents.

My godparents lived behind their store. Fred was retired, having sold his inventory a few years earlier. They continued to live in the building and Fred used the store as a den where he spent his leisure hours listening to soap operas and other programs. The store was located in the first block of Alameda Avenue, with other stores and used car lots. This was a step up from the projects. The business owners were Anglos.

I spent many months adjusting to a new life again. I had nightmares; I would wake up in the middle of the night and walk around, *una sonámbula*. My godmother said I would go outside in the back yard and call for Carlos and María. She would walk behind me so as not to wake me because it was considered bad to do so. When I returned to the house, I would go and sleep at the foot of their bed. Of course, I never remembered the next day. I would remember dreaming all night long about being in the railroad yard searching for María or Carlos to rescue me from the millions and millions of railroad tracks.

The school I had to attend was Beall School on Raynor Street. It was only two or three blocks from the store. I couldn't believe that the *condenado*, damned, Franklin Canal was right next to school. That canal was part of all poverty in the city no matter how far you moved. I was afraid of being new in the school, so my godmother walked me to school every day and walked me home at lunch and in the afternoon. After a month, I regained my confidence and asked my godmother not to walk with me anymore. It disappointed her because I provided her first experience of mothering. They were childless.

There were many rules for living with my godparents. I went from a great deal of freedom to almost none. I was constantly called down for behavior that had been meaningless in my previous circumstances. María and Palm took no notice of my childish behavior. My godparents on the other hand had many expectations that were repeated constantly to me. When I ate, I could no longer use tortillas to pick up food or make scoops out of them for my beans and rice. I had to use forks and spoons. And, I could no longer use *pachuquismos*; my godmother said that I had to use proper Spanish. My godfather also wanted me to learn American ways of expressing myself. It was like being born all over again. I was very uncomfortable until I got used to their serious personalities and strictness.

My godmother wanted me to be a perfect child and to learn how to be a lady. She wanted to teach me to crochet, to do needlework, and to paint delicate flowers. I wanted to paint big bright flowers and to use broad strokes with the water colors. She would tell me stories of ghost appearances when she lived in Mexico. She didn't realize how fearful I was. I tried to be brave but she was very impatient when I would gather all my religious medals before I went to bed. Fred's expectation was that I be smart but cute. "The Man Who Broke The Bank at Monte Carlo" and "I Wonder Who's Kissing Her Now" were two songs that he taught me to sing. He also taught me a lullaby, such as it was. It was a popular song of the day: "Chibaba, Chibaba". I liked the song by Perry Como because it sounded as if some of the words were *Chihuahua* and *enchilada*. And Fred loved to teach me riddles and songs that served only to confuse my knowledge of English.

What I liked about living with my godparents was that I was living with a couple: a husband and a wife. That was good for me. I had known them all my life and yet I didn't know them at all in the beginning. I had to learn how to please them as individuals and as a couple.

Fred, my godfather, was a ruddy-complexioned man from a small German settlement fifty miles east of St. Louis, Illinois. He told me many times that when he was eighteen he had decided that the greater the distance between him and his relatives, the happier he would be. So he decided to follow Horace Greely's advice to go west. He set out at the turn of the century to find employment in his trade as a watchmaker. He came to El Paso after a brief trip to the Northwest. He liked Oregon and after a trip to San Francisco planned to return to the Northern California city. But he left San Francisco just three days before the big earthquake of 1906. That settled that dream. After a few years, he went back to the midwest and married a German-American from his home town. She was not happy in El Paso or being married to him and they eventually divorced in the 1920s. He remained single for many years until he met my godmother, a pretty, twenty-year-old woman. By then he was over fifty and had gone into business for himself. He married her and took her out of the Second Ward poverty.

Many times he told me it was hard for him when World War I broke out because he was so obviously German. He was very self-conscious. He tried to go to the war but his feet had been ruined by tight shoes during the gay nineties. Actually, his feet were so deformed that the Tony Lama Store made special shoes for him for the last thirty years of his life.

Martha, my godmother, was a dark, cinnamon-complexioned woman originally from Torreón. She had come to the United States as a teenager with her uncle and his family: she was *arrimada*, taken in by the family because she was an orphan. She had no status in the family and because she had had a hard life before living with her uncle, she accepted her position in the family. Before joining them, she had been with a man and a woman who physically abused her when she did not work up to their expectations. Once when she broke an earthen bowl, the man cut her forehead with a piece of the broken bowl. She was very self-conscious of the deep scar on her forehead and it was one of the reasons she wore hats. I felt terrible when I looked at her scar. I did so when I knew she wouldn't see me looking at it. Whenever she would slap my arm for doing something wrong, I knew what would happen next: she would cry and kiss my arm again and again. I tried to avoid making her so angry that she would hit me and then suffer so much for having done so.

Martha didn't have any education and she regretted it. When her uncle and the family came over with the railroad, they lived first in Arizona. Martha and her cousins went to school the first day. When they spoke Spanish, because, of course, they didn't know English, the teacher made them kneel on a bunch of pebbles in the corner for a long time as punishment. They didn't go back the next day because they knew that they would be punished again. Eventually, they came to El Paso and lived in the tenements near where María lived. Over the years Martha had taught herself to read Spanish and with Fred's help, she learned to read enough English to pass her citizenship test, which made her very proud. On days we were together either to paint dainty flowers or crochet, she would also give me a lesson in government, which she had learned for her citizenship test. She had an old civics book that Fred had bought her. It had a beautiful color picture of the U.S.S. *Constitution* that I liked. Martha made me memorize the preamble to the Constitution. As I would say it she would mouth the words and if I didn't say the right sequence she would say a word or two to prompt me. I remembered how the boys had tried to teach me the Pledge of Allegiance. I loved Martha speaking English words! And I knew the different government powers before I knew fractions. Becoming an American citizen in 1946 was the biggest thing in her life next to marrying my godfather. Whenever she visited her aunt and uncle, the neighbors would tease her about having changed her citizenship. She didn't care what they thought. But she never spoke English because she was shy; she was afraid someone would laugh at her.

Carlos would visit me about every two weeks. He would come on Saturday and spend the whole day with me. I would watch through the big window in the store for the streetcar to stop. As soon as I saw him I would run outside and jump up and down for sheer joy. Sometimes, I would start crying because I was so filled with emotion at seeing a person from the life that I had left behind. He in turn was so happy to see me that he couldn't stop talking into my face. Finally, we would go inside so that Carlos could greet my godparents. They were polite to him but I knew my godmother was jealous of my love for him.

Carlos and I would spend the day outside in the backyard talking and telling each other what was going on in our lives. He would bring me messages from my father and the other boys. After lunch, my godparents reluctantly would let us go to the serials at the Mission Theater or sometimes we would go to Washington Park to swim. He and I would explore Alameda Street. Coffee Joe's, a novelty shop, was a favorite of ours because there were many things to look at. There never seemed to be enough time for us on those delicious Saturdays in 1947. I sometimes think that I couldn't have survived the move to my godparents' home if it hadn't been for my Saturday visits with Carlos. There were also the occasional Sunday visits with Palm. I knew he just didn't have the energy to work all week and visit every Sunday.

"Yoya, are you happy here?" Carlos would ask me every time he visited.

"Oh, yes. It is nice to have a home and to have two people to watch over me. There is always food and they have nice things. My godfather is very serious but also kind and gentle. My godmother is very strict because she wants me to grow up to be a respectful *señorita*. Besides, it is what my father wanted."

In July 1947, my adoption was finalized in the judge's chambers downtown behind Liberty Hall. My father and my godparents talked to the judge and the judge asked me if I wanted to be Martha's and Fred's child. I looked at Palm and he smiled at me and I looked at the judge and I answered yes. I looked to the door and wondered if María would enter and yell a big NO! She didn't.

I learned a great deal about trust the year I lived on Alameda Avenue. Because I lived in a storefront there were many opportunities to encounter the street people of that time. There were always the transients, the drunks, and the mean ones. One day on the way home from school, a man stopped me and asked me for directions to town. I stopped and innocently proceeded to tell him how to get on the streetcar. He smiled throughout my directions and I was confused but I did my best to help him. Then he asked me if I wanted to see his big worm. I didn't understand and didn't answer. Then he pulled out his penis and asked me what I thought about it. I ran and almost got hit by a car as I crossed Alameda Avenue. I could hear him laughing and asking me to come back. There were always strange people on the streets and I learned simply to avoid interaction.

Beall School was another place I learned about trust. The children there were like me, immigrants or children of immigrants—one hundred percent Mexican, all of them. The school was better equipped than the two other schools I had attended in the Segundo Barrio. But there were the same problems and abuse that some administrators and teachers employed: belittling and shaking.

That fall some of the children had lice, often a guest of poverty. The teacher would yell and say disgusting things to those children found with the uninvited parasites. I had had lice when I lived in the Second Ward with María, but she handled the problem and after a while I was free of them.

One cool morning, I remember because I had on my favorite navy blue sweater—the teacher told us to line up against the blackboard. We lined up like *borregitos*, like little lambs. Trusting our teacher, we laughed and just waited to see what the surprise was going to be. A few minutes later, someone came in with spray guns like those used on trees or dogs. The person moved up and down the line of children against the blackboard, spraying our hair. Some children started crying but I was scared tearless. When they got to me, I objected, saying that I didn't have lice. That didn't matter, I was sprayed anyway. When it was over we went outside and were allowed to stay longer for recess that morning. At lunch, I went home and by this time my eyes were almost swollen shut. My godparents, whom I now called my parents, were beside themselves.

"What happened to you?" my father asked. His ruddy complexion became redder. "What is wrong with your eyes."

"They sprayed us because some children had lice," I answered very sad. I told them the whole story and how they hadn't cared if we protested.

My father rushed to the telephone book and looked up the number of the school. He asked for the principal, a very unpleasant man, and wanted to know why they had sprayed me. I watched as he listened to the response. Then my father told them that they had no right to spray me or any other child. He talked back and forth with the principal and then hung up. Martha immediately wanted to know what he had said. The principal had said that there were several children with lice and because lice jump from person to person, they had to spray us all. The principal said that lice posed a health problem because they could enter a child's brain and cause harm. My father insisted he had no right to spray, but the principal said he did. Fred wanted to do something about it but Martha told him to let it go. That didn't make me feel very good. The reason they got away with it, Fred said, was they knew the poor Mexicans wouldn't do anything about it. Nevertheless, it wouldn't do any good to complain, Martha added. I was proud that my father had stood up to the principal.

The new year came around: 1948. Fred and Martha couldn't stand life at the store ever since I had come to live with them. They were aware of the rabble outside and they were fearful for me. Also, the insecticide incident had soured them on the neighborhood. Fred decided we had to move. He bought a little house in Five Points, about two miles away, which was to be a new world for me.

PART IV

A HOME

17 Pershing Drive

We moved to Five Points right after the new year began. I spent a great deal of time following Fred around because we enjoyed each other's company. He showed me all his tools and how to use them. He built a bench for me in the empty space in the Oldsmobile behind the front seat. He was an artist with his hands and even invented things. We would take early morning walks, which he talked me into by saying we would be just like Mr. Truman and the newsmen. He didn't like Truman because he was a Republican. Since he didn't work, Fred listened to soap operas in the afternoons—*The Right to Happiness, Stella Dallas,* and *Lorenzo Jones.* On these soaps there were trinkets and jewelry for listeners to purchase. He would order them for me and I kept them in a little wooden box that he'd made for me. In 1949, I would find a good use for them.

My parents and I still had some adjustment problems. My mother wanted to make me over, so I accommodated her. When we moved to Five Points, she didn't want me to wear braids any more. She said that only girls from ranchos wore braids. So, she cut my hair and curled it like Shirley Temple's, only I didn't look like her. The curls were sitting on my scalp because my hair was too short. My mother didn't comb them out so they looked like chocolate Tootsie Rolls on top of my head. She dressed me in organdy dresses with bows and ribbons as if I were going to a party every day. The children in the school laughed and embarrassed me. When Carlos came to visit, I thought he wouldn't stop laughing.

"Yoya, I'm sorry," he said later when we were alone outside playing with Martha's ducks. She had three of them. One was very big and her favorite. I named one Roy Rogers after my favorite cowboy but it made Martha angry that I gave him that name. She loved Gene Autry. I told her we could call the big one Gene Autry. The third duck was a female and she was the mother of my Roy Rogers. Because of her personality she was called *la bruja,* the witch.

"You don't look like you," Carlos said. " Where is the *chaparrita* that I used to know?"

"I just want to make them happy," I told Carlos. "They won't let me be a Catholic anymore. My mother and father hate the religion. They say it is the curse of Mexican people. I have to start going to a Protestant church."

"I'm sorry, Yoya. I feel responsible." Carlos was truly unhappy. "I know you will be fine here. But I am sorry that you are having to give up so much of you. Martha is very picky, isn't she?" he asked.

"She is funny also. I love when she tells me the story about when she and Fred went to New Orleans. She was so shy that she wouldn't go out to eat with him. She was afraid people would make fun of her because she is so dark. So, she took corn tortillas and she ate them while Fred went out to eat." We laughed and laughed.

"Just like a girl from the *rancho!*" Carlos laughed.

"Yes, but I can't be a girl from the projects any more," I said sadly. "I do so want to please them. They have forbidden me to tell anyone that I am adopted. They said that people would treat me as less if they knew."

Carlos and I spent the rest of the afternoon talking and visiting. I took advantage of his visit because he didn't come very often. The time we spent together helped me.

"Mañana" was a big hit in 1948. Singing with a Mexican accent, Peggy Lee complains about a window being broken and getting wet. But the rain will stop, she sings, and it won't matter that the window isn't repaired. Everyone sang it. It seemed out of place on American radio as much as I seemed out of place in Five Points. I asked Fred about the song.

"It's just about the American idea of when to do work as compared with the Mexican idea of when to do work," he explained. I was still confused.

"I don't understand." I secretly thought that Peggy Lee was imitating how I talked. I didn't want to ask that.

"Americans believe that things should be done as soon as they can be done. Mexicans do things when they feel like it." He laughed after he said that and then became serious.

"Why would she make fun of it in a song?" I asked.

"It's just a song, Gloria. Don't be so touchy," he replied in a firm voice. He wanted to end the conversation.

"I think she is making fun of Mexicans," I said, inspired by the fact that we were talking by ourselves. "Listen how she sings the song. If Tin

Tan or Cantinflas sang a song imitating gringos, I would think that they were making fun of them."

At this point, Martha must have heard us talking and she came into the room. The conversation stopped. I was not allowed ever to question or argue with my father. Plus, we were in his room, which was small and contained items that were very manly and sentimental to him. Many were objects from his old home in Illinois. Martha made it clear very early that he was always right. After I buried him in 1959, I would go back to his grave and wish we could finish one argument.

In 1948, Anglos had ideas about Mexicans that were not very flattering. A common symbol for Mexicans was the *campesino*, a rural person usually depicted sleeping with a big *sombrero* over his face. This was the subject of pictures of Mexicans as well as ceramic book ends. There were many other ideas that described Mexicans as lazy. It was difficult to build relationships when such ideas prevailed. It took me that entire year to get over the feeling of being a guest or an outsider.

I never dreamed that moving just a couple of miles would have made such a difference, but it did. I went from the barrio schools to Houston Elementary, which in 1948 was middle class and integrated. The differences sometimes made me uncomfortable and I made adjustments for many months.

One main difference was that my Houston class was about fifty percent white and fifty percent brown. Both languages were present, one being underground. In fact, it surprised me that the Anglos only spoke English. Although it was not that I felt there was a reason to for them speak both. Only Mexicans needed both. Some of the Syrian kids spoke Spanish well.

The Anglo kids asked you questions without reservation. Whatever occurred to them, they would ask. The Anglo kids talked loudly and seemed more sure of themselves. Since I was a new kid in the middle of the year, I attracted some attention. I was asked, usually by a group of them as they giggled: Do you think in Spanish or English? Do you dream in Spanish or English? By the end of the year someone had found out that Fred was German and the question then was: Do you eat sauerkraut with chili? What really provided fun for them was to ask me to pronounce chocolate or church. I didn't mind because it made them laugh and I had gotten used to it.

Another situation I had to get used to was the interaction between boys and girls. They competed together as well as cooperated together.

They yelled at each other and it was all right; they didn't think it was disrespectful.

I made friends with the shy ones and mostly played with the Mexican kids. I had never been around Anglo kids and I was fascinated by them and yet shy around them that first year. My English was still not very good.

Not speaking good English was a drawback for me in the new environment and it didn't help that at home I continued to speak Spanish with Martha. Fred would try to speak English all the time but it wasn't possible because of Martha. But our house was on Pershing Drive and there was a theater one block from my house. Movies were nine cents. I was allowed to go after school. My parents thought that if I saw movies, my English would improve. I went to the movies because I didn't have anyone to play with and I was lonely. Fred and Martha were used to being alone and I felt like an outsider with them, too. It's hard to believe that I went to the movies four times a week.

I was sick a few times that year. In October, I was sick as a dog with a bad cold at school. It was a Friday and we went to P.E. at the end of the day. We danced on Fridays and I loved the Virginia Reel as much as I loved the *Jarabe Tapatío*. Nothing was going to keep me from that class. Arithmetic was right before gym and I had managed to hide my illness all day long. Miss Dove Husbands, a tall elderly woman who wore long straight brown dresses and black, high top laced shoes, was the best teacher but was never friendly. She had a proverb or saying written on the board every day. She wanted to teach us more than arithmetic. I thought I was home free because she was so cold and distant. I kept my head down so that she wouldn't see my bright red cheeks. Almost at the end of the class, Miss Husbands stood up and walked over to my desk. Her cold hand went on my forehead and I knew the worst was about to happen.

"Young lady, you are sick!" she said in soft voice.

"No, Miss Husbands, it is hot in here," I quickly replied.

"No, you are sick! Go to the principal's office right this minute." She ruined my day. The principal sent me home; there was no Virginia Reel that week. At home, Martha made a hot toddy with a shot of whiskey, lemon, and some sugar. She gave me a full treatment of *apretones*, squeezes, from head to toes. She was very good at them. They made my achy body fell so good. I drank the toddy and slept for hours and I got well.

In October my father's uncle Robert, who was an old German in his eighties, came to live with us. He was angry at his children in Illinois

because he had turned over control of his farm when he thought he was
dying. When he recovered the children refused to return the farm. In his
anger, he left Illinois and arrived in El Paso on the train. He stayed with
us for about a year. He was the picture of the farmer from the old country, with a big mustache, a red complexion, and an accent that was hard
for me to understand. He wore blue overalls and farm boots. He had
come to the United States about the middle of the last century and spoke
German all the time. At any meal, you would find the four of us eating
and carrying on conversations in a mixture of languages. Martha would
speak Spanish. I would speak Spanish and English depending to whom I
was speaking. Fred would have to speak English, Spanish, and German.
His uncle Bob would speak whatever he wanted: English or German.
He was robust, with the appetite of a young man. He carried around a
cigar box with "his papers," which consisted of his deed to his farm and the
litigation that he was lodging against his children. All this made him a
little crazy and he would forget to do things. It annoyed my parents.
The old German would spend time with me showing me his papers and
teaching me German phrases. I remember thinking that I had enough
problems learning English phrases.

   I learned a great deal that year about dealing with Anglo children and
a German farmer. I learned to become thick-skinned to criticism about
my accent in school. The whole interaction between me and everyone
else was very similar to the complicated Virginia Reel that I loved to
dance, and about which I dreamed at night. In my dreams I danced with
everyone, including Uncle Bob, my parents, and all the kids in Houston
Elementary. There were so many patterns and steps. In order to keep up,
I had to learn and adjust quickly or I would find myself out of the dance.
And, I did not want that to happen.

   Christmas season in 1948 found me with my parents and Uncle Bob.
I followed them around because I had no one to play with and I liked
being with people. My mother and father had each other. My father
had my Uncle Bob and I had Uncle Bob whenever I would subject myself
to a German lesson or learning a new song in German. He would smile
a big broad grin that displayed his yellow teeth and his gold caps. He
chewed tobacco, which added a brown tint to the smile. As I repeated
and learned the song, he would grin and say: Ya! Ya! He would tell Fred
that I was intelligent. Fred loved to hear that. By Christmas Eve, I had

learned "Silent Night" and "Oh, Christmas Tree" in German. I now could sing of the Christmas joy in three languages. When I sang the song for him, Uncle Bob got lost in a place in his memory and I knew he was back in Illinois. His eyes became red and teary.

We spent Christmas week indoors because of the weather and because these grownups liked to be indoors. At night we would play cards on the dining room table. Uncle Bob took card playing very seriously. He would cuss in English and in German if he lost. It would embarrass Martha but Fred was unaffected by his anger. I would become uncomfortable and go to bed to read fairy tales. I would snuggle and create that magic atmosphere. If there was one thing I learned after I was adopted, it was how to deal with loneliness. There was no one to tell me stories. I filled my free hours with movies, the radio, and my duck Roy Rogers.

Christmas Eve was very different from *Nochebuena* in the projects. I went with my parents to deliver gifts. We went to St. Vrain Street to take presents to my father and my brother Carlos. I saw Pelón and the other boys. They were glad to see me but they seemed different, except for Pelón. He took me around to visit the neighbors. When we return to Palm's apartment, Martha was uneasy. She made me uncomfortable. I found myself very self-conscious with Palm because Fred and Martha were now my parents. I wanted to sit on Palm's lap and visit with him alone like in the old days. But that was not possible, nor would it ever be again. When I reached up to kiss him as we were going out the door, Martha seemed upset.

"Papí, I love you," I said as I started to cry. I didn't know why I was crying. He was upset too. He wished me a Merry Christmas and said he would be seeing me soon. He promised to visit when the weather was better. I never again would wish him a Merry Christmas. He died that May. But this *Nochebuena* I had no hint of that. As we drove away, I cried silently sitting on the wooden bench behind the front seat of the Oldsmobile coupe as Christmas carols played on the radio. The visit had saddened me and the soft sounds of the music put me to sleep.

The winter of 1949 was the worst of my childhood. Ask anyone alive that year how hard it was. It crossed the nation from the west with its icy breath and snow, destroying property and killing people and animals. "Baby, It's Cold Outside" and "I've Got My Love to Keep Me Warm" were very popular songs that year. I attribute their inspiration to the winter at the beginning of the year. It was 1949, the last year of the cold war before it heated up again in Korea and President Truman was still in office.

When New Year's Eve came around, I tried to stay awake until midnight, but I failed. My father had to carry me to bed while they celebrated by drinking whiskey and *champurrado*. The next morning I was angry that they had not awakened me to ring in the new year. It started to get very cloudy but we went to the Sun Carnival Parade down on Montana Street anyway. Soon, the storm began.

I got up the next day and looked outside and saw the magic of snow. A real storm had left more snow than I had ever imagined. The whole world seemed without color, as if someone had stolen it all while we slept. My place at the kitchen table looked out at the street. I didn't want to move my eyes from the window. Fred made oatmeal and sat with me while I ate. He drank coffee, smoked his pipe, and read *The El Paso Times*. Breakfast every morning was like that. I would either eat my favorite breakfast of cold enchiladas or if there weren't any, Fred would make me oatmeal. He liked making breakfast for me. He would put raisins in the oatmeal and a dab of butter. We were both early risers. Martha and Uncle Bob loved to sleep in. The smell of his sweet tobacco, which varied from time to time, is part of my memories of childhood. Fred had a whole rack of pipes and a humidor that held the tobacco and once in a while he would put a slice of apple inside to moisten the contents in the El Paso climate.

I started out for school that snowy Monday morning. I was never allowed to wear pants to school and actually only had one pair. Martha did not consider pants appropriate for girls. No one did in those days. This morning Fred said I could wear them. If the school didn't like it, he told me to tell them to call him. I put on my green, black, and white checkered coat and I walked to school. It was dark because the sky was so full of clouds. Five Points was buried under tons and tons of snow. The wind had blown the snow into huge, high drifts. This was a winter wonderland indeed! When I crossed Piedras Street and looked in the direction I was to walk, I was scared for a few minutes. There were no cars in the street and no other kids walking to school. But I wanted to go to school because I knew how boring it would with the grownups at home.

Houston Elementary was built on a high piece of land that sloped sharply down to Grant Street. It made me think of the tower of Babel in the Bible. The snow on the sloping grass gave it a magical look as if I had arrived at some imaginary place. The iron rails and the windows were supporting snow everywhere.

When I entered the school each classroom had only a few children in it. When I got to mine, the teacher became angry when she saw me.

"Why did you come to school?" she asked. "Didn't you hear the radio this morning? No one was to go to school."

I sat at my desk and in a few minutes some other children came in. I was relieved. I didn't want the teacher to be angry just at me. She was not happy because they couldn't send us home—the snow was still falling outside. At lunchtime, they served us sandwiches, which I loved because I never ate sandwiches. I liked American food. All we ate at home was Mexican or German. I even liked the smell of the cafeteria. I didn't understand why the kids who had to eat at school didn't like it. The whole morning had been an adventure for me! And that afternoon was to bring a new person into our classroom who would strip the last veil of innocence from my childhood.

After lunch, a new girl named Barbara and her mother appeared at the classroom door. She was a beautiful blonde with blue eyes. She looked just like a *muñeca*, doll. And, because I was the only girl in class that afternoon, the teacher called me over and introduced the girl to me. I was happy to welcome a newcomer to my class. I remembered what it was like for me the January before so I treated her like a guest and showed her where everything was. She told me that they were new to El Paso. I told her many things about Houston School and Five Points.

"Why do you talk different?" the new girl asked.

"Oh, you probably think I talk different because I speak Spanish also," I offered.

"Oh, are you Spanish?" she asked.

"Yes, I speak Spanish," I answered, not going into who we are. We rushed back to the room because I didn't want the teacher to be angry and embarrass me in front of my new friend. That night I told Martha about my new friend and how I looked forward to seeing her next day.

In the morning, the world was still covered by the blanket of snow but everyone was back in school. I looked for Barbara. She was with the most popular girls in the class by the time I got there. She waved at me and said hi, then she went off to the drinking fountain with her new friends. I was so disappointed. After that whenever I tried to talk to her, she didn't have time for me.

That afternoon, Martha put on some old pants of my father's and we went outside to play in the snow. My father came out and took a picture

of me with my duck Roy Rogers in my arms. He sent copies of the
picture to Palm and to Palm's son in San Antonio. I asked Fred to tell
my half-brother that I had finally learned to speak English. Many years
later I would see the picture when I visited him.

The *charreada*, rodeo, is another Spanish contribution to the New
World. It became the custom of settlers in that area of the United States
that was part of Mexico until Santa Anna sold Mexico out. The whole
idea of the *charreada* was to give people a chance to see men playing and
wrestling with animals. The rodeo came to El Paso the first week in
February. It had since 1929. Perhaps that time of year, near the end of
winter, was when playing and wrestling ran in the human blood.

The streets of El Paso had banners announcing the big event.
It usually started on Friday and there were activities in town as well as in
school. *The El Paso Times* and *The Herald Post* would run features on the
rodeo. Rodeo was truly a West Texas phenomenon. And this particular
February I felt like a Texan through and through.

Houston Elementary, like all the schools in El Paso, had "Go Western
Day." All the children would dress up as cowboys or cowgirls. They
could chose from cowpoke wear to drugstore cowboy wear. Or they
could simply wear a hat and call themselves ranch hands. All the children
who had them wore boots, gun holsters, and cowboy hats.

This year, for once, I wasn't embarrassed by my outfit. The year
before Martha had refused to buy me anything to wear and I had felt so
left out. But it didn't matter because I had only been there a short time.
No one noticed. For rodeo 1949 I was dressed like a cowgirl, *una charra*.
I had a brown, real-leather skirt and vest. I wore a red shirt and I had
a black silk scarf around my neck. My boots were brown and they
looked just like the ones Dale Evans wore in the movies. I wore a
brown felt hat, too, that went along with my outfit. I loved the way I
looked and I couldn't stop admiring myself in the mirror when I tried
the whole outfit on. Looking in the mirror almost made me late for
Go Western Day.

"Do I look *bonita*?" I asked Martha, and she smiled and said yes.
I waited for more, but it didn't come. Then I asked Fred and he smiled
and held his pipe in his teeth as he simply nodded. Then I asked Uncle
Bob in German if I looked pretty and he said with a big broad yellow
grin, "*Ya, du bist schön*! Yes, you are pretty!" Why was it so hard to tell

me I looked pretty? I was anxious for reassurance because there was always a contest at school for the best dressed in various categories.

At school, I found out that I looked like a lot of the girls there. Some were dressed in prairie looking outfits and wore bonnets. One girl had on a frilly dress that looked like she worked in a saloon. The boys loved her outfit. The boys that were dressed the best strutted around, pulled out their toy guns, shot each other, and then blew on the gun. We all thought we were true cowboys and cowgirls.

By afternoon, everyone was wild and almost beyond control. One Syrian girl, who was a little wild on ordinary days, was berserk! The teacher, who was tired of screaming at her by this time, resorted to tying up the poor girl. She and a couple of the cowboys tied her up but she didn't seem to mind because she was the center of attention. When the teacher's back was turned, the cowboys did an Indian pow wow dance around the tied up girl. It upset me because I liked her and I was afraid they might do that to me because I was a little *chiflada* myself!

When the contest was conducted, you could count on your friends to applaud. The most popular kids knew that they stood a good chance. The teacher didn't want to do it that way. She asked the patrol boys in the seventh grade to come in and judge. They were given a paper with what they were to judge for each category. I liked this method because I knew I didn't stand a chance if I had to depend on being popular. Anyway, I didn't win. The pretty new girl, Barbara, won. She and her friends were very happy. I was glad for her, but I wished she was my friend. José, who was dressed as a real cowboy with chaps, pistols, and *espuelas*, spurs, won easily in his category. He looked like a *charro*, a Mexican cowboy.

When we went to music class we sang all western songs—"My Darling Clementine" and "Home on the Range" The teacher asked me and some other Mexican children to sing "*Allá en el Rancho Grande*". We sang it with gusto because it was the only time we could sing out loud in Spanish without being punished.

When I got home, Martha was disappointed that I hadn't won a prize. But there was good news waiting. Uncle Bob's grandson and his wife, who were on their way from Illinois, were expected to arrive in a few minutes. I could hardly wait, but Uncle Bob was not very happy. He kept saying that the children of the enemy were coming and it wasn't going to do them any good. Fred had told me the day before that the grandson wanted to take Uncle Bob back to Illinois to live with him. And, from the way he said it, I got the impression that my father was ready to send him back. Of course, he would never say that.

I was outside sitting on the swing with my father and Uncle Bob when the blue car stopped in front of the house. Two very fair young people emerged; I was so excited. They were introduced to me and my father, who had left Illinois before they were born. They shook my hand, but I felt clumsy because I didn't have much experience greeting in English. They were so friendly; it was like a party for me. They hugged and sweet-talked Uncle Bob, who was not the friendliest of grandfathers. He was suspicious of them. Eric, his grandson, and Ursula, his wife, told Uncle Bob that they had wanted to visit him and convince themselves that he was fine. After all, El Paso was on the other side of the world.

"Ya! *Das* is true" Uncle Bob laughed and showed his gold teeth. "I am fine even though I have been a little *krank*, sick."

"Uncle Bob, that isn't true!" My father became defensive. "You have been in good health. Eric, he eats like a farmer; does that tell you that he is *krank*?"

We went inside and my father introduced Eric and Ursula to Martha, who looked so shy and so embarrassed I thought was going to die. They were looking at her very closely and she managed a hello. I became aware of her discomfort and I ran over to stand by her. She looked at me in relief.

"My mother's English is rusty like Uncle Bob's is when he is *krank*," I said as I grabbed her hand. I was surprised how dark she was when Ursula's hand met hers in a handshake. It was truly like the song said: Martha had *piel canela*, cinnamon colored skin. I stared at the contrast. They looked like chocolate and vanilla next to each other. Martha squeezed my hand to bring me out of my trance. Everyone was talking and chatting.

My father said that we could go to Juárez if they felt like going out for dinner. They agreed enthusiastically; I loved being with young people. They freshened up and I changed into my Sunday dress, which had a red velvet top with a taffeta skirt. I put on my black patent leather shoes with white socks. I admired myself, pulling my hair back from my face be-cause it was so wild from the cowboy day. I touched my ears, glad God had given me ears that stayed down. In the living room, we sat around and talked for about a half an hour. It was wonderful to have so much noise in the house. Uncle Bob decided that he did not want to go to

Juárez. My mother fixed him his favorite supper of limburger cheese, dark bread, and stewed tomatoes. I was glad to be free from the smelly cheese. The rest of us left for Juárez in their car.

We had supper at the Cafe Central. Afterwards we went across the street to have some drinks at the Tivoli Bar. Everyone had a couple and then we took a stroll of the strip. Martha bought me a little doll for having been so well behaved. She was drunk. I kept an eye on her because she started giggling and not being herself.

On the way out, we saw a large group of Mexican peasant men assembled in an area at the immigration station. Eric asked who they were. My father answered that they were *braceros,* farm workers that were going to the United States to work for a certain length of time. Then Eric shook his head and said he had heard of the program.

Eric and Ursula dropped us off at the house and went on to a hotel. We all fell asleep quickly, but the next day Martha was sick. My father said she had a hangover. I went to her bedroom and she was embarrassed. She asked me if she had done anything the night before that wasn't polite. I said no, she had been very polite. Then she complained of a headache and I began to tease her. I put the new doll in front of my face and I sang *"La Borrachita,"* "Little Drunk One." I poured some 7Up into two wine glasses and offered her one. I toasted her and sang the song again. Martha laughed and laughed, holding her head and asking me to stop. I said I would if she would baptize my new doll. She agreed. We laughed and laughed as I made the doll act as if she was drunk. Martha looked at me and seemed to see me in a different light. It made me feel good; our relationship changed that day.

The next day, Eric and Ursula left after convincing Uncle Bob to return the following month. They told him he could live with them and fight his children from their home. He could win if he were closer, they said. The young couple thanked my parents and told me that they had enjoyed meeting me and that I was a sweet little girl. They gave me a string of pearls and I didn't stop thanking them until they drove away from the curb.

On Monday, February 14, Valentine's Day, we had another fun day at school. Over the weekend, like many other children, I bought the small valentines that you punched out and that came with tiny envelopes. I wrote one for everyone in the class. I would sign the ones to the girls, but not the ones to the boys. On their valentines, I would put something silly like: "Guess who?" "From me!" "Someone who likes you!" I got a nice Valentine and a Bit-O-Honey candy bar for Barbara. When we were in class we all dropped the valentines into a big box that the teacher had made for the class. Our boards and walls were decorated with pictures of valentines, hearts, and cupids. At the end of the day we all got our valentines when the teacher pulled them out of the box. I gave Barbara her valentine and the candy. She thanked me, but when I looked over after a while she and her friend were sharing the candy. I could see them pulling at the candy and a nut fell out. I wished she were sharing it with me.

There was also a sweet girl named Jane in my class who was always friendly to me. Her name was the first I had learned in English in my reader: Dick, Jane and their dog, Spot. I was so glad to have a friend named Jane. She had curly red hair that she wore pulled back in an effort to control it. Her mouth looked like a rose bud especially this Valentine's Day because her lips were chapped. She didn't live far from me and in January I went to Sunday school with her. She took me around and introduced me to her friends. Protestant religion seemed very sociable and more personable than the Catholic Church that I was used to. She came over to my desk and gave me a valentine with a bag of pastel candy hearts attached that said: I love you! and Be mine! I was happy but embarrassed that I hadn't given her any candy with her valentine.

18 *Céfiro*

Céfiro, or Zephyr, is the west wind. He resides in the little tip of the right wing of Texas where the Río meets New Mexico. In the spring of 1949, Zephyr gently started the day by running around Mount Cristo Rey, just full of himself. Then he skipped through the villages of Anthony, Texas, and Anthony, New Mexico, and chased the coolness of the day along the Río Bravo or Río Grande right up to Juárez. He tore around Mount Franklin as if it were a little tail to wag. By the power of his own energy, Zephyr became a pale rider atop a golden palomino and he challenged the oxeye-daisy sun in the bleached sky to a race across the land. Chasing the ghosts of Indians past and running against a phantom mule train, he created his own rodeo. As Zephyr grew with the warmth of the day, he strutted and drove that palomino steed as fast as he could go and reached Fabens only to decide it was time to return to play in El Paso until the sun showed the yellow and orange signs of languishing and seeking out the horizon. Then Zephyr raced, devil-may-care, to the horizon to meet the blazing orange aftermath of the vanishing sun. Like a tired little *chamaco*, he went off to bed on the mesa to be ready to start again in the morning.

March arrived to the joy of everyone. The days became warmer and the warm glow of daffodils and the pastel colors of spring offered promise. I was finding a routine for myself. The week at school was more comfortable and Saturday afternoons I went to the Pershing Theater. On Sundays I found going to Protestant Sunday School with Jane, my friend from school, interesting and certainly a break from the boredom at home. Martha, Fred, and Uncle Bob hibernated on Sunday, even though they didn't work at a job during the week. It was frustrating for me to have everyone sleeping late and taking naps on top of that.

The day after Ash Wednesday was Palm's birthday. Martha and Fred took me down to visit him. They didn't tell me until we stopped at our

178

lamp post that Palm was sick. I walked inside nervously and found my father in the living room in his bed, which had been brought down from upstairs. I was frightened and ran to his side. I hugged and kissed him and asked him what was wrong. He said with a laugh, the only thing wrong with him was a hard life and bad living. His cowboy music was playing softly on the radio. We visited a while and I felt sure that he would be well soon. I went outside and sat on the curb with Carlos while Palm talked with my parents. My brother told me all about the neighborhood and listened to my stories about Houston School.

"Yoya, I have some bad news for you," Carlos said in a tone I knew only too well. He looked at me and seemed to be searching for something inside his head. "We haven't told Palm because we don't want to upset him." He was stalling.

"*Por Dios*, Carlos! Tell me, I am not a baby anymore!" I said in a loud voice. "Tell me."

"López died last month. He had tuberculosis and he died from one day to the next." He finally said it. I started crying. My whole past life was crumbling right before my eyes.

"Palm doesn't know?" I asked.

"No, we don't know when to tell him," Carlos said quietly. "Padre Luna will decide when. Palm gets depressed easily these days." My older brother, Oscar, had gone into the army, leaving Carlos with all of Palm's care.

"López told me that he would never die. He said *cosa mala nunca muere*. The bad never die," I cried. "I knew he wasn't bad."

Carlos and I returned to the apartment as soon as I regained my composure. Martha looked at me knew something was wrong. I kissed my father and I asked him to take care of himself.

"You have to have many more birthdays, Papí," I said.

"Oh, *mi'ja, cosa mala nunca muere!*" he said, laughing. I couldn't believe my ears and couldn't get out of there fast enough. Once in the car, I started crying again and I told my parents about my grandfather. It upset Martha to see me cry.

This March brought a new friend to the neighborhood. Linda moved in behind us on Douglas Street and although she was in my grade, she ended up in another class. We walked to and from school every day. She and her parents had moved from Ysleta. Her parents had met when her stepfather was in the *bracero* program in 1946. Linda's father had died in a farm accident. We had that in common: we both had lost a parent.

At school, I didn't play with Linda. Instead I played with Jane and tried to make friends with Barbara, but she was not interested in being friends with me. Once in a while, she would stop and talk. I would do anything she told me to do: sharpen her pencils or hang up her coat, even though I saw her friends laughing at me.

On April 1, 1949, Uncle Bob left. Fred and Martha took him to the train depot. I didn't expect it to be painful to say goodbye and I never thought he would be so emotional. He wouldn't speak English, only German. I understood some and Fred translated the rest. I asked him to speak English, but Fred pushed me. I realized that Uncle Bob was having a hard time. He said that someday when he had his farm back, he would send for me. Then I could see his farm, the big silos, and all the farm animals. I never saw him again. It occurred to me that I never realized how much I cared about someone until I lost them.

Two weeks later we went to William Beaumont Hospital to see Palm. Because my older brother was in the service and my father was so poor, the army hospitalized him at Fort Bliss. They let me see him only because he was so sick, but I refused to believe things were as bad as they seemed. We chatted and I had to leave when the nurse asked me. I hugged my father and told him that next time I wanted to see him on St. Vrain Street. I never saw him alive again. I wouldn't think about Palm and his illness. Maybe I imagined it would go away if I didn't think about it.

> *Céfiro* or Zephyr
> Whichever you are
> Gently blow reality far
> Let me think
> What I want to be
> Let me fly away
> On your wings.

If any single symbol was appropriate for my childhood, it would be the *sube y baja*, the see-saw. It seems that I was either up or down, or on my way up or on my way down. And, as in the see-saw, there was always a human being on the opposite seat. Sometimes I would find myself held up by the person in the other seat. Other times, I could try to stay on the ground by pushing down hard. Most of the time the ups and downs were natural, but many of them were unpleasant.

At school we were practicing for the May Festival. All the grades were going to give presentations on May 12. Our class had the Virginia Reel and another dance to perform. Every time we practiced I tried to dance with Barbara. It was so much fun. The teacher had warned us that there was no excuse for not being present for the festival. She told us that if we were absent we would receive an "F" in P.E. I wondered who would want to miss it? Little did I know that destiny had something else in mind for me. On May 12, I got home and wanted to bathe and get ready for the festival. I ran into the house and had just stepped into my room when I heard Martha call me. I went to her bedroom.

"Gloria I have something to tell you. But I don't want you to cry." She was upset.

"What is it. Did I forget to do something?" I asked.

"No. Palm died this morning," she said. I looked at her and waited. Then she repeated it again as my insides were bursting. But she had said I couldn't cry. I stood very still.

"Did you understand what I said?" she asked.

"Yes, you said my father died this morning," I answered.

"You can't go to the festival," she told me.

"I know," I said. "I have to go to the bathroom."

I went in and I sat in the chair by the window. Palm is dead. I can't cry. I can't go to the festival. I don't remember how the rest of the evening went. All I remember is that I couldn't cry.

The next morning we went to the funeral home. Carlos and Padre Luna met me at the door. Apparently someone had told Padre that they were going to bring me. I shook Padre's hand and I told him I was glad to see him. Then we went into the chapel. Señora Olga, Flaco, Pelón, and Señora Luz were sitting in the pews. I looked at them and I didn't say anything. I went up to the casket and I looked at the body. I saw only an old man with a mustache. I knew it wasn't my father. Padre Luna came up next to me.

"Are you all right, Gloria?" he asked.

"Yes, Padre. I'm all right but this isn't my father," I answered him. "Padre, this is not Palm. This is some poor old man."

"Gloria, it is your father," he said in a gentle voice.

"*Dispenseme Padre*, but this is not Palm." I was angry. I looked at Padre. "Look at him. My father never wore a mustache and he was not this old," I insisted.

Padre took me to the pew where my parents were. Martha was annoyed because she did not like priests. He told her I was having problems recognizing my father. Fred looked at me and said in a gentle voice,

"Gloria, it is your father. I would never lie to you." His voice upset me. "He is thinner and has a mustache. I don't know why they didn't shave it off." As I heard him say those words I realized that he was telling the truth. I grabbed Padre's arm as we walked alongside my parents.

"Please, Padre, it isn't so!" I cried. "Please ask God to give him back. It's not fair! I have lost all that once was my life. Please Padre, ask him to give him back."

"Gloria we all have to accept what God gives us. He has not abandoned you. He gave you your godparents to care for you."

"Padre," I whispered to him. "*No nos despedimos.* I didn't get to say goodbye. Is this God's way? Is it punishment for me to never to say goodbye to the people I love so much? Padre, it isn't fair."

Padre stroked my head and talked to me for a long time. Carlos tried to console me. I went back to the casket and I still could not believe it was Palm. But I had to believe that those people who loved me would not lie to me. They said that it was my precious Palm in that casket and I had to try to believe it.

Carlos went to live in Chihuahua with my Uncle Juan. He would return in a few years and go to Boys Town, the orphanage. I would miss him very much in the years after my father's death.

Palm was buried in Evergreen Cemetery next to the fence at the back just before the last exit. Palm's son from San Antonio, the one I had met when I couldn't speak English, paid for the funeral and the brown granite headstone. During the funeral I felt as if I had a head cold. I could barely hear people when they talked to me.

That night, the nightmares returned. Once again I searched the railroad tracks for Palm. I found Luis and López. The three of us searched and searched but we couldn't find Palm. Padre Luna finally found me and he talked me into leaving the tracks. He would say, leave your father with God. And I would answer, all I want to do is say goodbye: *Adiós para siempre, adiós.*

19   El Sol

If there ever was a metaphor for El Paso and Juárez it is the sun. El sol resided in El Paso for the whole year except for five days in 1949. That summer we had bone-drying humidity and there were only nine inches of rain. Summer started in June and lasted until the World Series in October. All that saved us from the heat were the cool evenings finally beginning in September.

Still the mornings in summer were the most delicious mornings in the world. They were mild and full of color, as any desert lover will tell you. But from midday until six in the afternoon, the atmosphere was stark and there was a haze created by the sun and tiny particles of sand suspended in the air. It was like peeling a lemon and having the light catch tiny particles of mist flying in the air. If there ever was a prayer sung by the Mexican worker it was Frankie Lane's 1949 song, "That Lucky Old Sun."

Time was different in those days for Mexicans than it was for Americans. The Mexicans just emphasized time differently. Morning in Mexican time was divided into *la madrugada*, early morning, and *la mañana*, morning. *La tarde*, afternoon, was that time until the sun set. In summer that made for a long afternoon. Time was more subjective than objective for me, as it was for many below the border. Time was savored like anything you didn't want to finish too soon. It was like that piece of candy or pie that you wish would replace itself as you consume it rather than disappear, as it always did.

The summer of 1949 was a healing time for me. My parents seemed to know that I was at odds with myself. I felt turned inside out. I blamed myself silently for leaving Palm but I never told them. I was angry with myself for not having shown him I loved him by visiting and kissing him more. I never realized it would end. I had to learn again that you don't know what you have lost until it is gone. All I had left were the ache and regrets.

The last week of school in the fifth grade was very busy. I got an
"F" in P.E. because I couldn't tell the teacher that my father had died:
Martha did not want people to know I was adopted. I tried to soften
the teacher's anger by offering to pick up paper.

Barbara had her group and I played with many of the children that
weren't in cliques. Barbara and Jane were the smartest girls in class.
They knew all the answers and they wrote beautifully, even though they
were both left-handed. My handwriting was like chicken scratch, according to Fred. Two weeks before school let out, Barbara and her friends
began to talk in a strange way. When I was near them, they talked to
each other in words I didn't understand. Then they laughed and laughed
at what they were saying.

"Ouyay igbay abybay!" said one to the other.

Jane was with me and she laughed. I asked her if she knew what they
were saying and she told me about pig latin. The trick was to take the
first letter of a word and put it at the end and add "ay". She was patient
with me and we practiced at recess and for a while after school. By the
end of the week I could understand and carry on a good conversation.
When next we were near Barbara's group, Jane started a conversation in
the new language with me and they were annoyed and stomped off. I felt
so good! When school ended, I taught Linda pig latin and we spoke it all
summer long. Martha heard us once and scolded me. She said if I didn't
stop talking like that she would not let me play with Linda. After that,
we didn't use it in front of adults. It was fun to have a secret language.

I played all summer with Linda on and around our block. We ex-
plored the neighborhood, went to the drugstore, acted out Nancy Drew
novels, and she went with me to my weekly piano lesson. I had been taking piano lessons for over a year and could play simple songs. Martha
didn't let me "bang" on the piano. My playing always had to have a
song or exercise in mind.

On the few days that it rained, Linda and I would stay outside so
we could smell the perfume of the wet ground. It was such a wonderful
smell. When it began to rain hard we went inside to listen to the radio.
We loved all the serials and there was always music to listen to both in
Spanish and in English. The radio was a daily companion for us. When
Linda spent the night, we would play the radio to guarantee our privacy.

All summer long I thought of how I could be friends with Barbara. I
wished that we could be friends in September. We could talk in pig latin

and share secrets. I planned on words we could invent so that no one would know what we were saying. She could teach me how to write neatly and not the blue polka-dotted messes I made with the long pen after I stuck it into the ink well. My beige sheet from my Big Chief looked like an accident. Maybe she could come and spend the night with me. Martha didn't let me spend the night anywhere. But she would let me invite Linda to spend the night with us. The next day, Barbara and I could eat Post Toasties just like Linda and I do when she stayed over.

At the beginning of the summer, Linda and I had two pieces of chalk we "borrowed" from our teacher. Once a week we would draw out a diagram for hopscotch. The two of us dropped to our knees at the garage and drew the diagram all the way into the street. The first square started at the curb and the circle at the top ended up being a half circle because of the garage door. If we were lucky, we got about three days play out of it. People seemed to respect it when they saw it and they would walk on it carefully. By the middle of the June we could only play outside until eleven in the morning. Then we came inside until six because it was too hot to play outside. We usually stayed indoors until we heard Uncle Roy read the comics on KTSM each afternoon.

Each week after we went to the movies, Linda and I would act out the whole film for the rest of the week. Generally, we would take up where the movie left off and add our own ending. I always insisted on playing the lead and Linda would play all the other parts. She would never complain. It was okay, I justified, because I knew more English than she did.

When Linda and I went to Memorial Park Library behind the railroad tracks were we lived, we found an answer to my problem of how to become friends with Barbara. We found a book on children's plays and the idea came to me. I would find a play in the book, and because I knew so much about acting from all the movies I had seen in the last few years, I would get the kids to act in my play. Barbara would be the lead. I would get the kids to participate by offering some of the trinkets that I had in the wooden box. I thought it was a perfect idea. When I told Linda about it, she questioned me.

"You just want to get Barbara to be your friend," she guessed. "Why do you want that *sangrona*, snotty girl, to be your friend? We don't need her."

"No, I just want a chance to direct a play," I answered.

The rest of August Linda and I made copies of the play. It had a heroine and hero. The hero would pose a problem. We couldn't stand the boys in our grade. But maybe José would be all right. We finished only four copies. And three of them I had to do; Linda thought it was stupid. Every evening I worked on the copying and every night I dreamed of directing Barbara in the play.

September arrived and we returned to school. The first two weeks were spent getting used to the new teacher. By the twelfth day, I finally could accept the change and school really began for me. Barbara and her friends were a group again. Jane and I were friends again. I showed her the play and she said she would be in the play for me. But I didn't have to give her any trinket: she liked to act. When I approached Barbara after practicing and rehearsing how to ask her, she liked the idea.

"What kind of trinkets do you have?" she and the Johnson sisters wanted to know. "When can we see them?" They all smiled and stared at me.

"Just things like necklaces, little watches, and lockets that were offered on the *Stella Dallas* or *Lorenzo Jones* show. I don't know which ones. My father loves those shows," I hurried to explain because I didn't want them to lose interest.

"Well, do you want to be in my play?" I got the courage to ask the big question. "What do you say?"

"Oh, sure. For trinkets we'll do anything," the sisters shrieked. "But, we'll only do it once. Right after school on Friday."

"Just once? What about rehearsals?" I asked.

"No, only once," they said together.

"Barbara, do you want to do it only once?" I didn't want to hear the answer.

"Yes, whatever they want." She smiled at them.

Well, you can imagine my disappointment, but once was better than nothing. I gave them copies of the play and I gave José a copy. He bargained for my decoder ring in exchange.

Friday came and I was so excited. I took my wooden box to school after I had hidden it outside the night before. I didn't want my parents to find out what I was doing with the trinkets. All day long I felt important and I could hardly wait for the last bell.

We met at the north part of the school. The kids wanted to see the trinkets. When they decided what each one wanted, we started the play. I would point to people for their parts. They half said them or they just mumbled. It was a disaster. They stopped looking at me for direction. They got the giggles midway through and the sisters just read the parts as fast as they could. And then they said they were through. They held out their hands for the trinkets and they ran off laughing. I was terribly upset but Jane comforted me. She said that they had only wanted the trinkets and they were stupid. I felt like a big fool.

That Saturday, Linda's father took us up to Scenic Drive. We first took a ride along the drive so that Linda could show me the house she was going to live in when she was rich. All the houses on Rim Road were the rich people's houses. They formed a tiara above all the humble houses below. At the high point of the drive you could park and look out at all of El Paso, Juárez, and some of New Mexico. Linda's father wanted to see the first evening of the full moon from there. My teacher said it was the harvest moon. We got there about seven and the sun was just about to set; a brilliant orange sky spread out to the west horizon. In a short time, the faint outline of the moon was apparent above the east horizon. I was surprised that both the sentry of the day and the keeper of the night were out at the same time. The sky was a blue purple stage and the mountains were knights in gray steel armor. The moon became more apparent as the sun approached the horizon. When the sun vanished, the bright silver moon reigned through the long night. The next three nights the moon became a big gold piece in the deep purple sky. As I looked at the lights of the two cities separated by a river, I thought about life in the desert and realized it was not simple.

20 October

De tin marín de lo pingüe
Cukara macara ti te re fué
Yo no fuí...fué ti ti
Chumbala, chumbala,
Que éste mero fué
Mi mama me dijó que
Devía ser Tú

On that sunny, dry October day in 1949, Linda was yelling out the Mexican version of one potato, two potato to pick the next lucky person. She said the chant, which doesn't translate into English well, as she banged her closed fist against the fists of the participants. When the sing-song finished, the selection was magically made. The Mexican love for consonants was clear in the rhyme. That love was Indian heritage.

Mine was the last fist to be hit. I pushed my hair back and charged in the direction of the *remolinito*, a small whirlwind that had sprung up spontaneously on the playground. There are always small whirlwinds in the warm afternoons of October. They were a sure bet when the cool night air and the warm sun of the day collided. The little wisps of wind appeared suddenly and rapidly spent themselves. They were light spirits full of sand, dust devils as they are called by many children, that danced and beckoned us to dance with them. We would jump up and down when we engaged those fickle ghosts. The jumping was to spare our legs the sting of the sand—sand bites. We kept our eyes closed. On the west side of the play ground of Houston School, a wind would start in the lower field, becoming strong by the time it reached the upper playground.

The sandstorms of the fall in El Paso were different from the spring sandstorms. In 1949, El Paso had few trees, few strong lawns, and a huge desert. A sandstorm that would start early in the afternoon would gain momentum in a short time. By the time I left school after three, the whole world was engulfed in a gritty red atmosphere. Every breath tasted of earth and sand.

The girls' dresses in October were the pretty ones of Easter and spring. But the bright pastel colors of those spring dresses were now faded. The waists of two of my dresses were at my lower ribs and the skirt part showed a white line where my mother had let out the hem in September. Sometimes, Martha would put a lace on this line so that it would disappear. There wasn't much a mother could do about the rib rub. The boys suffered equally from their summer growth. Their shirts were short as were their high rise pants. *Brinca-charcos*, puddle jumpers, was what we called those pants. There was no need in September or October for all new clothes because winter was just around the corner and we would need sweaters then.

The games on the playground this October were seasonal, including baseball. The World Series in the first week of October was eagerly awaited—the Dodgers versus the Yankees. The boys became preoccupied with the series and completely stayed out of our way. Their huddles were all about the games and the scores; nothing else seemed to exist for them. The girls were into jacks and "say-say-say" because they could be played in the shade of the building if it was too warm in the afternoon.

On October 16, 1949, began the biggest adventure that I ever had while living in Five Points. That day was a Sunday and it was cool with a slight breeze. Linda had gone to lunch with her parents at the Paloma Cafe in the Second Ward to celebrate her father's birthday. My parents gave me permission to go to the movies at 4 o'clock. They wanted to take a nap. Plus I had annoyed my mother with my imitation of the "Shadow" after I listened to the program at three. I stepped into the kitchen and in the wobbly voice of the Shadow I said:

Who knows what evil
Lurks in the hearts of men?
The Shadow knows.

That bit of acting got me in trouble. Martha hated the sound of the Shadow's voice. It scared her and I loved it. But, she said I could go to the movies as long as I didn't stay there past dark. In mid-October, it got dark around six thirty and in those days, you could stay in the theater until you felt like leaving. She didn't have to tell me twice. I set out for the movies.

I don't know what, but something made me walk past the Pershing Theater. I found myself going up to Houston Elementary. But, I didn't go to the school. I kept walking up until I got to Elm Street, which was lined with beautiful homes. When they built Five Points, they built a section near Memorial Park with beautiful expensive houses that belonged to upper middle-class Anglos. They did the same across Piedras street on Elm Street. This area was called Manhattan Heights. We lived on Pershing Street, where there were modest homes inhabited mostly by on-the-way-up Syrians, some Mexicans, and my family. Our house was a modest two-bedroom California style red-brick cottage like hundreds of others in El Paso.

Once on Elm Street, I started up the street with a specific destination in mind. Two weeks before, Linda and I had walked through the neighborhood when we were planning the play. We came upon a house that had movers in front of it. We stopped and watched them load the truck, much to the annoyance of the movers. It was fun watching beautiful expensive furniture come out of the grandest house on Elm Street.

"Now that is a house, Linda. This house is prettier than the houses on Rim Road," I told her. "You can live on Rim Road and I'll live on Elm Street."

She agreed and we stayed in front of the house until the movers loaded everything up and they even waved at us as they left. We took one more look at the house and then left.

I just wanted to look at the house again. When I arrived, I could tell that it was still empty. I walked around the house and then I went across the street to get a different look at it. Because it was Sunday, there was no traffic or people in the street. I returned and peered at the south side of the house. I noticed a small window slightly open. I don't know why I did it, but I glanced around and then went to the little window that had no screen and climbed inside. Once in, I was terrified at what I had done. Oh well, I just wanted to look. I walked around and was surprised at how beautiful the interior was. It was probably built a long time ago. The emptiness gave the house a magical atmosphere as did the front windows, which were shaped like arches in a church. The ceilings were very high and the wooden floors were golden. There was one room that had big windows from the floor up to the molding. The sunshine flooded in and bounced off a big white piano, the only piece of furniture left in the house. The beautiful wooden floor was the stage for the beautiful instrument. I opened it and played a few keys before I got nervous. Then I walked around and tried to imagine how it would be to live there. After that, I left by the window, just like I had entered. I left it slightly open. I was shocked by what I had done, but I didn't regret it. I went back to the school and I thought about what I had seen. Then, a plan occurred to me.

When I got home, I called Linda and asked her to meet me at the trash cans behind the Baca's house. There I told her about my entry in to the big house. She was shocked by my childish prank and at the same time fascinated by the details of the house. Then I told her my plan. On Halloween, if the house was still empty, we could go there. We could get José to come with us and we could really have an adventure.

"The house is haunted, isn't it Gloria?" Linda asked scared.
"That is why it is empty."

"Tish, haunted!" I snapped back.

That night I planned our Halloween escapade and I said twenty prayers: ten Our Fathers and ten Hail Marys. I felt anxious and yet it was so exciting.

Halloween was a funny idea to me. I had always been afraid of ghosts and devils, as you well know. It was something I believed one minute, perhaps not so later, but I know I didn't like the idea of ghosts and devils. Still, believing in them at twelve years old created some excitement for me that was special to Halloween. There was a little thrill to scaring myself.

Each day the week before Halloween, José, Linda, and I went by the house on Elm Street at lunch. It was still empty and we could tell that the window was open, even from a distance. I worried that someone might go into "our house". Each time, José and Linda would think of reasons why the house was empty.

"I bet someone died in the house and he walks around with his head cut off," José said, "just like in the Legend of Sleepy Hallow."

"No, I think there is an evil woman living in the basement. You know, Gloria, that all these houses have basements just like yours and mine does," Linda said. "And, at night, she comes out and plays the piano all night long."

"No, I think that the piano belonged to someone who everyone in the family loved, but the person went away and never returned." I added my two cents. "The family left the piano so that if the person returns it's there for them to play."

On the Friday before Halloween, José, Linda and I met at the north side of the school during recess to figure out who was to bring what. Linda and José would borrow their fathers' flashlights so that we could see inside the dark house. While we were standing there, one of the Johnson sisters went by and appeared to be looking for something. Soon, I realized she was listening to our conversation. She came over when she saw me looking at her.

"What are you all planning?" she asked.

"What business is it of yours?" answered José.

"All right, José! I just want to know," she answered as she looked at us in an unusually friendly way. "It's just that Marie is sick and Lulu is being punished and they won't be able to go trick-or-treating with us Halloween night. It's more fun if there's a bunch of us."

"Well, go with your sister and Barbara!" José said.

"Well, we are going together. I just wanted to know if you had something you were going to do and if we could come along," replied the mischievous brown-haired sister. She was the older one. The blonde sister was shy and quiet.

"Well, you can come with us. You, your sister, and Barbara," I answered because it meant Barbara would be with us! "But, we can't tell you what we are going to do until Halloween. Let's just say that there is a secret and we are going to find out what it is," I said mysteriously.

"Tell me, I won't tell," she pleaded. "Cross my heart and hope to die, stick a needle in my eye if I tell."

"If you keep what we have told you secret, then, on Monday afternoon, we'll tell you more." I set the rules. "You go talk to your sister and Barbara. Let me know what you want to do."

After school, Barbara came running up to me to ask me what the secret was. She promised and crossed her heart that she wouldn't tell anyone. I said that I knew she wouldn't tell but it was a secret and that if they kept quiet we would meet on Monday and include them on our adventure.

"OOOOOh! Just like a Nancy Drew mystery!" Barbara shivered. "I promise you, Gloria, we will keep quiet. Cross my heart." She narrowed her eyes and whispered her oath of silence.

I felt so powerful. The sisters and Barbara were dying to know what my secret was. I just knew that it was going to be a wonderful Halloween. Saturday and Sunday, Linda and I talked and talked about Halloween. We planned every step and vowed to stay out of trouble with our parents so that they would let us go trick-or-treating. Martha was not happy with the idea. On Sunday, I kept my radio low so as not to upset her. She wasn't even aware that "The Shadow" came on and off. All I did was mouth the words of the Shadow and looked at the direction of her bedroom. That evening, she wanted to talk about Halloween.

"How do I know you will be safe?" she asked.

"Martha, what is going to happen to her?" Fred asked.

"Well, it is dark. Someone might grab her!" Martha said.

"I am going to be with Linda, José, and some other children from school. We're going up Elm Street to trick-or-treat at the rich houses. I'll be home by nine," I answered calmly. Fred nodded and winked at me. He meant to tell me that there was no problem. He would talk to Martha and it would be all right. Then I promised to go with her on the Day of the Dead to the cemetery. I wanted to see Palm's grave.

Monday afternoon we met at school by the monkey bars. The Johnson sisters, Barbara, José, Linda, and I huddled together for privacy and for warmth. The air was very cold that afternoon because a Norther had moved in the day before. I told the Johnson sisters and Barbara that we were going into a haunted house on Elm Street. They loved the idea! The piano was a big interest. We all swore that we would not tell anyone and then we all crossed our hearts at the same time. And, if anyone told, we could all beat them up the next day. Then we shook hands. We agreed to return by quarter after six under the monkey bars.

At five, I started checking the outside every few minutes. I was checking to see if it was dark yet. The sunset was beginning. The sun set around a quarter after five. I went out to the back yard again and I heard dogs barking. I could hear the commotion the sparrows were making in the only tree we had in our yard. Across the street, I could hear more sparrows fighting for a place to sleep in the neighbor's big old mulberry tree. I thought to myself: if you have to fight for a place in the tree, you have to fight! As I had that thought, several more sparrows flew in and the whole commotion in the tree started again. I chuckled.

A few minutes before six, I checked myself. Since it was so cold, I was wearing my pants, my red reindeer sweater, and an old sweater of Fred's with patches Martha had sewn on to make it look like a hobo's sweater. I couldn't wear any of his old coats because they were too big. Fred made me a stick and put a sack at the end stuffed with paper. He gave me an old hat with a piece cut out of it to make it look real. Then Martha painted a mustache and big eyebrows on my face. I begged for some lipstick so that the wind wouldn't chap my lips.

The Halloween sky had the remnants of the bright orange-red of a Mesilla Valley chili. That color of sky always made me homesick, though for what, I didn't know. I looked up at the stars that were coming out and I walked to Linda's house. There a white-sheet ghost came out and away we went to school. We met everyone there. I became the leader and they were quick to follow my directions. The sisters were dressed in cat outfits that their mother had made. One was white and the other was black. They had tails that stood straight up. Barbara was dressed as a ballerina. She carried a wand and she had a tiara on top of her blond hair. José was dressed in old clothes and he had a very ugly mask on his face. Determined and silent, we left for our adventure up Elm Street.

There were not many children out because of the cold weather. When we got to the block, I pointed the house out to the sisters, who then rushed to Barbara and told her. We walked past it so that we could see if anyone was around. There was no one around. It was probably dinner time for most people. We quickly moved in the dark to the south side of the house to the window that was opened. I went in first, then Linda, then Barbara, the sisters, and José was the last one. He had problems getting in because he was bigger than all the girls. Inside the house, we turned the flashlights on and pointed them at the floor as soon as we were away from the window. We whispered to each other and then someone laughed.

"Why are we whispering?" asked the blonde sister. "We are alone." Then we all started laughing. We walked around on tiptoe as if we were afraid we were going to wake someone up.

"Look, there is no one here! What are we so afraid of?" the other sister said. "This is so funny!" Then we started laughing again.

"But, if the house has a ghost, we have to be careful until we know where it is," Linda said. Everyone was quiet for a second. José stopped and he looked at Linda with his right hand on his hip.

"There is no such thing as a ghost, Linda!" he barked.

"Let's go into the music room," I suggested. I showed them the way and then we went into the room that now seemed so dull in the dark. Barbara shone the light on the piano and we all made little sounds of surprise and delight. Everyone looked it over and Barbara lifted the cover to play some of the keys. She looked at me and asked me if I wanted to play chopsticks with her. The other kids danced around the empty room. After a while, we decided to check and see if there was a basement. We found the entrance off the kitchen. Everyone used a flashlight and we all went down into the basement except José, who thought he better stay upstairs just in case. The truth was that he didn't like basements. But we didn't care because it was a good idea someone stay upstairs. We came back up and took one more look around our haunted house before leaving through the little window. This time, I shut it because I knew I would never return and I didn't want anyone else to get in. We went trick-or- treating and then decided to walk back to school because it was so cold. The moon above was a fingernail-tip of gold. It was as if God were putting his thumb into the earth's atmosphere to check the temperature. All of us had to be home by nine. At school, we dumped our treats out and traded with each other for the candies we liked.

I went over to Barbara and asked her if she had a good time.

"Oh, it was fun. I wish I lived in a pretty house like that," she answered. "I wonder who will live there?"

"I don't know," I answered. Then I decided to see if Barbara would play with me. "Barbara can you come and spend the day with me on Saturday? We can play and I can show you all the hiding places Linda and I have."

"No, I can't," she answered and she must have seen that I was waiting for a reason. "I have too much work to do on Saturdays. I have to help my parents clean house and go shopping."

"Well, can I come and visit some afternoon after school?" I asked. "I can help you with your housework."

"No," she answered.

"Not ever?" I continued to ask.

"Gloria, my mother does not want any Mexican kids around. You can't come over," she answered.

"You don't have to tell her I am Mexican," I said as I was trying to understand what she meant. "Your mother doesn't have to know," I said, still confused and uncomfortable.

"Gloria, the minute you open your mouth, she'll know you are Mexican," she answered, somewhat annoyed at my persistence.

"Why doesn't she want any Mexicans around?" I asked.

"Because a few years ago, she had a very bad experience with some foreigners. And she doesn't want anyone who is not American around," she answered as she turned around and yelled at the girls to hurry up. She said goodbye as I watched her leave. I was stunned. I couldn't be friends with Barbara because I was a Mexican. I didn't understand.

Linda and I walked home. We shivered and stuck close to each other. All I could think about was that there was a problem because I was Mexican. I didn't want to think anymore. I was tired and I just wanted to go home to bed. Maybe I could figure it out the next day. My mother and father were listening to the radio as I walked into the living room. I stood at the door after I closed it. I looked at my mother as I had never looked at her before. She was Mexican and a part of what I had always known. Somehow I was different than I had been two hours earlier.

21 If

If one is uncertain or has doubts, the subjunctive tense reflects it. Here is the key to the Mexican mind as I knew it: *Si Dios quiere*, if God wishes, and *Si Dios manda*, if God wills it, reflected the tentativeness of life and destiny. In 1949, the subjunctive sentence announced suspended reality. There was an understanding that life contained elements of dependence on God, the government, or the environment. The use of the subjunctive was almost an arithmetic formula.

If the Moors had not invaded Spain in 711, the Spanish would not have felt the pain of conquest and the anger of subjugation. They would not have spent 781 years fighting and driving the Moors out of their land. They would not have experienced a need to subjugate in the name of religion. And they would not have developed a need to conquer. They might not have listened to the Italian Columbus with his crazy idea that the world was round and that riches lay beyond the sea. The Spanish followed the lead of the Portuguese in their pursuit of spices and gold. They had not planned on running into the Americas.

If the Spaniards had not come to this part of the world and subjugated the indigenous populations, I like to think that the Indians would have roamed this hemisphere until the end of time. If there had not been doubt and uncertainty in Montezuma II's mind, he would not have hesitated to murder the invaders of his world. If Spanish had not been the language that prevailed, perhaps destiny would be clearer. And, if the Mexicans had not lost so much to the North Americans, perhaps the hyphenated term, Mexican-American would not have been necessary.

The truth of the matter is probably that some other country would have done it. It just happened that the Spaniards in 1492 had a need for gold and they were risk takers. In 1848 the American colonists in

Mexican territory wanted the land, so they prevailed. The subjunctive depends on fate, timing, and determination.

November 1, I awoke sick. I had a fever and I felt awful. I complained to Martha, who was quick to scold me for having gone trick-or-treating and for having eaten so much candy. I didn't contradict her, although I hadn't had one piece of candy. She said that I could stay in bed for the day. She asked me if I was just trying to get out of going to the cemetery with her. I quickly answered that I wasn't. Martha came over and started to give me a treatment of *apretones*. I looked at her dark brown hand and I remembered the conversation with Barbara. As Martha squeezed my shoulders, I grabbed her hand and I looked at her skin trying to find an answer in it.

"What are you looking at?" she asked in a puzzled voice.

"I'm just looking at your *piel canela*," I answered. "*Amá*, you told me that your father was French. That's true?" I asked. She nodded a yes answer. "And your mother was Mexican." I didn't ask if her mother was Indian because Martha was very touchy about her Indian blood.

"Yes, why?" she answered annoyed. "Why do you ask?'

"Well, because you are dark, *mi negra*, my beloved. And I wondered what happened to the French in you." I smiled so that she wouldn't be offended. She wasn't.

"I guess Mexican blood and color is stronger than French. My mother said that my father, Blanchett, was olive complexioned. I have more Mexican than French." She sighed. "That's all right. In my rancho, it wasn't popular to be French."

"So you don't claim to be French in your rancho?" I asked.

"That's right. I am Mexican," she answered quickly. I envied her sureness at that moment because I wasn't there completely.

In the afternoon, I walked around the house looking at everything as if it were new to me. I felt as if I were a guest inside my body. At supper, I listened to the conversation between my parents and realized that Fred spoke English and Martha spoke Spanish. But I already knew that, I thought to myself.

By bedtime, I said goodnight to my parents and I told Martha that I really wanted to go to the cemetery with her. She was pleased. Then she looked at me in a strange way.

"Gloria, did something happen to you last night?" she asked.

"Did you hurt yourself? I feel something is wrong," she said as she looked at my father who just shook his head. I went over and kissed him and said to myself: Bay Rum after-shave.

"No, I just don't feel good," I answered. "But, tomorrow, we'll go to the cemetery. I hope I don't get into trouble for missing two days of school." Actually, I didn't care. I didn't want to see anyone. I didn't care if I ever returned.

I went to my room and I made sure that the door was closed. Martha and Fred did not like me to close the door. They said my room would stay warmer if I left it open. Actually, I think they just wanted to hear me if I walked in my sleep.

I turned my radio on and, as I listened to Margaret Whiting sing "Far Away Places," I looked at my face in the mirror. I looked at my eyes and wondered whose eyes I had. Then I inspected my dark brown hair. And my freckles seemed to take over my whole face. I wondered whose full mouth I had. Who did I look like?

I had a hard time sleeping. All night long I felt as if my body was asleep and my brain was awake. I wanted to get up but my body was too heavy. My brain kept trying to lift my head but it wouldn't move. I could see the room and the door and I wanted to get up to go to the door, but my body would not wake up. It was a horrible night!

The next day I went into the kitchen and Martha was already awake. She poured me a cup of coffee and promised to heat some enchiladas for me. I smiled and nodded agreement. The enchiladas tasted like paper and I felt as if I would never swallow them. When she asked me if they were good, for a moment I didn't know what she was talking about. Then I looked at the enchilada and answered that it was very good.

We hurried to gather empty coffee cans and some scissors and left for the cemetery. We all got into the Oldsmobile. I sat on the bench and looked at the empty world until we arrived at the Evergreen Cemetery. We went to some of the relatives' graves and then we came to Palm's. I was surprised when I looked at the tombstone and read his name. This was the first time that I had seen the tombstone. I read it in my head: Palm, 1871-1949. Martha came up next to me.

"It's a nice stone, isn't it?" she asked.

"Stone?" I asked without thinking.

"Yes! What is wrong with you?" she asked.

"I was just thinking," I mumbled.

"Are you all right?" she asked. She seemed to realize something. "Does it make you sad to see it?"

"No, I'm just thinking. *Amá*, Palm was a gringo?" I asked.

"Yes. He was an American," she corrected.

"Does that make me an American?" I asked.

"Well, yes!" she answered.

"So, I am an American?"

"Yes, but your mother was a Mexican." She said that proudly.

"So, I am a Mexican," I asked.

"Well, yes, but you're an American, too," she answered.

"If my father had not married my mother, would I have been a Mexican all the way?"

"Gloria, I don't know what you would have been." Then she thought. "Well, your mother was a Mexican and she lived in Mexico and she would have probably married a Mexican. But, I don't know if you would have been you." She laughed. "If we had not adopted you, when your father died you probably would have gone to live with your uncle Juan in Chihuahua like Carlos did. Then, I guess you would have been Mexican." She started fixing the flowers that she had brought for Palm. I wondered quietly if where you lived determined who you were.

"You said that you are Mexican. But your father was French. Are you not French, too?" I asked.

"I am, but I do not choose to be. I choose to be Mexican because that is what is comfortable to me and being French is not. I chose to become an American citizen and that is what I am today," she answered in a matter-of-fact tone. She was thinking about something else. "I never knew my father. At least you had your mother until you were five. All I had were the stories my mother told." She was becoming sad.

By the time Fred returned, I had planned my afternoon. I was feeling so bad that I had to go find Padre Luna. He had to talk to me to help me work things out.

"Dad, I think that I should go to school this afternoon. I am afraid that the teacher will give me another 'F' like she did when I was absent for Palm's death last May." I presented a good excuse.

"This has made you sad, hasn't it, Gloria?" Fred asked. "I'm sorry. Your dad would be so happy to see how well you are doing in school."

"Yes, let's get back so that she can go in the afternoon," Martha said. I could hear the sadness in her voice. She had told me the year before

that every November, after she comes to the cemetery, she gets sad.
I could see it starting.

I rushed through lunch and ran out of the house after kissing both of
them goodbye. It didn't even scare me that I was about to be dishonest.
I had a bigger need—to see Padre Luna. I carefully went to the corner of
Piedras and Pershing and looked back to see if either of them had come
out onto the porch. Realizing that they would have to have the vision
of Superman to see that far, I ran down Piedras until I got to Alameda.
I didn't even notice how far it was. All I was thinking about was getting
to the Second Ward.

At Alameda, I took the steetcar until I got to the street where the
church was. Inside the church, I looked around. I had not been there in
more than two years. I looked lovingly at the walls. The stations of the
cross were the sweetest sight I had seen in a long time. I went down the
aisle between the two rows of pews. I genuflected and blessed myself like
I used to when I went to church there, then I slipped into the pew near-
est the confessionals. I knew father would be very busy today, but I
hoped to catch him if he came out into the church. I prayed and asked
God forgiveness for lying to my parents. I told God that I had to find
mi lugar, my place, my comfort spot. I gazed at the saints. The blessed
mother and the crucified Christ were almost too painful for me to look
at. I looked instead at St. Anthony.

After about twenty minutes, Padre Luna came out with a couple.
The woman was crying and the man was talking to Father. I guess they
have troubles, I thought. I do too, I said under my breath. Padre looked
at me and for a second he didn't see me. Then his eyes widened. He turned
to the couple, whom he led out of my sight. I knew he was walking
them out. Knowing Padre, I was afraid that he would spend a long time
comforting the couple so I started a new set of Our Fathers and Hail
Marys. But to my surprise he was back in an instant. He came to me and
when he did I started crying.

"Gloria, *mi'ja*? What is wrong, my child?" he asked. He looked right
into my face.

"Oh, Padre, I'm so happy to see you," I answered.

"Are you all right?" He pressed my hand for an answer.

"Yes Padre, I am all right. It is my soul that isn't." He looked at me
and motioned for me to follow. We went along the side of the pews and
out to the church office. He sat in a big chair and I sat across from him.

It seemed unreal to me that I was there. I looked around at the wonderful religious things in the office. They were the same ones I had seen for so many years before I went to live with my godparents.

"Gloria, what is wrong?" he asked. "Are you still confused about your father's death?" He remembered my anguish at my father's funeral.

"No, Padre. I know you say it was my father. I have to accept it," I said, even though in my heart it still wasn't real. But that wasn't why I was there.

"Padre, I did something very bad. I went into a *casa ajena*. I pretended that it was haunted and my friends and I went into it on Halloween night. I know it was wrong, and I want your forgiveness." I rushed out my confession. "I have already said hundreds of Our Fathers and Hail Marys."

"Gloria, you went into someone's home?" he asked concerned.

"It was empty and we did no harm. We just wanted to pretend the house was haunted," I explained, waiting to be scolded. He said nothing for a long time.

"Gloria, why are you here today? Any priest could have heard the confession you just made," he told me. "What is the real reason you are here?"

"Padre, I do not know who I am any more. My life has been so full of change and I don't know who I am." I cried into my hands because I was embarrassed. "First, I was Palm's daughter and now I am someone else's daughter. *No puedo hallar mi lugar.* I can't find my comfortable place."

"Yes, it has been hard. For a twelve-year-old, you have suffered much loss and change," he said in a soft voice.

"What else, Gloria? I feel there is something else. No one has hurt you. Like Eduardo tried to?" He asked what was worrying him.

"No, Padre. It is a *tontería*, a silly thing, but I must ask you about it," I said as he nodded and waved his hand in a gesture to continue. "I asked this little Anglo girl who I like so much. . . . I wanted to be her friend and I even wished she was my sister. I asked her if she could play with me and she said that she couldn't. She said that her mother does not want any Mexicans around their house because some foreigners had hurt her. And, I don't understand," I said softly to him.

"It is hard to understand, Gloria." he said. "It hard for anyone to understand why they have to pay for the harm others do. It may just be an excuse. But, it still doesn't make it easy to understand." He sighed. "You know, Gloria, my parents were Spaniards from Barcelona originally. They were wonderful parents and I loved them so much. The first time someone said to me that being Spanish was wrong, I was shocked. I had never imagined that being who you were was wrong. I looked at my parents and I didn't see any difference from the rest of the *pueblo*. But, as I learned my history, I realized that the harm the first Spaniards did to the *Mejicanos* was the harm I had to pay for. I was a Mexican because I was born in the Republic, but I was a Spaniard to those whose wanted to see me as a Spaniard." He sighed again, this time more deeply. "It didn't make sense to me at twelve anymore than it makes sense to you at twelve."

"Padre, which am I? Am I Mexican or am I American?" I wanted a simple answer. "Which one do I say I am?"

"Gloria, you are both. You have both bloods in you. And that will be a problem for you all your life if you let it." He looked sternly at me. "Would you prefer that I said that the left side of you is Mexican and the right side of you is American? Or that your head is American but you heart and lungs are Mexican?" He laughed and I laughed too. "*Mi'ja*, people are going to accept you or not. You are going to have to deal with the prejudices of people from now on. You are strong!" He got up and poured some water for us. He handed me the glass and I felt safe in his presence.

"Gloria, there are only two things in the world that never change: love and hate. Everyone knows them. They learn them from their parents and their group. And, many times, children can't choose which they want to feel. They are told every day of their lives who they can love and who they must hate." He coughed and looked at me. "You will know which one they feel by how much they accept you. Don't worry, the good always find each other."

He looked at me seriously, as he had in Juárez with his brother and sister on *Sábado de Gloria*. "Pure good is only of heaven. Pure bad is only of *el infierno*. Here on earth, human beings have to struggle with both. Sometimes we don't do so well. But at other times . . . we make the right choices."

Padre and I sat and talked a little longer. Then we went into the confessional and he heard my full confession. I spent the next half hour praying. I went and knocked on his door and I thanked him. He blessed me and said I knew where I could find him if I needed to. I would never seek him out again. The next year he left for a new church in East Los Angeles.

The rest of the month, I still felt confused, even though I knew what Padre said was right. But my head said Padre was right and my feelings said I was in pain. Whenever I was with my parents, I walked behind them. I didn't want to be seen with them. And, every night, I prayed to

God to help me stop feeling that way. At school, I was upset by the slightest thing. I didn't feel right and it would be a while before I did.

December is ambivalent in El Paso. It wants to be cold and it wants to be sunny. The air may be truly frigid, but if you're in the sun, you can become warm. Once in a while there is precipitation. But that is not the nature of the desert. With the dry air as pristine as it was in the 1940s, you could see a glorious display of stars and planets on any given December night while lying on a *colcha*, a blanket, on the cold ground. If the moon was full, the experience was truly religious—a desert night mass. Because the desert could be so cold, the only vegetation was the desert flora, which basked in the hot sun and shivered on the cold nights. You could predict the weather in December in El Paso. It would be cold in the shade and hot in the sun.

The trees that survived in the El Paso desert lost all their leaves by December. They were small versions of big trees you saw in travel books of Washington state. It seemed as if overnight someone pulled the tree out of the ground and shook the dirt off the roots and stuck it back into the ground upside down. Like brittle bones, the branches were naked and exposed as they reached out for God to help them. They looked raw in the West Texas sun. You could see everything that had happened to the trees: the growth spurts, the scars from pruning, and their spider web-like branches. They could not hide anything. There was nothing that could protect them. Exposed were the abandoned nests of sparrows that were hidden by the leaves in the summer. The leaves that fell off the trees were dead and dry in the street. The restless December West Texas wind would whip them up to a standing position and make them dance in a ring-around-the-rosy and then release them just as quickly.

Ring a round the rosy
A pocket full of posies
Ashes, ashes,
We all fall down

I felt like a desert tree that December of 1949. I felt vulnerable and exposed. Gone were the leaves of illusion for me. My roots were exposed and the winds of time ran through me. I was aware that everyone could see who I was. Apparently, the only person who had not seen it was me. I found myself on a quest for a comfortable place.

The month started slowly and I had no enthusiasm for anything. I noticed every reference to Mexicans or Anglos that anyone made. It was like the time I learned the word "environment" in geography class. After I learned it, I heard it all the time. I wondered why I had not heard it before. It was always there, I just had not noticed it. It was like finding a post in front of you. You were unaware of it until you ran into it. How could you not have seen it?

Early in December I walked home after school with Amad. He was a funny and cheerful boy, always laughing and telling jokes. During the talent shows we had in school, he would do anything to get attention. The Friday before, Amad had arranged for a friend and he to tell a joke as their talent. The funny part came when his friend slapped him very hard as part of the joke. Amad didn't mind. All through the rest of the class, Amad sat there with a big red hand imprint on his face. That was funnier than the joke. I laughed every time I looked at him.

This afternoon we were walking together by chance. I avoided him many times because he wanted me to be in his talent presentations. I didn't want to be in them; I liked just reading a poem or singing with a group. Somehow we got into a conversation about which church we went to and I told him that I went to the protestant church with Jane but that I was born a Catholic.

"Once a Catholic, always a Catholic!" he answered proudly.

"Oh, are you Catholic?" I asked not ever having thought about what religion Arabs were.

"Yes, I, too, was born a Catholic," he said, his black eyes bright with pride as I smiled at him.

"I never knew Syrians were Catholic. I thought they had a special religion."

"We are not all Syrian! Not all people who speak Arabic are Syrians. I am Lebanese and that is not Syrian!" he said angrily and he scared me. He reminded me of the little whirlwinds that spring up so rapidly you wonder where they came from.

"What is the difference?" I innocently asked and I found out soon that I would regret the question.

"*Tonta!*" Amad said in Spanish, which he spoke as well as he did English. I was impressed that he knew three languages. "Lebanese are better than Syrians. It's like it is better to be Spanish than Mexican."

He laughed because he knew that would make me mad. I punched him and laughed because I knew he was just pulling my leg, as Fred would say.

"I don't understand. Syrians and Lebanese are Arabs who speak the same language, but you think you are better than Syrians?" I asked again wanting to get the difference.

"Actually, Gloria, my mother is Syrian. It is a shame to my father's family that she is." He talked seriously for a moment. "I love *mi prietita*, my dark one. My mother just laughs when some one in my family says something nasty about Syrians. And, it makes me mad sometimes too. But, I am a Lebanese man and I have to defend my father's people."

"You seem so happy, Amad. How can you be happy with so much confusion about who you are?" I asked in a soft voice. The tone shook Amad out of his serious mood and he twirled an imaginary mustache. He was flirting with me.

"*Eh teene bawsi habibi!* Give me a little kiss honey!" he said in Arabic. I had heard it often from the other Syrians.

"*¡Ya mero!* That'll be the day," I answered as usual.

In the middle of December, I was sitting with Jane one afternoon. She had come over and we were in my room listening to the radio. We were sitting on the floor, our backs against my bed. I was feeling very tired and I decided to talk to Jane about what had happened to me with Barbara. I told her the whole story. As she listened, I realized she understood what I was saying. I told her about my trip to Padre's and how I felt so unhappy and unlike myself.

"It's like I am walking beside myself, like I am not together," I complained.

"I know that you have been very different since Halloween. And I knew it had something to do with Barbara," Jane said. She took a big sigh and then she looked very serious.

"Gloria, my father was killed in the Bataan Death Walk in the war. When my mother told me, I was so furious that my father wasn't coming home. Instead, the government gave us medals," she said very sadly. I felt so bad as I thought of the losses in my life. I had never told Jane about my past life. And it would be years before I would.

"I hated the Japanese. I wanted to kill the whole nation of them. All through the war, I hated them with all my guts," she said in a painful voice. "When we bombed Hiroshima and Nagasaki, I was happy that

Japan had been bombed. Then when my mother explained to me that innocent people like us were killed by the bomb, I was surprised."
Jane stopped: she had just ran into her post. "I realized that killing all those innocent people would not bring my father back or bring back the Japanese the Americans killed in the war. They had to do what they were supposed to do. I stopped feeling so angry." She sighed.
"Maybe Barbara's mother has not stopped being angry."

We played the whole day. It made me feel good that I had told Jane. I had so much trouble telling anyone how I felt. I thought I always had to be strong, and even if it hurt, I had to pretend that it didn't. Halloween seemed a little farther away today, but I knew it would never go away. On Halloween, I found out that there were things you couldn't put away, like the little jacket María made for me and that I kept in a drawer so it wouldn't remind me of having lost her.

22 Christmas

A long, long time ago—millions of years ago—giant reptiles and dinosaurs roamed West Texas and Northern Mexico. The land was rich and
full of vegetation. The dinosaurs were huge, especially around the Río
Grande. In the area of El Paso and Juárez, there lived two enormous
animals: one was a lizard and the other was a dinosaur—they were a
mixed couple. She was the dinosaur named Teja and he was the lizard
named Méjico: they were in love. They also loved the river and the immense
solitude and they played and frolicked in the warm sun. Eventually
the vegetation began to disappear and soon only cactus grew. One afternoon, Teja and Méjico took a siesta after a long, lovely, loving time together.
The large, rounded Teja went to sleep north of the Río Grande river.
The sharp, pointed Méjico went to sleep south of the Río Bravo,
the same river.

Cihuateteo, the Aztec spirits of women who died in childbirth and
the daily carriers of the sun from high noon to sunset, pleaded in vain to
the Aztec Gods for the lives of Teja and Méjico. During their long sleep,
Tlaloc, the rain god, and Quetzacoatl, who created the Aztecs and gave
the Mexican people the gift of corn, considered Teja and Méjico's im-
pending lack of food and made their sleep a final one. Then hating to
see the playful couple disappear, Quetzacoatl and Tlaloc turned them
into stone. They became the grey and brown mountains that are known
as Mount Franklin to the north and the Juárez Sierra in the south.
I like this explanation, even if the scientists don't agree.

Méjico is a very defined and masculine mountain. He was petrified
while sleeping on his stomach. In the 1940s and 1950s he appeared to
be asleep on a vast plain that resembles the plains of the moon. As the
twentieth century ends, this plain has become filled with shacks and
people from the interior. Méjico is surrounded by the dust, smoke,
and smog from the *colonias* of the Aztecs' descendants.

208

Teja is a pretty, soft-looking stone mountain with a great deal of color. The part visible from the Santa Fe Bridge looks like her head. Her west side has a natural tattoo of a red thunderbird, which becomes red with passion at sunset. It is as if for a brief quarter of an hour she tries to wake and look at Méjico, her blue king sleeping to the south. The color of the mountains depends on the light, the time of day, and the weather. You can see what they are really like on a silver day in El Paso.

In 1949, Teja also carried some white tattoos that were made by the citizens of El Paso. These were the forerunners of graffiti that would plague Teja for decades to come. Back then, these authorized tatoos were proud displays of letters from each high school and for the College of Mines. The letters were lighted by the students on football game nights. If you wanted to know who was playing, all you had to do was look to the mountain.

About mid-December, Conrey Bryson of KTSM radio told us to look to the mountain. The El Paso Electric Company would light the electrical marvel on the east side of Teja's head. The star decoration that looked like diamonds from afar would be lit throughout the Christmas season until Epiphany in January. The lighting of the star would mark the beginning of the best holiday for most El Pasoans.

The Christmas carols on the radio reminded me of past Christmases with my father. Then I recalled the holiday I had spent in Chihuahua with María. It was now one of the sweetest memories for me. I didn't linger long on the memory, though. I did not want to become sad.

The Sunday before Christmas, Linda's father took Jane, Linda, and me to see the lights on Rim Road. The rich people put out nice decorations. It was a magical drive overlooking the lights of El Paso and Juárez. We sang Christmas songs and told each other what we wanted for Christmas. I was happy and glad to be with my friends. When we went back to Linda's house to have chocolate and cookies, we started planning the week.

"On Friday the church group will go caroling down and up Pershing Drive. We will sing all the songs in the little booklet they gave us. Linda, you and Gloria can meet me at the church," Jane informed us. It was as if she was announcing my death sentence. Caroling up and down Pershing drive? Oh, my God!

"Oh, I don't think I want to go caroling, Jane!" I said.

"Why? You love music and singing," she said.

"Oh, I don't know. It'll probably be too cold," I said.

"Nonsense! We'll have our coats on."

"I don't want to go, Jane!" I whispered when Linda left the room. "If they come caroling to my house, my parents will come out," I said to a puzzled Jane. "Then they'll see that Martha is Mexican. I can't stand to have someone else say something to me about being Mexican!"

"Gloria, are you serious?" she asked and I motioned to her to be quiet because Linda was coming into the room. I certainly didn't want her hearing about my problem.

When Friday came around, I still didn't know what to do. I wanted to go caroling but I was afraid of what someone would say to me when they saw my mother. I tried to tell myself that it didn't matter, but it did. I decided that I would just say I didn't feel well. When Linda came over to get me, I told her I didn't want to go. She said that she couldn't go if I didn't. Please would I go? When I saw the disappointed look in her face, I got my coat.

At seven o'clock, the group of carolers huddled together in front of the church. The leader gave us last minute instructions. It was cold and I was shivering hard. Then we started walking down Pershing Drive. I sang but thought all the time that soon we would come to my house. I wanted to stay and sing, and yet I wanted to run away. Jane kept looking at me and smiling. She is such a good person I thought. The good people always find each other, Padre had told me. I had to believe that. For a minute, I hated myself for being so scared and sensitive. But as we approached my house, I felt myself becoming more afraid. I looked around and saw that all the kids were Anglo except for Linda and me. I looked at Jane and she smiled. Calm down, I said to myself. Then instead of singing I started saying my Hail Marys. After twelve of them, I felt calm again. The next block was my house. My legs felt like big weights. I thought, I'll leave the group and run through the alley until they have passed my house and then I'll stay home. But I could see Jane's eyes fixed on me. She got closer to me as I tried to drop back from the group. Her wind-tossed, curly red hair formed a halo above her hair. She looked like an angel.

"What do you think you are doing?" she asked me.

"I can't, Jane. I can't have them looking at me as if I am a vinegarroon." I said that because I couldn't imagine what they might think. "I am going home by the alley. I'll talk to you later."

The group was moving up to the middle of my block. No one seemed to notice that we had dropped back. Jane stopped and looked at me.

"Gloria, if you don't come with me and the group, I swear to God that I will never, never, speak to you again as long as I live!" She looked at me and even in the dark, I could see the tears forming in her eyes. It hurt me. She waited and then she said, "What makes you think they don't know you are Mexican! I know they know. Last week, I heard someone talking about you and I listened. The boy called you the pretty half-and-half señorita. He didn't mean any harm! Everyone knows you are Mexican. Everyone has heard you say 'church'!" she said as she laughed. Then I laughed. I looked at her and because I respected her so much, I decided that if she thought I was all right then I didn't care what anyone else thought. I put my arm through hers and we ran to catch the group. We caught up with them just as they reached my house. The singing brought my parents out and I looked at them and it didn't matter anymore. Up on the red porch were the two people who loved me enough to give me a home. The two represented all that I came from and all that I was. It was as if Palm, López, Fred, Martha, Francisca, and María were up there reminding me that there was a lot to me. I understood and I didn't want to be sad anymore. And like the sparrow in the mulberry tree in the evening time, I wanted my place with them even if I had to fight for it and regardless of the commotion it caused. I looked around at the group and there was nothing to see. The kids were all singing and enjoying themselves. I found my voice and I sang with them my favorite carol, "Holy Night."

I looked at Jane and Linda and for the first time in what seemed a long time, I felt good. I sang and sang. As we moved to the next block, I said a quiet prayer to the Virgen de Guadalupe. I breathed in deeply and inside my head, I said *"Feliz Navidad"* to the world.

New Year's Eve came around fast. Martha and Fred said I could go to the midnight movies if Linda and Jane went with me. They also said I could invite them to eat dinner with us, as well as spend the night.

We went to the movies and we yelled and cheered when the New Year came in. It was a special New Year . . . 1950! I had lived a long life in the 1940s. This was a new decade.

Later, when we were in my bedroom, we talked for hours. We talked about everything. We giggled when we thought that in the next ten years we might get married. Then we asked each other what we wanted in a husband.

"I want a rich man who can buy me a house on Rim Road," Linda said. "He has to be tall and handsome!"

"Jane, what about you?" I asked.

"I want a man like my father was," she said thoughtfully. "He was strong and very kind. That is how I want him to be."

"I want to marry a man who can sing like a *mariachi* and dance the two step like a Texan," I said as I performed a somersault and stood up and yelled like a *mariachi*. Linda and Jane laughed as I repeated my cry.

"AyyAyyyAyyAyy!"